# CRITIQUE
# THE STAKES OF FORM

T0375124

# CRITIQUE
# THE STAKES OF FORM

EDITED BY
SAMI KHATIB, HOLGER KUHN, OONA LOCHNER,
ISABEL MEHL, BEATE SÖNTGEN

DIAPHANES

GEFÖRDERT DURCH DIE DEUTSCHE FORSCHUNGSGEMEINSCHAFT (DFG) – PROJEKTNUMMER 2114
FUNDED BY THE DEUTSCHE FORSCHUNGSGEMEINSCHAFT (DFG, GERMAN RESEARCH FOUNDATION)—
PROJECTNUMBER 2114

ISBN 978-3-0358-0240-5

LAYOUT AND PREPRESS: 2EDIT, ZURICH
PRINTED IN GERMANY

WWW.DIAPHANES.COM

# Contents

## Writing Differently / Writing the Self

## The Scene as Form

**Sami Khatib, Holger Kuhn, Oona Lochner,
Isabel Mehl, Beate Söntgen**

# Critical Stances

## An Introduction to *The Stakes of Form*

Seldom has critique been as controversial as it is today. On the one hand, new technologies and distribution channels have given rise to an abundance of unexpected critical or quasi-critical practices. On the other hand, the theoretical foundations of critique have come under massive pressure—and so too, it seems, has the modern project of critique in general. Recently, the question of what can be regarded as a critical act and which actors, expectations, and criteria might play a role in such an act has not been an isolated matter of discussion, but rather a fundamental issue in sensitive debates world-wide. A generalizing systematic and theoretical reflection is inadequate to explain what constituted critique at different times, what constitutes it in the present, and what it can and intends to be. It is only by ascertaining critical practices, their formal and material basis, their medial and technological contingency, and the precon-ditions of a critical act—the ways in which it is received and its horizons of expectation—that critique can be understood in concrete terms: as a situated phenome-non, as an attitude or stance that manifests itself in a wide variety of ways, be it verbally, textually, visually, or gesturally through art, activism, or theory. For critique is always already a culturally situated praxis that neverthe-less needs to claim comprehensive validity and a binding nature in order to be effective. Criticized phenomena are inextricable from the forms and media of their (re-)pre-sentation. Such (re-)presentation constitutes the object as it appears in a given critique, and it determines the specific effect of the latter. (Re-)presentation is therefore the point that crystallizes various forms of critique, such as those assembled in this volume.

To repeat, at the moment when critique is put into practice, it is inseparably linked to the forms, media, and effects of its (re-)presentation.[1] Critique does not simply reconstruct the object to which it refers. Rather, methods of (re-)presentation, styles, and media emphasize particular aspects of the object,[2] put it in a new light, and make it something that can be criticized in the first place. It is no coincidence that, regarding this emphasis on the dependence of critique on (re-)presentation, rhetoric plays a significant role, and not merely as a theory of persuasive (re-)presentation techniques. After all, rhetoric also teaches us how to comprehend the procedural qualities of these very techniques.[3] Critique expresses itself through specific—and more-or-less reflective—modes of (re-)presentation: of singling out, framing, and elucidating, which constitute the object of the critical act as such. On the one hand, this perspective reveals the processual nature and the specific situation of a given critique. On the other hand, this focus on (re-)presentation also evokes the venue in which cri-

---

1 See Tilo Wesche, "Reflexion, Therapie, Darstellung: Formen der Kritik," in *Was ist Kritik?*, ed. Rahel Jaeggi and Tilo Wesche (Frankfurt am Main: Suhrkamp, 2009), pp. 193–220.

2 See Christian L. Hart Nibbrig, ed., *Was heißt "Darstellen"* (Frankfurt am Main: Suhrkamp, 1994); Louis Marin, *On Representation*, trans. Catherine Porter (Stanford CA: Stanford University Press, 2001); Dieter Mersch, ed., *Die Medien der Künste: Beiträge zu einer Theorie des Darstellens* (Munich: Fink, 2003); Dieter Schlenstedt, "Darstellung," in *Ästhetische Grundbegriffe*, ed. Karlheinz Barck et al. (Stuttgart: Metzler, 2010), vol. 1, pp. 831–875; and Michael Gamper and Helmut Hühn, eds., *Zeit der Darstellung: Ästhetische Eigenzeiten in Kunst, Literatur und Wissenschaften* (Hanover: Wehrhahn, 2014).

3 See Roland Barthes, *The Rustle of Language*, trans. Richard Howard (Berkeley: University of California Press, 1989), pp. 83–89; Paul de Man, *Allegories of Reading: Figural Language in Rousseau, Nietzsche, Rilke, and Proust* (New Haven: Yale University Press, 1979); and Anselm Haverkamp, *Metapher: Die Ästhetik in der Rhetorik* (Munich: Fink, 2007).

tique stages its respective object. Not only does critique showcase represented circumstances and objects in a particular light;[4] it also implicitly or explicitly thematizes the techniques and methods of critical (re-)presentation, which are in turn complicit in the constitution of the object as it appears in the act of critique.

The German term "Darstellung" merges critique's referential mode with its ways of actually constituting its object. To address and to hold up this ambivalence, we generally translate "Darstellung" here in its double function as "(re-)presentation." Even though critique so obviously depends upon (re-)presentation, many forms of critique, down to the present day, overlook this condition or acknowledge it but cast it aside. This mistrust or suspicion likely springs from the unreflective assumption that the term "representation" implies an immediate referentiality to its object, an expectation that the actual *form* of medial presentation cannot but undermine. Considered to be an alienating praxis that distorts the object that is to be represented, representation and its media have been and continue to be held responsible for estranged social relations. Adorno's modern critique of the culture industry, Debord's critique of the spectacle, the turn against rhetoric in favor of "naturalness" in the eighteenth century, Rousseau's critique of the theater: they all object—in one way or the other—to the alienating mediality of representational practices.[5]

---

4    See Andrea Allerkamp et al., eds., *Gegen/Stand der Kritik* (Zurich: Diaphanes, 2015).

5    See Jean-Jacques Rousseau, *Letter to d'Alembert and Writings for the Theater*, trans. Allan Bloom et al. (Hanover NH: University Press of New England, 2004), pp. 251–352; Friedrich Nietzsche, *The Birth of Tragedy and the Case of Wagner*, trans. Walter Kaufmann (New York: Random House, 1967), pp. 153–192; Guy Debord, *Society of the Spectacle*, trans. Ken Knabb (London: Rebel Press, 2005); Sven Kramer, "Benjamin und Adorno über Kunst in der Massenkultur," in *Massenkultur: Kritische Theorien im interkulturellen Vergleich*, ed. Rodrigo Duarte and Gerhard Schweppenhäuser (Hamburg: Lit Verlag, 2003), pp. 21–41; and Beate Söntgen, "Das Theater des Herrn Diderot findet im Innenraum statt: Zum Rahmen wahrer Darstellung im späten

In various ways, they thus perpetuate Plato's rejection of the representational arts and the theater, which are suspected of deceiving and alienating individual subjects (understood as passive audience members) and society at large through their forms and media of (re-)presentation.[6] It is usually forgotten in all of this mistrust that any critique of representation articulates itself, too, through certain forms and media of (re-)presentation.

Every (re-)presentation alters that which it leads before our eyes; along with its object, it also alters the perception and effect of what it shows. This concerns the form(s) of critique on multiple levels. First of all, it concerns the formal configuration of critique—that is, the question of its specific grammars, genres, styles, idioms, and narratives,[7] not to mention the question of the interplay between texts and visual elements, and between language and tone. With the recent rise of diverse online cultures, this spectrum has been broadened by hybrid forms of digital critique.[8] To what extent

18. Jahrhundert," in *Theaterfeindlichkeit*, ed. Stefanie Diekmann et al. (Munich: Fink, 2012), pp. 127–146.

**6**  See Plato, "Republic," in *Plato: Complete Works*, ed. John M. Cooper (Indianapolis: Hackett, 1997), pp. 971–1223; Jacques Rancière, *The Emancipated Spectator*, trans. Gregory Elliott (London: Verso, 2011); Claus Pias, "Falsches Spiel: Die Grenzen eines Ressentiments," *Maske und Kothurn* 54:4 (2008): pp. 35–48; and Juliane Rebentisch, *Die Kunst der Freiheit: Zur Dialektik demokratischer Existenz* (Berlin: Suhrkamp, 2012).

**7**  See Reinold Viehoff, "Literaturkritik als literarisches Handeln und als Gegenstand der Forschung," *Wertung und Kritik: Zeitschrift für Literaturwissenschaft und Linguistik* 18:71 (1988): pp. 73–91; Samuel Weber, "Criticism Underway: Walter Benjamin's Romantic Concept of Criticism," in *Romantic Revolutions: Criticism and Theory*, ed. Kenneth R. Johnston et al. (Bloomington: Indiana University Press, 1990), pp. 302–319; Jörg Huber and Dirk Baecker, eds., *Ästhetik der Kritik oder verdeckte Ermittlung* (Zurich: Voldemeer, 2007); and Martin Saar, "Genealogische Kritik," in Jaeggi and Wesche, *Was ist Kritik?*, pp. 247–265.

**8**  See Geert Lovink, *Zero Comments: Blogging and Critical Internet Culture* (New York: Routledge, 2008); and Thomas Anz, "Kontinuitäten und Veränderungen der Literaturkritik in Zeiten des Internets: Fünf Thesen und einige Bedenken," in *Digitale Literaturvermittlung: Praxis, Forschung und Archivierung*, ed. Stefan Neuhaus et al. (Innsbruck: Studienverlag, 2010), pp. 48–59.

do these feedback loops between new technologies and distribution channels create novel "languages" of critique and thus new critical effects?[9] And how do such new forms alter our perspective on what came before?

Every critical process sets processes of participation and reciprocal transmissions in motion. Form is always a decisive component of the way in which judging voices situate themselves (subjectively or anonymously) in relation to the object of critique. The effects of affective and linguistic transmission, for instance, thus provide the object with room to resonate instead of keeping it at a critical distance.[10] Recently, over the course of digitalization and globalization, new forms of social participation and intervention have emerged that pose fundamental challenges to the traditional understanding of critique.[11]

Moreover, areas of competence have started to merge, as in the example of artists and curators, who are now both active as critics.[12] What are the consequences of this for critical writing? And how, in both art and critique, has the conception of form been changed by interferences between artistic production, digital media, and new configurations of capitalism?[13] At this point, a model comes to light that might apply to a variety

9   See Michael Sanchez, "2011: Art and Transmission," *Artforum International* 51:10 (2013): pp. 294–301.

10  See Beate Söntgen, "Distanz und Leidenschaft: Diderots Auftritte vor dem Bild," in *Sprechen über Bilder, Sprechen in Bildern: Studien zum Wechselverhältnis von Bild und Sprache*, ed. Lena Bader et al. (Berlin: Deutscher Kunstverlag, 2014), pp. 33–50; and Stephanie Marchal, "Für eine 'Farbenlehre der Worte': Julius Meier-Graefe und die 'neue' Kunstkritik," in *Wie Texte und Bilder zusammenfinden: Vom Mittelalter bis zur Gegenwart*, ed. Renate Kroll et al. (Berlin: Reimer, 2015), pp. 125–136.

11  See Andreas Ziemann, *Soziologie der Medien* (Bielefeld: Transcript, 2006); Timon Beyes et al., eds., *ParCITYpate: Art and Urban Space* (Zurich: Niggli, 2009); and Eric Kluitenberg, *Legacies of Tactical Media – The Tactics of Occupation: From Tompkins Square to Tahrir* (Amsterdam: Network Notebooks, 2011).

12  See Barnaby Drabble and Dorothee Richter, eds., *Curating Critique* (Frankfurt am Main: Revolver, 2008); and Beatrice von Bismarck et al., eds., *Cultures of the Curatorial* (Berlin: Sternberg Press, 2012).

13  See Armen Avenessian et al., eds., *Form: Zwischen Ästhetik und künstlerischer Praxis* (Zurich: Diaphanes, 2009).

of different critical processes: Forms and formats are the condition that determines both *how* things are perceived and *that* they are perceived at all. This is not only true, most obviously, of the artistic phenomena of critique, but also of all forms of critique that address social relations. The fact that today's socio-economic developments are worthy of critique goes hand in hand with the forms in which critique itself is produced and disseminated.[14] In light of the medial and organizational multiplicity of current critical expressions and alliances, the diagnosis that critique has been "disarmed"[15] might perhaps simply apply to the diminishing relevance of certain types of critique, which were associated with a specific set of intellectual forms and people.[16]

If, in this volume, we focus the question of (re-)presentation on the problem of form, this may at first seem like a limitation. After all, the concept of form is associated just as closely with rigid and fixed configurations as it is with dichotomies that treat form as either the opposite of content or as the opposite of materiality. Whereas form plays a rather indirect role in many discussions—in the critique of hylomorphism,[17] for instance, or in approaches that, drawing upon Deleuze and Guattari, tend to think in procedural categories ("to form, to transform, to reform, to inform, or to perform"[18])—it acquires a different contour in works that, in their awareness of the problematic nature of formalism and the concept of form, pose questions about which of form's aspects can be salvaged for the present and why this might be possible.

---

14  See Meg McLagan and Yates McKee, eds., *Sensible Politics: The Visual Culture of Nongovernmental Activism* (New York: Zone Books, 2012).
15  Luc Boltanski and Eve Chiapello, *The New Spirit of Capitalism*, trans. Gregory Elliott (London: Verso, 2005), p. 36.
16  See Bruno Latour, "Why Has Critique Run Out of Steam?" *Critical Inquiry* 30:2 (2004): pp. 225–248.
17  See Erich Hörl, ed., *Die technologische Bedingung: Beiträge zur Beschreibung der technischen Welt* (Berlin: Suhrkamp, 2011).
18  Quoted from Birgit M. Kaiser and Kathrin Thiele's article in this volume (p. 96).

Exemplary in this regard are recent discussions of form that have been held by historians of art and images. Above all, their contributions to form and formalism have validated the self-reflexive potential of form and its fundamental relevance to aesthetics, the theory of perception, and the theory of the arts.[19] The recently published anthology *Formbildung und Formbegriff* reflects on the way that form has been thought about in modernity; there, the editors see a fundamental difference between the "procedural creation of form" [*prozesshafe Formbildung*] and "apparent form" [*erscheinende Form*]. In their view, this distinction is of the utmost significance throughout all of modernity, and it is also applicable beyond the realm of art and aesthetics, be it from the perspective of epistemology, subject formation, society, or ethics—and, above all, wherever the discussion at hand concerns the possible forms of the "right life" (in Adorno's terms).[20]

In general, it can be stated that there has been a dynamic and fluid understanding of form since the end of the eighteenth century, as is evident from the topoi of rupture, delimitation, fissure, and opening as well as from antithetical concepts such as Schlegel's *Antiform* or Bataille's *informe*.[21] However, these diverse attempts "through demolition to continue building on the formation," in Benjamin's terms,[22] also demonstrate

---

19  See, in particular, Avenessian et al., eds., *Form: Zwischen Ästhetik und künstlerischer Praxis.*

20  See Markus Klammer et al., "Formbildung und Formbegriff: Zur Einleitung," in *Formbildung und Formbegriff: Das Formdenken der Moderne*, ed. Markus Klammer et al. (Paderborn: Fink, 2019), pp. 9–31, here p. 9.

21  The concept of formlessness does not imply a lack of form but rather a deformation caused by the separation of form and material. See Friedrich Balke, "Mimesis und Figura: Erich Auerbachs niederer Materialismus," in *Mimesis und Figura: Mit einer Neuausgabe des "Figura"-Aufsatzes von Erich Auerbach*, ed. Friedrich Balke and Hanna Engelmeier (Paderborn: Fink, 2018), pp. 13–89, here p. 43. See also Georges Didi-Huberman, *Formlose Ähnlichkeit oder die fröhliche Wissenschaft des Visuellen nach Georges Bataille* (Munich: Fink, 2010).

22  Walter Benjamin, "The Concept of Art Criticism in German Romanticism," in *Selected Writings: Volume 1, 1913–1936*, ed. Marcus Bullock and Michael W. Jennings (Cambridge MA: Belknap Press of Harvard University Press, 1996), pp. 116–200, here p. 165.

the dependence of every articulation on forms of presentation,[23] which in turn, as Bettine Menke shows in this volume with reference to Benjamin, remain provisionally dependent and constitutionally contingent upon the formlessness from which they emerged. Yet in order for an object or phenomenon to be articulated, seen, and comprehended in the first place, it needs for at least a moment a fixed (if still dynamic) form, which is in turn at risk of being torn apart by the autonomy of the object and by the visibility of the constitutional conditions of its form. Symptomatic of this renewed interest in the dialectics of form and formlessness is the recent renaissance, in the German research landscape, of Erich Auerbach's concept of *figura*. In the classical and early Christian rhetorical tradition, *figura* not merely designated a fixed form but rather included the process of figuration or formation. In fact, it emphasized the latter even more than the rigid form itself,[24] and this in turn led to new forms of thinking and interpretation oriented toward the *figura* and its mutability.[25]

For critique and its dependence on (re-)presentation, this aspect is relevant to the extent that both the "becoming" of critique and the conditions under which its object is produced are revealed through form. Thus Auerbach proceeds from the notion that "reality has to be figured

---

23  Here and in the following, wherever we refer to Benjamin's specific use of the German term "Darstellung," and the context within which it is used, we translate it as "presentation," complying with recent translations of his work.

24  See Gabriele Brandstetter and Sibylle Peters, eds., *De figura: Rhetorik – Bewegung – Gestalt* (Munich: Fink, 2003); and Balke and Engelmeier, eds., *Mimesis und Figura*.

25  Balke illustrates this with the example of the opening scene from Virginia Woolf's *To the Lighthouse*, which evokes the author's writing process. The six-year-old James Ramsey cuts images out of an illustrated catalogue and puts them together to form new constellations. This act of cutting out images, according to Balke, "is the occasion for the production of *figurae* [...], for which Mrs. Ramsey then offers a highly idiosyncratic figural interpretation." Balke, "Mimesis und Figura," pp. 73–74.

so that we can recognize and understand it as such."[26] The object formed in the act of critique develops and is indeed constituted as a specific form of reality; like Auerbach's *figura*, it has, as represented reality, a particular potential for expression, interpretation, and generating affect[27]—a potential that applies equally to the (re-)presentation itself, its form, and the phenomenon under critique. The term *form* thus allows for the relationship between critique and its object to be pointedly described as one that is mutually constitutive and also reveals itself as such. This focus on the question of form thus contributes to Christoph Menke's idea of aesthetic critique, according to which the act of critique is performatively reflected in its conditions, possibilities, and limitations.[28] Menke's concept, which is sensitive to the question of (re-)presentation, further opens the notion of form to the repeatedly problematized authority of the criticizing and evaluating subject, whose (ideally self-reflexive) stance manifests itself in the form of his or her critique.

The considerable extent to which the idea of a modern, world-generating subject was and remains tied to the term *form* has recently been underscored by Sam Rose in his book *Art and Form*.[29] Instead of concentrating on the idealistic and transcendental dimension of this idea, Rose focuses on the communicative aspect of form. In his opinion, form articulates and preserves

---

26  Hanna Engelmeier, "Die Wirklichkeit lesen: Figura und Lektüre bei Erich Auerbach," in Balke and Engelmeier, *Mimesis und Figura*, pp. 89–112, here p. 94. See also Erich Auerbach, "Figura: Neuedition des Textes von 1938," in ibid., pp. 121–188, here p. 140: "*Figura* is something real and historical that represents and announces something else that is also real and historical."

27  See Balke, "Mimesis und Figura," p. 26. Balke describes how, in Auerbach's work, *figura* and figural interpretation transcend their theological context and become an instrument for understanding the world without recourse to prophecy. Ibid., pp. 29–31.

28  See Christoph Menke, "The Aesthetic Critique of Judgment," in *The Power of Judgment: A Debate on Aesthetic Critique*, ed. Daniel Birnbaum and Isabelle Graw (Berlin: Sternberg Press, 2010), pp. 8–29.

29  Sam Rose, *Art and Form: From Roger Fry to Global Modernism* (University Park PA: The Pennsylvania University Press, 2019).

historically specific manners of production, reception, and use. Moreover, if it is thought of in terms of structure and organization, it should be understood less as a world-generating *organon* than as a medium of contact that exhibits its own becoming.

Comparable notions of communicative formalism can also be found in art criticism itself, which has indeed created new forms of writing that endeavor to evoke that which is expressed through the form of a given work, or that seek to bring to light, by means of a specific use of form, that which the act of giving form has pushed into the background—aspects that this book's section on "Writing Differently" thematizes as well. Thus, if attention is directed toward the use of form, one sees that the latter exhibits a complex and active engagement with the outside world—with an object of critique, in our case—and that it does not engage in such a way as a naturalizing representation, but rather as a critical enactment of presentation.

In her book *Entgrenzter Formalismus*, Kerstin Stakemeier has recently offered an entirely different perspective on the modern concept of form.[30] According to Stakemeier, the conceptual rendering of form in the twentieth-century history of art can only be understood in light of its alliance with the ideology of aesthetic autonomy. The various understandings of form, in her opinion, are thus closely related to the disciplinary tendencies of bourgeois capitalist society, and contemporary artistic practices are able to destabilize and loosen the strictures of this regulatory order. Stakemeier's three main targets of destabilization (the individualization of the subject, the reproductive aim of desire, and the equation of freedom with the bourgeois subject) are each addressed in this book's section on "Forms of Work / Forms of Life." Traces of Stakemeier's ideas concerning

---

**30**  Kerstin Stakemeier, *Entgrenzter Formalismus: Verfahren einer anti-modernen Ästhetik* (Berlin: b_books, 2017).

forms of "anti-social life,"[31] which is suppressed by the logic of capitalism and colonialism and by this logic's conception of a free bourgeois subject, can be found, for instance, in Birgit M. Kaiser and Kathrin Thiele's article, albeit from a different theoretical standpoint. From an ecosophical perspective (in Guattari's terms), they examine the transformations of critique in light of worldwide interrelations and global historical upheavals.

Although this book has gained much from Stakemeier's work, we do not share her opinion that every instantiation of formalism in twentieth-century art can be understood as a reversion to bourgeois art and its aesthetics of autonomy or that form is always paralyzed by the (value) concept of art, which would make the self-abolishment of art desirable.[32] Rather, the dialectic that has developed in the case of art between rigid form and boundless formalism—between apparent form and processual formation—has furnished us with a heuristic instrument for analyzing not only the critical practices within the world of art but also the multifaceted manners of critical articulation that each of this book's four main parts addresses.

## Form of Critique

In the "Epistemo-Critical Prologue" to his book *The Origin of German Tragic Drama* (1928), Benjamin diagnosed that philosophical writing has "to be confronted anew at every turn with the question of presentation [Darstellung]."[33] However, as long as philosophy projected the identity of object and presentation within the total form of its system, it seemed as if "among the tasks of the philosopher" there has never been "a place

31  Ibid., p. 33.
32  Ibid., pp. 23, 43.
33  Walter Benjamin, *Origin of the German Trauerspiel*, trans. Howard Eiland (Cambridge MA: Harvard University Press, 2019), p. 1.

for concern with presentation."[34] Benjamin's critique of this system went hand in hand with his ruminations on the question of presentation: How can unsystematic thinking confront the danger of slipping into arbitrariness? Which presentations make it possible to avoid the schematizing and unifying effects of systems of philosophy? From his critical interpretation of early Romantic thought as being "systematic without a system,"[35] Benjamin—and Adorno in his wake—developed a manner of thinking in terms of constellations. Through the medium of the essay, both writers created a place for this open form of philosophical writing. They developed a perspective that went beyond the opposition between systematically guaranteed validity and unsystematic arbitrariness—a perspective that redefined the relationship between truth, history, and presentation.

A central insight that the chapters in this section owe to Adorno's and Benjamin's ideas concerns the critical and crisis-ridden historicity of forms of thinking and action. Regardless of whether it is understood in transcendental or formal-logical terms, form is not a mold but rather a historically congealed constellation of social relations that manifests itself in art, literature, the economy, politics, and unconscious structures of subjectivity. In order to ascertain the historicity of forms, philosophical writing can rely neither on the apparent immediacy of individual stories of suffering nor on the false objectivity of a meta-historical perspective; rather, it has to develop, from the materiality of historical forms of thinking and objects, an immanent manner of presentation. The methodological challenge of such a manner of presentation consists in the immanent reference to a dual historicity: the historicity of one's own forms of presentation and presentational media cannot claim to be indepen-

---

**34**  Ibid., p. 8.
**35**  See Sami Khatib, *"Teleologie ohne Endzweck": Walter Benjamins Entstellung des Messianischen* (Marburg: Tectum, 2013), pp. 55–61.

dent of the historicity of the presented forms, for the historicity of presentation cannot historicize itself in the presented. In theory, the act of thinking cannot betray its own historicity, and thus it cannot map the historicity of the forms of its objects on a meta-historical system of coordinates. In Benjamin's words, this methodological problem can be described as the doubling of a historical "nucleus of time lying hidden within the knower and the known alike."[36] In theory, the historicizing act can never betray the historicity of its objects, because the nucleus of time of what is theoretically known applies simultaneously to the forms in which it is critically known, interpreted, read, and presented. In Fredric Jameson's terms, this challenge of critique can be formulated as follows: If critical thinking truly ought to follow the imperative "always historicize,"[37] it cannot simply disregard the historicity of the temporal locus of "always."

Heiko Stubenrauch's contribution addresses this challenge with a precise reading of Adorno's understanding of the dialectics between the resistance of presentation and the labor of presentation. Presentation is not external to its historical object; rather, it impinges upon it and constitutes it in the first place. The media of presentation thus also pose questions concerning objects of thought and their historical forms. At first, conceptual "access" is opposed by this problem of presentation. In Adorno's concept of presentation, Stubenrauch recognizes a core idea of non-identical thinking, which strongly rejects the idealistic temptation to conflate thought and its object. The chapter traces the "resistance of presentation" through various central stages of Adorno's praxis of theoretical writing. The praxis of philosophical thinking, according to Adorno, cannot overcome individual suffering in and

---

**36** Walter Benjamin, *The Arcades Project*, trans. Howard Eiland and Kevin McLaughlin (Cambridge MA: Belknap Press of Harvard University Press, 1999), p. 463.

**37** Fredric Jameson, *The Political Unconscious* (London: Routledge, 1981), p. ix.

from society. The dialectic between individuals suffering from the non-identical difference of the objective and the presentation of social objectivity does not resolve itself; rather, it leads to the differentiation between presentation and the presented. Instead of suppressing and theoretically switching off one's own suffering, the labor of presentation accepts this suffering and transforms it into the capability of differentiation. This capability, in turn, has its own nucleus of time, which, in a parallel reading of Adorno and Freud, Stubenrauch does not psychoanalytically trace back to the suffering of the subject. Instead, he makes the social-critical claim that it derives from a historical formation of capitalist society: "If I lend a voice to suffering in the process of presentation and search for the reason of this suffering in society (instead of letting it turn into rage against difference), I search for it in the relations of production which prevent the emancipatory potentials of the forces of production from unfolding."[38]

Eva Geulen's contribution likewise confronts this challenge of critique through the medium of Adorno's thinking, but her focus is on a dialectical interpolation of expression and suffering as well as semblance and mimesis. Despite what is often maintained in Adorno research, she claims that mimesis, in his writings, is neither the compulsion to make oneself similar nor the art of imitation. Rather, mimesis denotes the ability to approximate oneself in the medium of form. Philosophically and art-theoretically, it is thus impossible to proceed from a symmetrical alternative between immediate expression and form-generating semblance or mimesis.[39] Adorno's project is therefore not to demonstrate the untruth of

---

38  Quoted from Stubenrauch's chapter in the present volume, p. 52.
39  See Geulen's chapter in this volume, p. 63: "Thus, mimesis does not mean that in art which imitates or is imitated; rather, it means its ability to make itself similar in the medium of form. In turn, there follows a sentence that radically transforms and displaces the relation of aesthetic oppositions between (immediate) expression and form-generated semblance or mimesis."

mimetic behavior but rather to preserve the mimetic impulse in the form of a reciprocal exchange ("quid pro quo"). In this sense, the problem of mimesis—the compulsion to approximate something and the suffering caused by this—translates into a necessary act of failure, whose critique is not an endpoint but rather the impulse for engaging with mimetic forms: "For the experience of a deceitful semblance is only possible if one previously attempted to make oneself similar. It is *this* impulse—not the right of suffering to authentic expression—which is, as it were, the motor of the inner-aesthetic dynamic between mimesis and expression."[40]

Sami Khatib's chapter elucidates the problem of the dual historicity of form and critique through a close reading of Marx's exposition of the commodity form. According to Khatib, Marx's "value-form analysis" in the first chapter of *Capital* pertains to the problem of presentation because the very form (the commodity form) that Marx attempts to present in theoretical terms is a historical form which, at the same time, derives its logical validity from its historically locatable genesis. In a psychoanalytically-informed reading, the chapter argues that Marx's value-form analysis ultimately has to do with the epistemological and ontological status of the unconscious of form. The commodity form is a historically congealed expression of specific social relations; at the same time, however, the validity of this form cannot be historicized with the same forms of thought that are also at work in social reality. The problem of presenting the unhistoricizable historicity of the commodity form, which is at first theoretical, ultimately proves to be a symptom of repression—the repression of the history of an inconsistent unconscious subject, the proletariat. In this way, "the unhistoricizable historicity of the commodity form structurally conditions and represses the negative history of an unconscious subject (the proletariat) without which the commodity form could have never come into being 'in the first place.'"[41]

## Forms of Work / Forms of Life

The series title "Critical Stances" is meant to suggest that we understand critique in a broad sense that is not limited to textual or visual articulations and practices.[42] Forms of life and work can also be regarded as critical practices, especially if such forms involve artistic or intellectual activity. For it is these forms that often reveal, in an especially poignant manner, the typically reciprocal transformations of work and life and their societal, social, and institutional effects. Events in life occasionally call for a change of habitual work forms and processes. It was not until Rachel Cusk became a mother that she felt alienated from the novel form and turned to a new sort of writing later known as "autofiction" (as in her book *A Life's Work: On Becoming a Mother*).[43] While struggling with breast cancer treatment and depression, the queer theorist Eve Kosofsky Sedgwick incorporated both into a book about desire, dependence, and death, drawing on the literary forms of the Platonic dialogue and the seventeenth-century Japanese prose form known as *haibun*.[44] Then again, work infects the ways we live our lives. The forms of experiencing motherhood, relationships, illness, or trauma change when they are also the object of our thinking.

---

41  Quoted from Khatib's chapter in the present volume, p. 92.
42  This is the series title of the books published by Diaphanes for the graduate program "Cultures of Critique" at Leuphana University, Lüneburg.
43  See "Woman as Subject or Exemplary of Her Kind: A Conversation between Maija Timonen and Rachel Cusk," *Texte zur Kunst* 115 (September 2019): pp. 70, 72.
44  Eve Kosofsky Sedgwick, *A Dialogue on Love* (Boston MA: Beacon Press, 1999).

Yet how can forms of life be identified as such, and through which forms are they made visible? In Rahel Jaeggi's terms, forms of life are an ensemble of mostly rule-governed practices that nevertheless have an enabling character precisely because of their relatively rigid nature. As frameworks that can be visibly demolished—and can thus open up new venues of activity—they add a new dimension to our question of form and representability. Following Adorno, Jaeggi examines the extent to which forms of life can still be criticized at all in light of cultural diversity, ethnic pluralism, and the modern conception of self-determination. On the basis of what values and norms, she wonders, can such a critique take place? To Jaeggi's question of how to describe and determine whether forms of life are good, successful, or rational, we add the aspect of the critical. In an inversion of Jaeggi's approach, our question concerns the ways in which forms of life, and with them forms of work, can be identified as critical.

In their contribution, Birgit M. Kaiser and Kathrin Thiele, who often work collaboratively, provide an account of the international research network "Terra Critica," which they founded in 2012. Treating global interconnectedness as an onto-epistemological starting point of critique, Terra Critica asks how critical practices can be performed when forms of allegedly distanced judgement, which have been habitual since the Enlightenment, have come under question. Kaiser and Thiele's points of reference are Virginia Woolf's *Three Guineas* (1938) and Félix Guattari's *The Three Ecologies* (1989). As reactions to extreme historical shifts, both texts engage in a critical practice that couples work with the implication of living within a multiplicity of relations. According to Guattari, such relations can be understood as *eco-sophical*.

Yet another perspective is offered by artistic forms of life and work, and especially the historical avant-garde, which—with its movement toward blending art and life and with the fraying (in Adorno's terms) of artistic genres, media, and methods—expanded the breadth of artistic work to include societal, social, and institutional structures, by reconfiguring private forms of life, work, and relationships. This gesture was readopted by neo avant-garde movements in the 1960s—from Fluxus and Happenings to postmodern dance—which often made direct reference to Dada and Duchamp. Current debates about art since the 1960s thus also treat it, above all, as a social and collaborative praxis in which individual forms of life are inextricably linked to artistic claims and methods.[45]

Oona Lochner's chapter focuses on the case of the American art critic, art historian, and educator Arlene Raven. Beginning in the 1970s and within the context of a (lesbian) feminist movement, Raven developed a style of writing that arose from the conditions and needs of her life while, at the same time, the forms of her life followed the trajectories of her theoretical work. Showcasing her relationships as the locus where her living and writing intersect, Raven emphasized that, as Sara Ahmed has recently argued, "feminist theory is what we do when we live our lives in a feminist way."[46] This idea also underlies Lochner's (re-)presentation of Raven's work: Following in the tracks of other writing mothers, including Rachel Cusk's *A Life's Work* (2001) and Maggie Nelson's *The Argonauts* (2015), Lochner reflects on how Raven's feminist practice interrelates with her own struggles between (family) life and writing.

That the rejection of habitual forms of life and work can often lead to the creation of alternatives is also a topic of Rosi Braidotti's feminist ethics of the nomadic subject, in which, under the provocative title "Powers

---

**45** See Matthias Warstat, *Soziale Theatralität: Die Inszenierung der Gesellschaft* (Munich: Fink, 2018); Sabeth Buchmann et al., eds., *Putting Rehearsals to the Test* (Berlin: The Sternberg Press, 2016); and Claire Bishop, *Artificial Hells: Participatory Art and the Politics of Spectatorship* (London: Verso, 2012).
**46** Sara Ahmed, *Living a Feminist Life* (Durham NC: Duke University Press, 2017), p. 11.

of Affirmation," she conceptualizes the relationship between critique and creativity.[47] In her contribution to the present volume, Beate Söntgen examines how such a form of critique looked at the beginning of modernity, in light of the example of Charleston Farmhouse, which was coinhabited by various members of the Bloomsbury Group. In this house, fluid work and living relations gave rise to a form of life that served as a counterexample to Victorian models of family and marriage—a counterexample that, in this artistically arranged house, which was characterized by appropriations and repurposing, found a facilitating framework. Here, a form-oriented attitude was revealed in this framework's communicative potential and in its ethical and political dimensions. Such a perspective blurs the lines between the avant-garde and aestheticism, and it suggests that both can be potential forms of social critique.[48]

## Writing Differently / Writing the Self

Critique is typically articulated in and through the form of language. Since the 1960s, within the broader environment of (writing about) art, more and more writing practices have been developed that create critical statements less through argumentation than through the programmatic use of disruptive, destabilizing, and open formal means. Writing practices that neither deny nor passively accept their dependence on (re-)presentation, but rather actively engage with this dependence, address their object through processes of mimicry, mimesis, parody, or inversion; they repeat, reflect, satirize, or exaggerate their object in order to affirm, reject, reinterpret, or reconstitute it. The "material turn" of art criticism

47  Rosi Braidotti, *Nomadic Subjects: Embodiment and Sexual Difference in Contemporary Feminist Theory*, 2nd edition (New York: Columbia University Press, 2012), pp. 267–298.
48  See Sam Rose, *Art and Form*, pp. 92–97.

during the 1960s and 1970s often had nothing to do with writers attempting to ape Romanticism or approximate visual arts and texts. This is made clear in Thomas Glaser's contribution, with reference to Roland Barthes' late-1970s interpretations of Cy Twombly's artistic works. Glaser traces an arc from early German Romanticism to the post-war writings of Walter Benjamin and Georg Lukács, and from there to Roland Barthes' idiosyncratic critical positions. These authors are connected by their period-specific opposition to an aesthetic conception of form that is based on the dualism of form and content.

The convergence of visual art and the practice of writing about it was also taken into account by the art critic Lucy Lippard when she retrospectively referred to her work as "art-imitative writing."[49] Writing about conceptual art, then about feminist art, she attempted to translate the aesthetics of both into a linguistic form. In a similar way, an abundance of new manners of writing, conscious of their being entangled with forms of (re-)presentation, developed within the context of feminist art criticism from the 1970s on. In particular, the thematicization of gendered everyday experiences and the deconstruction of topoi—for instance the topos of genius as a naturalization of male domination[50]—provided a new arena for radically different writing practices. The latter allowed the first-person narrator—together with her attitudes, reflections, and emotions—to enter the critical scene in a visible way in order, at the same time, to destabilize this very form of narration.

The 1970s and 1980s in particular gave rise to a massive increase in art magazines, books about artists, and catalogs that opened up space for new forms of texts

---

**49**  Lucy Lippard, "Freelancing the Dragon: Interview with the Editors of Art-Rite," *Art-Rite* 5 (1974); reprinted in Lucy Lippard, *From the Center: Feminist Essays in Women's Art* (New York: E. P. Dutton & Co., 1976), pp. 15–27.
**50**  See Linda Nochlin, "Why Have There Been No Great Women Artists?" *ARTNews* 69:9 (1971): pp. 22–39.

with clear political objectives. These heterogeneous texts, which often go by the name "art writing," even became the subject of new courses of study, such as the MFA program of that very title that was directed by Maria Fusco from 2007 to 2013 at Goldsmiths College, London.[51] In addition, art magazines have shown an increased interest in storytelling, as is clear from *Texte zur Kunst*'s recent issue on "Literatur" or *Flash Art*'s recent issue on "Stories."[52] For our specific context, we are less interested in theoretical and philosophical examinations of art writing—such as David Carrier's analysis of texts by Clement Greenberg, Rosalind Krauss, Michael Fried, and others[53]—than we are in forms of writing (often by poets and non-academics) that circulate primarily in the artistic community before entering the academic realm.[54] This type of writing approaches

---

**51** In 2011, Maria Fusco, Yve Lomax, Michael Newman, and Adrian Rifkin published eleven manifesto-like theses on art writing. The latter are reprinted in Maria Fusco, *Give Up Art* (Los Angeles: New Documents, 2017), pp. 13–15. Similar graduate programs to that at Goldsmiths College include the program "Art Writing" (formerly "Art Criticism and Writing"), directed by David Levi Strauss at the School of Visual Arts in New York, and the seminar "Pure Fiction Class," led by Mark von Schlegell at the Städelschule in Frankfurt am Main.

**52** See *Texte zur Kunst* 115 (September 2019); and *Flash Art* 309:49 (2016).

**53** See David Carrier, *Artwriting* (Amherst: University of Massachusetts Press, 1987).

**54** Maria Fusco has since distanced herself from the term "art writing," preferring instead "interdisciplinary writing": "I feel that 'art writing' is a redundant phrase now, it's not so useful anymore. The value of having a phrase like 'art writing' at the time of the Goldsmiths MFA was a bit like ringing a bell and saying to people, 'We're doing this here! Do you want to be involved in it, do you want to do it together?' By doing it together we could all make it a bit better. I strongly believe in that idea, hence doing things through practice, embodying the rigor and originality of scholarly activity as practice. But now, much in the same way we might have talked about time-based artists or new media artists in the past, it's no longer a relevant term. It's not completely irrelevant, but it has lost much of its use value and gained more symbolic value. Phrases are very useful for building a constituency of people who are interested in challenging the practice, but now I think that 'interdisciplinary writing' is a clearer, more nuanced phrase; 'art writing' now has a smack of antiquity about it." Quoted from https://www.artandeducation. net/schoolwatch/229480/writing-as-a-visible-practice-an-interview-with-maria-fusco (accessed January 10, 2020).

art in literary and interdisciplinary forms, often with an explicitly feminist and social-critical agenda. Often, its writers are female authors or poets who, like Lynne Tillman, Gary Indiana, and Eileen Myles, developed new forms of writing alongside art. In 1984, Marcia Tucker, then director of the New Museum of Contemporary Art, New York, described a shift in the development of art criticism from the disembodied and authoritarian third person singular toward a more personal and subjective tone, which embraced the imaginative and creative.[55]

The uses and effects of such critical writing conscious of its form have been diverse, and they have gone beyond self-reflexive observations about the interrelated nature of objects, authorial subjects, and (re-)presentation. What manners of (de)subjectivation take place in such writing practices? How do they alter critique's claims to validity? Do they disempower or replace the dominant (re-)presentational form of the argument and therefore, if possible, the entire critical gesture? What forms of agency or experience are generated by the application of these various rhetorical, poetic, and aesthetic methods? Where and how do the political effects of such interventions manifest themselves in these various forms of (re-) presentation?

In her essay in this book, Isabel Mehl focuses on an explicitly critical approach from the broad field of art writing. In this approach, the act of underscoring the subjectivity and situated nature of the art writer emphasizes the fact that the critical and creative practice is ambivalent, and rejects the notion that it is possible to speak "from a distance" or "from the outside." Mehl cites Chris Kraus as one of the pioneers of the act of combining criticism, autobiography, social analysis, and feminist practice. Kraus assumes the role of a situ-

---

**55** See Marcie Tucker, "Preface," in Brian Wallis, *Art After Modernism: Rethinking Representation* (New York: New Museum of Contemporary Art, 1984), p. viii.

ated critic who observes things closely and is aware of her surroundings, her mood, and the distractions of her mind. These ideas are further explored in a conversation between Mehl and Kraus—whose book series "Native Agents" includes works by Indiana, Myles, and Tillman, among others—in which the two discuss contemporary modes of art criticism and the significance of description to the critical undertaking.

Two specific models of (re-)presentation-conscious and critical writing can be found in the contributions by Lynne Tillman and Masha Tupitsyn: close reading and editing. Tillman's descriptions of works by the artist Carroll Dunham invoke the relation between the description, interpretation, and explication of art in literary, associative forms. Tillman contrasts the "unavoidable linearity" of language with visual composition, which is characterized by spatial simultaneity. Yet what, in general, are we able to see, and why? The critique gives Dunham's art—with its forms, colors, and textures—room to resonate, and Tillman evokes through her use of language a specific and situated type of writing alongside art.

For her part, Tupitsyn artistically edits the stories of others in order to develop, from her close observation, (repeated) readings, and editing, a different critical perspective on the narratives at hand. Central to understanding her process is the differentiation between nostalgia and mourning, a distinction that she defined as follows in an interview: "Nostalgia is often about the fetishistic melancholia of forgetting. Mourning allows us to be critical of the time we live in and aware of what has changed, what is being lost, destroyed, and what that does to relationships, communities, ecologies, ideas."[56]

---

56 Quoted from an interview with Masha Tupitsyn by Felix Bernstein: https://www.artforum.com/books/masha-tupitsyn-discusses-picture-cycle-81280 (accessed January 11, 2020).

Editing and reshaping are also at the core of Maria Fusco's take on critique, even if such acts involve violence (violence, in her case, against her own wayward body). The excerpt printed here from her experimental play *ECZEMA* describes living with a skin disease that causes her to scratch herself constantly. Her irrational "desire to edit [her] skin" by picking at it is her desperate critique of being governed by the itch. However, as her scratch-editing in fact only worsens her condition, it also becomes a metaphor for resisting (supposedly) rational academic thinking and for acknowledging the "bodily and affective imperatives" of thinking itself.

## The Scene as Form

Under the conditions of its practical implementation, critique intervenes with its object and defines it by means of (re-)presentation. By tailoring and framing an object, critique establishes specific strategic fields and is simultaneously a venue that produces different perceptions.[57] Critique therefore creates, for both its object and itself, an altered and heightened form of visibility, which is in turn its condition of possibility.

It is in this sense that we understand critical praxis as a "scene." The cultural-theoretical use of this term designates a process that enables its own performative approach to be reflexively (that is, visibly) observed and thus ultimately critiqued itself.[58] In the stage design of

---

57  See Michel Foucault, "What is Critique?," in Michel Foucault, *The Politics of Truth* (Los Angeles: Semiotext(e), 1997), pp. 41–81.

58  See Rüdiger Campe, "Die Schreibszene, Schreiben," in *Paradoxien, Dissonanzen, Zusammenbrüche: Situationen offener Epistemologie*, ed. Hans Ulrich Gumbrecht and Ludwig Pfeiffer (Frankfurt am Main: Suhrkamp, 1991), pp. 759–772; Gerhard Neumann, "Einleitung," in *Szenographien: Theatralität als Kategorie der Literaturwissenschaft*, ed. Caroline Pross et al. (Freiburg im Breisgau: Rombach, 2000), pp. 11–32; and Beate Söntgen, "Bild und Bühne: Das Interieur als Rahmen wahrer Darstellung," in *Räume des Subjekts um 1800: Zur imaginativen Selbstverortung zwischen Selbstaufklärung und Roman-*

**30**

classical theater, the Greek word *skēnē* designates not only the stage itself but also the changing room of the actors and thus the place where roles are changed.[59] Thus understood, every "scene" of critical (re-)presentation always reflects, beyond its formational and defining function, its "behind": that which predetermines it.[60] The notion of the "scene" therefore underscores the perforated nature of critique, which hints at the world "outside" of its conditions of (re-)presentation and thus becomes part of the critical process. That is to say, critique is not only "scenic" when it intervenes theatrically, for instance in an urban public sphere. Rather, its scenic nature is a structural feature of critique in general. Critique must, however tentatively, establish frameworks in order to define, categorize, and expose its field of interest, and regardless of the medium in which it operates, it always allows this framing process itself to come to light. With the concept of the scene, the productivity and inherent dynamics of critique can thus be understood as a performative and self-exhibiting phenomenon. Moreover, the concept of the scene allows critical (re-)presentations to become legible as "constellations,"[61] as configurations that bring together sets of problems and link them to a network of interpretations, speculations, connections, and to other scenes of critique.[62]

It is only by making its conditions and functions visible in "scenic" and historically as well as geographically

*tik*, ed. Rudolf Behrens and Jörm Steigerwald (Wiesbaden: Harrassowitz, 2010), pp. 53–72.

59  See Josef Früchtl and Jörg Zimmermann, "Ästhetik der Inszenierung: Dimensionen eines gesellschaftlichen, individuellen und kulturellen Phänomens," in Ästhetik der Inszenierung, ed. Josef Früchtl and Jörg Zimmermann (Frankfurt am Main: Suhrkamp, 2001), pp. 9–47.

60  See Bettine Menke, "On/Off," in *Auftreten: Wege auf die Bühne*, ed. Juliane Vogel and Christopher Wild (Berlin: Theater der Zeit, 2014), pp. 180–188.

61  See Benjamin, "The Concept of Art Criticism in German Romanticism"; and Sigrid Weigel, *Entstellte Ähnlichkeit: Walter Benjamins theoretische Schreibweise* (Frankfurt am Main: Fischer, 1997).

62  See Jacques Rancière, *Aisthesis: Scenes from the Aesthetic Regime of Art*, trans. Zakir Paul (London: Verso, 2013).

situated constellations that critique is able to have a generally valid and binding effect: as the venue of an ongoing and constantly renegotiated conflict that, in specific cases, can be situated in precise historical contexts, as is clear from the history of theater itself. In their contributions to this volume, which make use of Walter Benjamin's ideas in different ways, Bettine Menke and Mimmi Woisnitza demonstrate how early twentieth-century theater can be understood as a critical praxis. Menke focuses on gestural theater as a form of creating distance, as an *act* directed against the naturalistic confusion that something needs to be said in order to be critical—an act whose political relevance lies in the awareness that it is theater. This is because gesture refers all that is shown back to the act of showing; it is not a form of expression or a representation but rather a form-giving act and not a given form. And the scene is, in Menke's terms, not itself either, but rather the venue of a separation that invokes that which has been separated—the unseen spaces from which it has emerged—and reveals that what has been shown is incomplete and fragmentary.

Mimmi Woisnitza also reverts to Benjamin's notion of gestural theater in her revision of Erwin Piscator's scenography as critical practice. Even though Brecht himself refers to Piscator as an important initiator in the development of the epic theater, Benjamin disparages the "Zeittheater" (most often associated with Piscator) as mere political "plays of ideas." Benjamin thereby obliviates, Woisnitza argues, the radical intervention that Piscator's staging practices posed for conventional forms of theatrical presentation at the time. His early experiments with proletarian theater had in fact turned the stage into a podium which, according to Benjamin, provides the grounds for the advent of the epic theater. Further, Piscator's eventual introduction of media technology as a stage element does not merely represent his time's (primarily) technologically-conditioned problems; rather, it is driven by a dialectic between the showing and the being shown of these very technological mechanisms (and the human agents among them) as well as of the constructive means of structuring the stage space.

The contribution by Sebastian Kirsch refines the question of the form of the scene by examining the exterior spaces that, in a historical perspective, were constitutive for early twentieth-century theater and remain so today. A central element of Brecht's theater and Benjamin's theory was their claim that the constitutive exterior space of the stage was the street. In their focus on the milieu of the street, however, they neglect another exterior space, which Kirsch traces back to the origins of European drama in classical antiquity. Whereas, in classical drama, the protagonist entered the *proskēnion* from the *skēnē*, the chorus entered the *orchēstra* at the beginning of the theater festival from landscape surrounding the *polis*. The chorus functioned as a living memory of the ecological relations and environmental conditions that precede the actions of the protagonist without his knowledge. The chorus thus formulates a type of knowledge that allows the modern project of critique to be reconceptualized from an ecosophical perspective (in Guattari's terms)—a perspective that Birgit Kaiser and Kathrin Thiele also refer to in their chapter. Even though this book concludes with a discussion of a historically distant phenomenon, it nevertheless brings into focus the urgent issues of environmental knowledge and ecological relations that years ago had prompted Foucault to ask his famous question: "What Is Critique?"[63]

---

**63** Foucault, "What Is Critique?" As Kirsch's chapter on the ecosophical conditions of the chorus in classical antiquity shows, the questions posed in this volume are connected to recent reflections on "critique and the digital," which is the subject of another book in this series. So-called smart technologies, ubiquitous computing, and increasing surveillance have redefined how the modern project of critique can still claim validity in the face of rapidly changing environmental conditions in digital milieus. See Erich Hörl et al., eds., *Critique and the Digital* (Zurich: Diaphanes, 2020).

## Acknowledgments

*Critique: The Stakes of Form* began as part of the conference "Critical Stances," which the DFG research training group "Cultures of Critique" hosted at the Leuphana
University Lüneburg in July 2018. The book is part of
the series "Crititical Stances" and will be accompanied by two other books: *Critique and the Digital* and
*What's Legit? Critique of Law and Strategies of Rights*.
We thank all participants for their contributions and for
the engaged discussions.

Catharina Berents supported both the event and the
publications with invaluable commitment. Mimmi
Woisnitza kept the whole project from falling apart dur-
ing the final steps. We wish to thank Stephanie Braune,
Jasmin Camenzind, Jonas Ehret, Maximilian Gebhardt,
David Mielecke, and Niklas Roth for manifold support.
The translators, namely Angela Anderson, Gérard A.
Goodrow, Jason Kavett, Valentine A. Pakis, Sebastian
Truskolaski and Aaron Zielinski, worked patiently with
both authors and editors on multiple revisions. Cathe-
rine Lupton copy-edited this volume with care and dili-
gence. Our sincere gratitude goes to Michael Heitz from
Diaphanes for his confidence in the series and all his
efforts to ensure its timely release.

Finally, we would like to thank the German Research
Foundation (DFG) for the generous funding that facili-
tated the entire venture.

*Translated by Valentine A. Pakis*

# Form of Critique

Heiko Stubenrauch

# How to Do
# Materialistic Dialectics
# with Words?

## Adorno and the Resistance of Presentation

> "I am the flower, and the gardener as well,
> and am not solitary, in earth's cell."
> Osip Mandelstam, *What Shall I Do*
> *With This Body They Gave Me*

When Adorno makes the final remarks in his 1958 lectures on *An Introduction to Dialectics*, they come as a surprise. He does not dismiss his students with a summarizing definition of dialectics. On the contrary, in the last session of the semester things suddenly become practical. The theoretical problems that dialectics entail and that had been treated in the weeks prior to this session—the mediation of part and whole, of concept and object, universal and particular—seem to lead to one practical problem: the "problem of presentation."[1] Adorno proposes a thesis that is both simple and radical. Only the practical work of the presentation of a thought can lead to a progress of knowledge. For whether I am thinking dialectically or not can only be decided if I "offer a resistance to [my] concepts through the process of

1    Theodor W. Adorno, *An Introduction to Dialectics*, ed. Christoph Ziermann (Cambridge: Polity Press, 2017), p. 211.

37

presentation," because "it is only the process of presentation which allows thought to go beyond the merely pre-given character that a concept already brings with it."[2] If I, however, save myself the trouble of the arduous work of presentation, my thoughts can't evolve. Attaining knowledge through thinking alone—a dialectics in the head—seems to be impossible.[3] To explain why knowledge is essentially bound to the activity of presentation, Adorno paints a confusing yet fascinating picture. The most far-reaching external contradictions, he claims, infiltrate the subject as suffering. While this somatic and unconscious suffering is unable to communicate with conscious thought in contemplation, in the process of presentation it can express itself as a resistance to thought. Only once I confront my thought with this internal resistance in the process of writing, can I continue thinking about the external contradictions. Only if I leap the internal hurdles while presenting, can external borders be surpassed. This is the picture that I want to elaborate on. Habermas famously rejected Adorno's "ideal of presentation" as a "philosophical thinking [that] intentionally retrogresses to gesticulation."[4] In contrast, I will put forward an interpretation of presentation as the core of a philosophical praxis that intentionally progresses by opening up to bodily and unconscious aspects of subjectivity. Instead of turning away from dialectics towards communication or recognition,

**2**  Ibid.
**3**  In this regard, Adorno resembles Heinrich von Kleist. He, too, denies the ability of attaining knowledge through pure thinking by recommending dialogue as a method of externalizing thought. His treatise "On The Gradual Construction Of Thoughts During Speech" starts with the following words: "If there is something you want to know and cannot discover by meditation, then, my dear, ingenious friend, I advise you to discuss it with the first acquaintance whom you happen to meet." Heinrich von Kleist, "On the Gradual Construction of Thoughts During Speech," *German Life and Letters* 5:1 (October 1951): pp. 42–46.
**4**  Jürgen Habermas, *The Theory of Communicative Action. Volume 1. Reason and the Rationalization of Society* (Boston MA: Beacon Press, 1987), p. 385.

I will draft a contemporary conception of materialistic dialectics as a labor of presentation.

## Collective thought and individuating suffering

Time and again, Adorno depicts subjectivity as being peculiarly torn. Initially, he assumes that we participate in society by thinking in concepts and by talking with other people. Every member of a language community understands something similar when hearing or reading the words we are taught. Only thus can we communicate. Even if I think on my own, I am like everybody else in regard to conceptual thinking. Strictly speaking, the idea that I am an individual when I think or speak turns out to be an illusion. With Wittgenstein, Adorno denies the possibility of a private language. According to Adorno, "language itself—through its generality [*Allgemeinheit*] and objectivity [*Objektivität*]—already negates the whole man, the particular speaking individual subject: the first price exacted by language is the essence of the individual."[5] The social character of language is not per se a problem. Yet if I am living in a society that doesn't allow for a fulfilling life, then, according to Adorno, I end up in a torn condition: I suffer, and as a suffering, isolated body I drop out of society, whilst still belonging to it as a thinking person. When I think, I am, paradoxically, part of the exact society that suppresses me, that excludes me and that makes me suffer. I speak the language and think the thoughts of a society that forces my suffering body to take on the role of an isolated individual,[6] a role that I am denied as a speaking and thinking being. My bodily experiences and my

5   Theodor W. Adorno, *The Jargon of Authenticity* (Evanston IL: Northwestern University Press, 1973), p. 14.
6   Suffering, according to Adorno, throws the subject "back on himself." Theodor W. Adorno, *Aesthetic Theory*, ed. Robert Hullot-Kentor (London and New York: Continuum, 2002), p. 63.

conscious thoughts drift apart. In my thoughts—which necessarily are a part of society—I can neither understand my suffering, nor can I communicate it properly. In a certain way, my own thoughts justify and reproduce my misunderstood bodily suffering through this inability. Here we can start to grasp in what way the confrontation with inner resistance is, according to Adorno, of the utmost importance for resolving external contradictions. The contradiction between the universal (society) and the particular (the individual) enters the subject as suffering and stretches it apart, so that it is more and more torn between the pole of universal thought and particular body. Opposing this movement and reversing it is the task of materialistic-dialectical knowledge. Thought must not continue justifying and reproducing its own suffering. Even if my thought can't fully articulate my bodily suffering, it at least has to be disrupted by this suffering. Even if my thought—i.e. society's thought—can't fully express my suffering—i.e. that I am suffering in this society—suffering can indirectly signal that I am not thinking correctly of the things that cause the suffering, thus urging my thought to rethink. *I cannot speak adequately of my suffering, nor can I understand it adequately, but what I can do is to "lend a voice to suffering."*[7] Instead of continuing to think in the same way and thus justifying the subject's suffering, thought should—in the moments when suffering expresses itself through impulses— reverse itself: "without abandoning it, we can think against our thought." (the quote goes on as follows: "if it were possible to define dialectics, this would be a definition worth suggesting.")[8] The contradiction that has entered the subject becomes virulent once the subject validates the suffering indicative of this contradiction

---

**7**   Theodor W. Adorno, *Negative Dialectics* (London and New York: Routledge, 2004), p. 17.

**8**   Ibid., p. 141

as a resistance against his or her own thought. As a resistance against one's own thought, suffering induces a process of rethinking, leading to publicly advocating the product of that process and demanding a change. External contradiction produces inner resistance; inner change in thinking produces external change. I pass back my suffering to the society that once gave it to me. I become the scene of its self-reflection. But as the argument appears to answer many questions, it also poses many new questions. If the functioning of thought is bound to the condition of submitting oneself to the general rules of language, how is this exact thought able to think against its own thoughts without jeopardizing its very functioning? How can the subject, by remodeling his or her thought, diverge from society and convince it of a different kind of thought, especially when we conceive of thinking and speaking as being constitutively social and assume that there is no private use of language? Does the social nature of language not only exclude the direct speech of suffering but also the indirect lending-a-voice to suffering?

## The death of the author is the birth of the dialectical mode of writing

Adorno claims that the task of writing an essay necessarily starts with a humiliating discovery. First, one has to admit that one is hopelessly bound to society due to conceptual thought. For the time being, I am stuck with using concepts in the way society has taught me to. According to Adorno, defining concepts and asserting that I mean one thing when I use one concept and another thing when I use a different concept, is just the pretense of a sovereignty in my use of language that, in fact, does not exist. The essay explicitly shows this, because it "introduces concepts unceremoniously, 'immediately', just as it receives them."[9] In an essay, I use concepts in the way anyone uses concepts. Yet the essay doesn't stop here. *For Adorno, the death of the author is the birth of a dialectical mode of writing.* Since I use the personal humiliation as an explicit starting-point, I can revolt against it throughout the course of the essay. "The essay starts with these meanings, and, being essentially language itself, takes them farther."[10] I take language as being universal and social, but I realize that I am presenting the object of practice that makes me suffer as an individual. I try to give my bodily affects, my unconscious suffering and my somatic impulses a chance to express themselves as resistance against the common conception of the object or the practice (to which I am attached with my thought and my language) within the process of presentation. I start with a common conception, yet I alter it throughout the process of presentation along the lines of the resistances and impulses that express themselves along the way. I don't use language only to argue, when I present something and struggle against the universal use of language. For through the mode of logical argumentation, I only interpret or unify thought in its existing form. I illustrate the consequences of the already-known and its internal contradictions in order to sublate them. The resistances that oppose my thoughts in the process of presentation, however, are no mere logical contradictions within the already-known; they are, if they are to be declared contradictions at all, contradictions between the already-known and the bodily impulses of suffering that oppose the already-known. When my presentation thus strives for an alteration of thought, it cannot prove its point by pure reasoning. Rather, I have to invoke *rhetorical* instruments. By presenting suffering, I have to, in a way,

---

**9**  Theodor W. Adorno, *Notes To Literature, Volume One*, ed. Rolf Tiedemann (New York: Columbia University Press, 1991), p. 12.
**10**  Ibid.

*persuade* my thought to defer and alter meanings and assume a new form that is proper to the object *and* the suffering that is its result. According to Adorno, it is only through rhetoric that presentation differs from the communication of "contents already known and fixed."[11] Therefore, both to me as the writer and to those who read the essay, one thing holds true: Neither the logical form of judgement, nor the compliance of a judgement with criteria previously stated by epistemology is sufficient, but the "fulfilling concurrence in the judgement in which we understand something is the same as a decision about True or False."[12]

Adorno thus gives us two important reasons to explain why the resistances evoked by suffering only communicate with thought in the process of presentation, and why the dialectical mediation of universal and particular occurs in the rhetorical labor of presentation. By forcing me to externalize my thoughts, the process of writing a text creates something that is opposite to my bodily and my unconscious affects, and against which they can rebel. When they are written down, my thoughts can become a target, which they cannot be as long as they're in my head. The text, in contrast, gives a beginning and an end to my thoughts, thus not only externalizing them, but also setting them in a temporality. Only then can my thinking be transformed by the resistances evoked by suffering without losing itself. In writing, my thought is able to change without becoming incomprehensible. Every transformation takes place between beginning and end. Despite semantic shifts and splits, the unity of the text prevails. Kant used the unity of consciousness as epistemological foundation and thus excluded every unconscious aspect from knowledge. Adorno expands the unity of consciousness by introducing the unity of text as a medium in which

11  Adorno, *Negative Dialectics*, p. 55.
12  Ibid., p. 64.

the conscious subject can learn from its unconscious impulses and evolve alongside the unconscious expressions of suffering.[13] He also suggests that Hegel's idealistic dialectics is bound to the unity of consciousness too strongly and therefore isn't seriously externalized in the text. It silences unconscious suffering, because it dreads the effort of presentation.[14]

## Capability of differentiation or rage against difference

In his work, Adorno talks about two different, almost opposite ways of dealing with suffering. I can either turn away from the suffering, turning it into a "rage against difference,"[15] or I turn towards it, turning it into the capability of differentiating. The first way of dealing with suffering can be depicted as follows: When I am not able to recognize my own weaknesses, and tend to repress my suffering because of a fear of losing control, I distance myself from it and, at the same time, from everything that is incomprehensible, strange, different and natural in myself. One of the central theses in Adorno's philosophy—that he already advocated in the *Dialectic of Enlightenment*—is that distancing myself from unpleasant aspects within myself might be possible, but that this internal distance cannot be separated from an external distance. Denying difference internally is necessarily accompanied by an anger towards that which

13  Reacting to Wittgenstein's argument of private language, Adorno could answer: Whereof one cannot speak thereof one must write. Using Adorno, Kant's theory of schematism could be expanded similarly: What one cannot schematize, thereof one must write, as well.

14  Adorno, *Negative Dialectics*, p. 163. On the relation between Hegelian idealistic dialectics and Adorno's negative dialectics see also Marc Nicholas Sommer, *Das Konzept einer negativen Dialektik* (Tübingen: Mohr Siebeck, 2016).

15  Max Horkheimer and Theodor W. Adorno, *Dialectic of Enlightenment* (Stanford CA: Stanford University Press, 2002), p. 172.

is different and strange in the external world. The fear of dealing with that which is different in myself causes a fear of dealing with that which is different on the outside. Theoretically, the anger towards difference is at work in the thought of identity that only perceives that which it already knows and denies the existence of the unknown. According to Adorno, the anger towards difference became practical in the anti-Semitism of the Nazis, who not only denied the existence of difference, but wanted to eradicate it. "It is not just the anti-Semitic ticket which is anti-Semitic, but the ticket mentality itself. The rage against difference which is teleologically inherent in that mentality as the rancor of the dominated subjects of the domination of nature is always ready to attack the natural minority, even though it is the social minority which those subjects primarily threaten."[16] The other way of dealing with one's suffering counters the anger towards difference by differentiating within the process of presentation. When I don't shy away from my suffering, but actually turn towards it, suffering can specify my presentation of the object or practice that evokes it. In this case, suffering creates differentiation instead of denying difference.[17] This is what Adorno implies in the *Minima Moralia* (which is an example of the labor of presentation itself), when he states: "The splinter in your eye is the best magnifying-glass."[18] At the beginning of a text, the existence of unrecognized suffering implies that the universal conception of a practice that creates suffering is *superficial*,

---

16 Ibid.
17 In this respect I disagree with Joel Whitebook, who claims that Adorno gave up the idea of a remembrance of nature within the subject [*Eingedenken der Natur im Subjekt*] after the publication of the *Dialectic of Enlightenment*. Joel Whitebook, *Der gefesselte Odysseus: Studien zur Kritischen Theorie und Psychoanalyse* (Frankfurt am Main: Campus, 2007), p. 39. In my reading, it is this very idea that Adorno takes up and specifies in his thoughts on presentation.
18 Theodor W. Adorno, *Minima Moralia: Reflections on a Damaged Life* (London and New York: Verso, 2005), p. 50.

for the simple reason that it creates suffering whilst not admitting to it. Accordingly, suffering tries to *deepen* our understanding of the universal conception the text starts with. Throughout the text, I try to historicize the concept of an object or a practice from the perspective of suffering, reconstructing it in another context, examining it in relationship to society, associating it with different aspects or theories, until my conception of the presented practice has changed and my suffering is temporarily appeased. "The author's impulses are extinguished in the objective substance they seize hold of."[19] It is yet again the essay as a textual form that can, according to Adorno, achieve this task: "The essay's differentiatedness is not something added to it but its medium."[20]

### Presentation and psychoanalysis

For Freud, the therapeutic situation consists of two people and two activities. On the one hand, there is the analysand, whose task it is to associate freely. Freud points out that his or her speech only *seems* to be senseless, irrelevant and obscene. In fact, the technique of free association reveals unconscious material. The process of free association deceives consciousness. Consciousness, which usually doesn't allow for unconscious and repressed thoughts to be uttered, is opened up. On the other hand, there is the analyst. His or her task is to interpret speech and discover unconscious thoughts hidden in plain sight. The unconscious and repressed thoughts appear whilst the analysand associates freely, and the analyst tries to extrapolate the causes of the repression in order to animate the healing process of the analysand. If there is a conflict between an individ-

**19** Adorno, *Notes to Literature*, p. 4.
**20** Ibid., p. 15.

ual drive and the collective moral demands, the analyst can bring this conflict to consciousness by his or her interpretation, thus enabling the analysand to alter his or her drive-aim [*Triebziel*]. For if the new drive-aim is not in conflict with the collective demands, the individual doesn't have to repress this particular drive. As a consequence, the suffering caused by repression is alleviated. In psychoanalysis, the analysand turns to his or her unconscious suffering by confiding in the analyst instead of turning his or her suffering into "rage against difference." Obviously, Adorno's model is informed by Freud's approach of presenting repressed thoughts in a process of interpretation. Yet Adorno's model is different from Freud's model in two very important aspects. Firstly, to Adorno I am both analysand and analyst. I utter my suffering whilst interpreting it. It is me who tricks my consciousness, when I expose my thoughts to the resistance of presentation to confront them with my unconscious suffering in my writing. It is also me who interprets this suffering by using its impulses to alter my conception of the object or of the practice that is its cause. The nature of the interpretation points towards the second difference. While Adorno agrees with Freud when he thinks that the conflict between individual drives and social demands adequately describes the cause of many forms of suffering, and that the transformation of this relationship is key to healing, he nevertheless resolves this relationship in a different way. The disintegration of individual needs and social reality, to Adorno, is a problem for which we have to formulate collective, not individual, solutions. In light of a conflict between drive and society, he accuses Freud of doing nothing but to advocate individual adjustment: "the subsequent absence of conflicts reflects a predetermined outcome, the a priori triumph of collective authority, not a cure effected by knowledge."[21] While psychoanalysis solves

21  Adorno, *Minima Moralia*, p. 59.

**47**

the conflict between drive and society by transforming the individual drive, Adorno advocates a social change to resolve this conflict. In light of suffering, I don't interpret the structure of drives and needs in order to adjust the individual according to collective conditions and norms, but I criticize society by interpreting it. In doing this I compel society to transform into a collective that's not in conflict with the individual and that allows for a collective life that is compatible with the individual drive. It is therefore only one person who does the therapeutic labor of presentation, whereas two people are involved in the psychoanalytic cure. Yet the goal is to open up this cure to everyone, by introducing suffering to a social process of self-reflection. In the process of presentation, I psychoanalyze myself while transforming psychoanalysis into a critique of society.

## Labor and labor of presentation

Where has my presentation of dialectics led to? I want to illustrate the result by highlighting the differences from Habermas. Having read the *Negative Dialectics*, he turns away from dialectical philosophy and introduces a *paradigm shift to communication*. Habermas wrongfully interprets Adorno's insistence on those contents of experience that can't be submitted to thought, and the subsequent impossibility of a dialectics in the head, as an impossibility of dialectics in general. Negative dialectics are thus, according to Habermas, nothing more than a dispirited exercise which displays the ambitions of dialectical knowledge "in their unworkability."[22] The concept of the nonidentical therefore would express an unattainable aspiration for truth and the failure of dialectics, consequently surrendering all cognitive competence to art: "In reflecting dialectical thought

---

[22] Habermas, *Theory of Communicative Action*, p. 373.

once more, it exhibits what we can only catch sight of in this way: the aporetic nature of the concept of the nonidentical."[23] Since I've interpreted negative dialectics as a labor of presentation, we can now see that Habermas wastes the potential of assuming a contemporary position in dialectics. It is true that the concept of the nonidentical refers to a limitation of thought by that which is not thought, and which therefore has the authority to object against the idealistic dialectics of Hegel that won't accept this limitation. Yet negative dialectics is no concession of dialectical thought's failure in general. Rather, it is only the reference to the nonidentical that allows for a conception of dialectical cognition as the *process of mediation between conscious-identical experience and unconscious-nonidentical impulses of suffering*.[24] This mediation takes place in the activity of presentation. Dialectical knowledge becomes practical, not impossible. When Adorno claims that the "freedom of philosophy is nothing but the capacity to lend a voice to its unfreedom,"[25] this capacity shouldn't be understood as defeatist or ironic, but as political. If negative dialectics were to lead to irony, Habermas's turn towards the paradigm of communication theory would be very understandable. In fact, he only vindicates the unconscious and misunderstood suffering that is lent a voice by negative dialectics and that is bound to fall silent under the paradigm of communication theory. By misjudging Adorno's relationship to Hegel, Habermas also misjudges his relationship to Marx and thus the political dimension of his theory. Negative dialectics mustn't be, as proposed by Habermas, understood as "renouncing

23  Ibid., p. 385.
24  Oftentimes Adorno's descriptions of the unconscious-nonidentical impulses of suffering remain vague. His characterizations seem to differ between preconscious impulses and unconscious symptoms. In order to further pursue a reading of negative dialectics as a labor of presentation, it would be important to clarify Adorno's notion of suffering.
25  Adorno, *Negative Dialectics*, p. 18.

the goal of theoretical knowledge, and thus [...] renouncing that program of 'interdisciplinary materialism' in whose name critical theory of society was once launched in the early thirties."[26] It is much rather a supplement to this program. Adorno does not turn away to depoliticized aesthetics. Instead, he expands a certain reading of Marxism by adding a moment of subjective critique that contains an aesthetic component because it proceeds in the medium of presentation. This is his response to a lack in Marx's theory he calls a "metaphysics of the forces of production"[27] and that he holds responsible for the "authoritarian perversions"[28] of real socialism. He calls upon us to challenge the relationship between productive forces and relations of production that was postulated by (early) Marx and reinforced by Engels. He warns us not to see a necessary connection between labor and technological progress on the one hand and social emancipation on the other. Adorno believes that it is both metaphysical and dangerous to think that the productive forces necessarily and all by themselves will one day uncover and collapse the inequalities of the relations of production, once they are an impediment to a progressing productivity. The belief in a necessary connection of these two he regards as being a relic of a Hegelian metaphysics of spirit that sneaked into Marx's theory and became a gateway to authoritarian tendencies:

This metaphysics of the forces of production is reminiscent of the Hegelian World Spirit and leads ultimately to the persistence in Marx of a highly dubious theorem of German idealism. We find it explicitly stated, above all by Engels in the Anti-Dühring. This is the assertion that freedom really amounts to doing consciously what is neces-

**26**  Habermas, *Theory of Communicative Action*, p. 385.
**27**  Theodor W. Adorno, *Lectures on Negative Dialectics*, ed. Rolf Tiedemann (Cambridge MA: Polity Press, 2008), p. 96.
**28**  Ibid., p. 97.

sary, something that is of course meaningful only if what is necessary, the World Spirit, the development of the forces of production is in the right a priori and its victory is guaranteed.[29]

To Adorno, the belief in productive forces that necessarily are emancipatory not only makes the case for the repression of the individual by the party as the medium that manages this automatic progress, but also leads to a blind belief in technology. This is where the labor of presentation enters the stage. It takes the place that opens up after rejecting these wrong beliefs, for if the metaphysical junction of unleashed productive forces and emancipation is dissolved, the junction can only be guaranteed by subjective critique. While social progress can neither be separated from labor nor from technological progress, we nevertheless need a moment of subjective critique in order to steer this progress and prevent repressive tendencies. "Productions that avoid it [the subject], that effectively want to make themselves technically autonomous, are obliged to correct themselves by way of the subject."[30] By appropriating Freud's psychoanalysis and using it as an instrument of social critique, Adorno responds to the torn connection between unleashing the productive forces and emancipating the relations of production. The unconscious and bodily suffering expresses those repressive tendencies that, against every "optimism about the forces of production,"[31] have not led to an emancipation of the relations of production, but to the stabilization of the unfree relations of production. In bringing suffering to a presentation, critique reflects upon the question of why and how the given relations of production prevent the emancipatory potential of the forces of production: "the spontaneity of the subject,"

**29**  Ibid., pp. 96–97.
**30**  Adorno, *Aesthetic Theory*, p. 42.
**31**  Adorno, *Lectures on Negative Dialectics*, p. 96.

**51**

Adorno claims, becomes "a *movens* of the objective dialectics of productive forces and conditions."[32] Adorno's
remodeling of Freudian therapy work into the critical
labor of presentation turns out to be an extension to
Marxian theory: If I lend a voice to suffering in the process of presentation and search for the reason for this
suffering in society (instead of letting it turn into rage
against difference), I search for it in the relations of production which prevent the emancipatory potentials of
the forces of production from unfolding. Labor thus has
to be accompanied by the labor of presentation, which
reflects and corrects the development of labor within
the relations of production. They depend upon each
other: labor, in this reading of Adorno, is blind without
the labor of presentation and its critical capacity, and
the labor of presentation is empty without labor and the
actual change it brings about.

*Translated by Aaron Zielinski*

---

32   Adorno, *Negative Dialectics*, p. 205.

Eva Geulen

# Expression and Suffering; Semblance and Mimesis

## (Notes on an Enigmatic Passage in Adorno's *Aesthetic Theory*)*

Since Rousseau, the following has held true: whoever does not suffer from culture does not have any. Those who do not want to know anything about the price of cultural accomplishments are philistines; those whose praise for culture does not also demonstrate their awareness of what Simmel conceptualized as the *tragedy of culture*[1] are barbarians. "There is no document of culture which is not at the same time a document of barbarism,"[2] Benjamin states categorically. After Rousseau, modernity fostered more than a mere sense of discontent concerning culture. Over time, it developed a veritable culture of suffering *from* culture, and hence a second order of culture and a second order of suffering. This culture of suffering, which belongs to those who suffer from culture, is no less essential to the reflection on culture than the demarcation of one's respective culture from the very *non* or *un*-cultures that those barbarians, philistines and other

---

*   This article has been published in a different version in German as "Leid-Kultur vs. Mimesis bei Adorno," in: *Spielräume: Ein Buch für Jürgen Fohrmann*, ed. Jürgen Brokoff, Elke Dubbels and Andrea Schütte (Bielefeld: Aisthesis, 2013), pp. 155–167.
1   Compare Georg Simmel, "The Concept and Tragedy of Culture," in *Simmel on Culture: Selected Writings*, ed. David Frisby and Mike Featherstone (London: Sage, 1997), pp. 55–74.
2   Walter Benjamin, "On the Concept of History," in Walter Benjamin, *Selected Writings, vol. 4: 1938–1940*, ed. Howard Eiland and Michael W. Jennings (Cambridge MA: Belknap Press of Harvard University Press, 2003), p. 392.

savages call home. Since Herder, these *non* or *un*-cultures have readily ignited phantasms of redemption because they could—and, indeed, had to—represent a freedom from suffering that was, for the tormented creators of culture, promised land and taboo in equal measure.

After Rousseau, it was especially Schiller who proved to be formative for the style of the culture of suffering [*Leidkultur*]. In his fifth letter *On the Aesthetic Education of Man*, he succinctly captured the co-evolution of culture and suffering: "Culture, far from setting us free, develops in every capacity with which we are cultivated merely a new need."[3] Schiller had already abandoned the pious belief in a culture—that of the ancient Greeks—which was still tied up with nature to such a degree that it was supposed to have escaped this aporia. The old ones may have been happier, but they certainly did not have culture—not least because they did not have Kant. Accordingly, Classicism was not really an option. "The critical path alone is still open";[4] although it is unclear whether this path really leads through a backdoor to some forgotten, forbidden paradise. After Schiller, and for the time being, one has to settle for a transitory aesthetic condition—albeit one that is pointedly free from suffering—in which the experience of freedom offered means, in the best case, an anticipation of a better future, and, in the worst case, its substitution. However, art—which, in Schiller, is still understood to be ambiguously therapeutic—cannot withstand the burden of suffering [*Leidensdruck*] in the culture of suffering [*Leidkultur*]. Art quickly becomes the latter's advocate—"[f]or beauty is nothing but the beginning of terror."[5] At no point in aesthetic theory since Baudelaire

3   Friedrich Schiller, *On the Aesthetic Education of Man* (London: Penguin, 2016), pp. 15–16.
4   Immanuel Kant, *Critique of Pure Reason* (Cambridge: Cambridge University Press, 1998), p. 704.
5   Rainer Maria Rilke, *Duino Elegies* (Berkeley: University of California Press, 1961), p. 3.

and after Schopenhauer has the constitutive connection between art and suffering been subjected to closer scrutiny than in Adorno.

Initially, however—after Schopenhauer and before Adorno—Nietzsche put an end to the ancients' nature-culture, and thus, as it were, significantly advanced the modern culture of suffering. According to Nietzsche, Attic tragedy was already born from the spirit of suffering. That is, the Greeks *required* tragedy in order to bear their disgust *at*/suffering *from* life [*Lebensekel*/*Lebensleid*]. This marks a caesura in the history of Western cultural theories. After Nietzsche, they can be split up into ideal types: into those which, like Christianity and Rousseau, trace the beginnings of culture to an expulsion from paradise and nature, in line with theories of decadence; and those which view culture as a measure for managing suffering, and are willing to accept collateral damage, in keeping with theories of compensation. Where wood is chopped, splinters must fall. These two models rarely appear in their pure form. Even in Nietzsche they present themselves as compatible variants. Moreover, and as a side-note, Nietzsche—as the father of decadence and aestheticism—promotes the artistocratization of the aptitude for suffering [*Leidensbefähigung*]. In this way, he draws a line, inter-culturally, between those suffering in a cultivated manner and those of whom Gottfried Benn would assert: "to be stupid and have work: [/] that is happiness."[6] The sentimentalist boundary between the pre-cultural Greeks—or, rather, between savages and cultivated peoples—now also runs through this culture itself: between cultural philistines, who are free from suffering, and the suffering carriers of culture. This motif persisted over the course of further differentiation. In Adorno, for instance, the mindless consumers of

6   Gottfried Benn, "Eure Etüden," in Gottfried Benn, *Sämtliche Werke, vol. 1: Gedichte 1*, ed. Gerhard Schuster (Stuttgart: Klett-Cotta, 1986), p. 292.

the culture industry are, for the most part, irreconcilably opposed to highly sensitive artists, even if—under these dire circumstances—the latter are inevitably capable of suffering more eloquently than the former.

Fundamentally, however, the ideal-typical distinction between theorists of decadence and theorists of compensation is thwarted by an altogether different factor. All suffering from culture shares a decisive trait in common with the overcoming of suffering *qua* culture, namely: the creation of distance. This is evident in the case of overcoming suffering through culture. But whoever suffers *in the horizon of culture*,[7] as Oelmüller once put it, has already begun to overcome his or her suffering by dint of this horizon, and by dint of designating culture thus. Given that this is the case, one might ask—heretically—whether it is even possible to suffer *in* or *from* culture, since the very articulation of any suffering in the course of treating it means its instrumentalization and presentation. Unproductive, mute suffering thus tends to be betrayed in the name of an inflated cult of expression. As Adorno knew, the fact "[t]hat it is spoken, that distance is thus won from the trapped immediacy of suffering, transforms suffering just as screaming diminishes unbearable pain."[8] But he also made clear that the sheer, immediate expression of suffering "tends toward mendacity, regardless of any aesthetic manipulation," because the latent trust that inheres in it—"by being spoken or screamed all will be made better"—represents "a rudiment of magic" (*AT* 117). Accordingly, the immediate expression of suffering is deemed to be pre-culturally archaic. It would be possible to systematically unfold the dialectical drama of aesthetic expres-

7   Compare Willi Oelmüller and Ruth Dölle-Oelmüller, *Grundkurs Philosophische Anthropologie* (Munich: Fink, 1996), p. 20, pp. 36–49. See also Willi Oelmüller, "Philosophische Antwortversuche angesichts des Leidens," in *Theodizee – Gott vor Gericht?*, ed. Willi Oelmüller (Munich: Fink, 1990), pp. 67–86.

8   Theodor W. Adorno, *Aesthetic Theory* (London and New York: Continuum, 2002), p. 117. (Hereafter cited as *AT*).

sion—and, more generally, of art—in Adorno, using this quotation as a point of departure. This drama concerns the expression of suffering [*Leidensausdruck*] as alleviation [*Leidenslinderung*] on the one hand, and on the other as a double, simultaneous, betrayal: of culture and of the suffering it causes. In a brief essay, titled "Experience of Suffering as Truth Condition" [*Leiderfahrung als Wahrheitsbedingung*], Norbert Bolz described the precariously paradoxical foundations of art, in Adorno, as follows: "the fact that art must not exist in the face of societal suffering, namely as transigent semblance, and yet must exist, namely as the only faithful expression of privation, determines its philosophico-historical place."[9] The *theologoumena* associated with this interpretation have been thoroughly investigated by now.

But the matter points back beyond Christianity. An age-old, magically mimetic *ur*-impulse asserts itself in the logic of subsumption, which is crude when compared with the Christian belief in miracles, and which Adorno and Horkheimer treat through the ambiguous notion of sacrifice in *Dialectic of Enlightenment*: suffering frees from suffering. It is good if we have suffered. For Adorno, Hegel's account of art as the "consciousness of plight" (*AT* 18) is ultimately justified, notwithstanding Adorno's critique of semblance and lies; the reason being that this archaic impulse survives in art in a manner that must of necessity remain alien to discursive modes of thinking and presentation, including philosophy (and not only the systematic kind). These modes deny their magical inheritance, on which the experience of the beautiful feeds, because it survives—and is remembered—herein alone. It is not necessarily good if we have suffered, but it is good under certain circumstances: art. This connection marks the starting point for what

9   Norbert Bolz, "Leiderfahrung als Wahrheitsbedingung," in *Leiden (Kolloquium Religion und Philosophie, vol. 3)*, ed. Willi Oelmüller (Paderborn: Schöningh, 1986), pp. 9–19, here pp. 15–16.

Adorno calls the "mournfulness of art" (compare *AT* 28), which is continued in the commonly cited shame of art as an "uncommitted crime."[10] For my purposes, the shift I have alluded to is significant: from the primacy of suffering, which Peter Sloterdijk did not hesitate to cynically call Adorno's "pain *a priori*,"[11] to the function of art as the cultural memory of a magical mimesis that has become homeless. Of course, mimesis is connected to anguish and suffering [*Leid und Leiden*] in myriad ways; but the question nonetheless arises as to whether suffering is Adorno's first and final word. Overstating matters, what I am getting at is the following: for Adorno, it is not pain which justifies art and its expression; rather it is art *as mimesis* which justifies pain *a posteriori*.

In what follows, I want to try and illustrate this in three stages or steps: First, it is worth briefly calling to mind the primal scene of art's cultivated, painful [*leidvoll*] enjoyment, as it is unfolded in the excursus on the Odyssey in *Dialectic of Enlightenment*. Second, I will attempt to determine the manner in which the basic model thus presented is modified and supplemented using the passages at the end of the excursus, which treat the death of the maids. Third, I will attempt to verify whether the resultant thesis concerning a primacy of mimesis over suffering also plays a systematic role in *Aesthetic Theory*, using some select examples. That is to say, I want to explore the entwinement of two motifs that have attracted considerable attention in Adorno studies, but which have rarely been brought to bear on one another, and which have—even less often—been treated as possible alternatives, namely the theorem of suffering [*Leid-Theorem*], and the problem of mimesis.

---

10 Theodor W. Adorno, *Minima Moralia: Reflections from Damaged Life* (London: Verso, 2020), p. 118.
11 Compare Peter Sloterdijk, *Critique of Cynical Reason* (Minneapolis: University of Minnesota Press, 1988), p. xxxvi.

(1) Odysseus' encounter with the Sirens is interpreted on two occasions in *Dialectic of Enlightenment*. First, in the chapter "The Concept of Enlightenment," and second, in the first excursus, titled "Odysseus or Myth and Enlightenment." The first presentation does not, initially, concern the primal scene of art as stemming from the division of labor and exploitation, as something that is practically without consequence and that, hence, induces an enjoyment suffused with suffering. Rather, it foregrounds the relation of the burgeoning subject to time. The first principle learnt by Odysseus, of whom it is said that he matured through suffering, is the tripartite division of time. He protects himself from the supremacy of the past by "banishing the latter beyond the absolute boundary of the irrecoverable and placing it, as usable knowledge, in the service of the present."[12] This marks the genesis of his famous cunning. Even though, in this context, the interpretation of the Sirens' irresistible attraction, as yet, does not posit any connection to art, the authors nonetheless put forward a surprising claim in the form of another phrase that follows immediately. It proclaims that, in the end, it is only art that satisfies "[t]he urge to rescue the past as something living" (*DE* 25). Art is called upon as the spell with which to counter rationalization. Thus, it is bound to the past; not as a repository of dead knowledge, which— by dint of its deadness—is practically available at any time, but rather as remembrance [*Eingedenken*], which keeps what is passed alive and rescues what is living beyond the tripartite division of time: a division, which, henceforth, is binding. As yet, the Sirens guard this past. They know "all that has ever happened on this fruitful earth." (Ibid.) At the time when Odysseus passes by these primordial monsters, their song "has not yet been

---

12 Max Horkheimer and Theodor W. Adorno, *Dialectic of Enlighten-ment* (Stanford CA: Stanford University Press, 2002), p. 25. (Hereafter cited as *DE*).

deprived of power as art." (Ibid.) It is only his double act of cunning, the deafening of his oarsmen and having himself bound to the mast, which transforms the Sirens' song into art: "The bonds by which he has irrevocably fettered himself to praxis at the same time keep the Sirens at a distance from praxis [...] In this way the enjoyment of art and manual work diverge as the primeval world is left behind" (*DE* 27). There is no further discussion of the wholly positive, indeed emphatic, relation between art and the past in the subsequent course of the argument.

The second interpretation, in the Odysseus excursus, reads the episode with the Sirens according to a contractual logic. The right of the past, for which all of the mythological figures in the Odyssey stand, is not abolished; rather, it is defused through a gap in the contract, for the right of the mythical figures, conceived of as the right of those who are stronger, lives exclusively from the unfulfillability of their contract. In the case of the Sirens, this contract does not preclude one from listening captivatedly to their song. There is only one sentence in which this contractual interpretation finds entry into aesthetic theory: "Since the happily hapless meeting of Odysseus with the Sirens all songs have ailed; the whole of western music suffers from the absurdity of song in civilization, yet the motive force of all art-music is song" (*DE* 47). If the first interpretation was of sociological provenance, concerning the social praxis of art, then the second ends with the theorem summarized by Bolz, which he locates at the basis of Adorno's aesthetic theory. Here too, there is no trace, until the end of the excursus, of an art which would not only stir up a sense of longing in the passer-by, but which would, rather, be an instance of fulfillment; an instance that would actually satisfy the urge to rescue what has passed as something living.

(2) This changes at the point where, late in their deliberations, the authors leave the allegorizing interpretative schema of burgeoning rationality in order to turn to the Odyssey as a linguistic artwork. As Adorno and Horkheimer show, the Odyssey does not dispense with the primeval world, whose downfall it demonstrates and carries out. The hero is no less bloodthirsty than the forces of the primeval world that he cunningly defeats. On the contrary, "[t]he vengeance wreaked by civilization on the primeval world has been terrible" (*DE* 61); what principally bears witness to this, aside from the mutilation of Melanthios, the goatherd, is the account of the gruesome death of the unfaithful maids on Ithaca. But in the instance of narration, the circle of violence and suffering is suspended at certain points. According to Adorno and Horkheimer, the dreadfully indifferent portrayal of the dying women is followed by "a statement reporting that 'For a little while their feet kicked out, but not for very long' [...] Homer comforts himself and his listeners, who are really readers, with the certified observation that the kicking did not last long" (*DE* 61–62). Yet it is this dwelling on the detail that the death of the maids cannot have taken long which forms a deferring caesura. It can be compared to the appeal of the expressionless, which, Benjamin believed, resounded in the utterance about the star that went over the heads of the lovers in Goethe's *Elective Affinities*.[13] The references to remembrance [*Eingedenken*] in this passage clearly point to Benjamin.

In being brought to a standstill, the report is prevented from forgetting the victims of the execution and lays bare the unspeakably endless torment of the single second in which the maids fought against death. [...] But in the

13   Compare Walter Benjamin, "Goethe's Elective Affinities," in Walter Benjamin, *Selected Writings, vol. 1: 1913–1926*, ed. Marcus Bullock and Michael W. Jennings (Cambridge MA: Belknap Press of Harvard University Press, 2004), pp. 297–360.

report of the infamous deed, hope lies in the fact that it is long past. Over the raveled skein of prehistory, barbarism, and culture, Homer passes the soothing hand of remembrance, bringing the solace of "once upon a time." (*DE* 62)

As a story, and *qua* caesura, the artwork holds on to what has passed as a speech on what is past. If the maids have suffered, it is good; not: it is good because, or after, they have *suffered*. It is not good because the Odyssey is a beautiful work of art, but rather when, and because, they *have* suffered. The caesura lends expression to the "endless torment of the single second," but, through what is said, this expression is interrupted by the logic of semblance. It consolingly claims that what will have been an eternity for any mortal will not have taken long. The narrator who speaks thus does not know nearly as much as the Sirens knew; but he knows how to give a past to suffering, which rescues it as something living. The authors permit themselves such an interpretation without ifs and buts. It is as free from dialectics as the sentence, in the first excursus, on art as the guardian of remembrance [*Eingedenken*] of a bygone, primeval period before the tripartite division of time.

Yet it is not art *per se* which is empowered here, but rather prosaic, narrative speech—it is only in the form of the novel that the epic is transformed into a fairy tale, as the final line of the excursus proclaims. It stands in contrast to the "mythical song" (*DE* 61) of the Sirens and to the diseased songs of art music. Against the appearance of a primacy of music as the epitome of art as such in *Dialectic of Enlightenment*, the privilege of prose returns in *Aesthetic Theory* as a theorem about the language-like character of all artworks. To conclude, I want to examine the status of the dialectic of expression and mimesis this entails with reference to a specific passage.

(3) As Adorno explains, both semblance/mimesis and expression/suffering are part of every (successful) artwork. Expression is "the suffering countenance of art-

works," (*AT* 111) which is strictly opposed to the semblance of beauty. Since, consequently, expression and semblance are "antithetical," they are dialecticized to the utmost in their substitutability (*AT* 110). From the start, expression has been on the side of dissonance. Dissonant expression belies semblance: In the case of the Homeric passage involving the maids as the disrupting caesura; in the other example as the narrator's assurance that the torment did not last long. At the same time, semblance has, for its part, stemmed from the mimetic comportment's primal stirring. "[S]ince the mimetic taboo," (ibid.) art appeared on the scene as the executor of this mimetic comportment's will, as Adorno frequently writes. In the work of art, Adorno claims, expression draws "demarcation lines against semblance." (Ibid.) Moreover, Adorno explicitly ascribes semblance and mimesis to "form in the broadest sense." (Ibid.) Thus, mimesis does not mean that in art which imitates or is imitated; rather, it means its ability to make itself similar in the medium of form. In turn, there follows a sentence that radically transforms and displaces the relation of aesthetic oppositions between (immediate) expression and form-generated semblance or mimesis. It is somewhat complicated:

> The unfolding of art is that of a quid pro quo: Expression, through which nonaesthetic experience [i.e. the living, E.G.] reaches most deeply into the work, becomes the archetype of everything fictive in art, as if at the juncture where art is most permeable to real experience culture most rigorously stood guard that the border not be violated. (*AT* 110–111)

*Quid pro quo* names a substitution: within this logic of substitution, the semblance that is familiar to expression becomes a primal image—a prototype, a model—of the fictive, i.e. of semblance itself. Expression (of extra-aesthetic life, which, for Adorno—here and elsewhere—

is identical with suffering), as it were, lends its traits to the problematic semblance (of the inner-aesthetic harmony of a formal framework). So far, so good. However, the following line is utterly enigmatic: "as if at the juncture where art is most permeable to real experience culture most rigorously stood guard that the border not be violated." (*AT* 111) The frontier that is guarded by culture, not art, can only be that frontier which separates the sphere of external life—and, hence, suffering—which has seeped into the artwork as expression, from the mimetic moment of inner-aesthetic semblance. More succinctly: it is culture that insists on the difference between life and art. However, art does not oppose this difference with an identity that is secretly given or longed for in a utopian fashion. It does not oppose it with the anticipation [*Vorschein*] of something better, but rather with the age-old logic of *quid pro quo*. Expression insinuates itself into the workings of mimesis and semblance and thus keeps the set of problems that stem from them in check. Adorno continues to surpass himself: "That quid pro quo not only neutralizes mimesis, it also derives from it." (Ibid.) This *quid pro quo* is not only a trick played on mimesis by expression, as the cunning by which mimesis asserts its dominance over expression and takes its place; rather, the *quid pro quo* proves to have been mimetic from the start. It is not so much proper to expression as it is a consequence of the mimetic. "If mimetic comportment does not imitate something but rather makes itself like itself, this is precisely what artworks take it upon themselves to fulfill." (Ibid.) Along with this, however, the fallibility of mimesis also comes to the fore—a fallibility that is, of course, different in kind than the disdain directed against it by culture. Mimesis is judged [*gerichtet* not *geurteilt*] in aesthetic experience: "that what makes itself like itself does not become truly alike, that mimetic intervention failed." (Ibid.) The mimetic mode of making-oneself-alike is doomed to failure. Yet it is precisely this flaw of all mimetic impulses which marks an indispensable opportunity for the *quid pro quo*. It only gets its chance when there is an attempt and a need to make oneself alike and to become similar—only then does the complicated dialectical machine, which Adorno is operating, get going.

To sum up: as the heiress of the Sirens' song, art satisfies the urge to rescue what has passed as something living. Philosophy and theology may also be driven by this urge; however, only art—in its unbounded positivity—can do justice to it, by rescuing, as expression, the extra-aesthetic, and particularly suffering. Finally, this privilege stems from an affinity to the mimetic, the impulse of which survives in art as semblance. Each time anew, however, this aesthetic experience of the mimetic is one of failure. Time and time again experience shows that semblance [*Schein*] is deceitful. It is only an illusion [*Anschein*]. Yet, in my opinion, Adorno is not really concerned with proving the untruth of mimetic modes of behavior, so much as with sustaining the mimetic impulse in the form of the *quid pro quo*. For the experience of a deceitful semblance is only possible if one previously attempted to make oneself similar. It is *this* impulse—not the right of suffering to authentic expression—which is, as it were, the motor of the inner-aesthetic dynamic between mimesis and expression.

After all, what is this dynamic's *quid pro quo* if not the infinitely productive, objectified logic of subsumption, stripped of its magical dimension? The logic of exchange, which reigns in art, means that—contrary to any rational logic—it is possible to substitute one thing for another, *quid pro quo*. This differs from the demonic logic of exchange outside, only through the experience of failed and failing mimesis. Its opposite would be successful identification, which would leave no room for the experience of failed mimesis. In this sense, the difference between art and the culture industry, which Adorno likes to posit, is not a difference in substance but in function: wherever one can, or must, experience that one is not similar, one is dealing with a successful work of art. But this failure to become similar is not a proof of truth. It does not serve to authenticate or privilege expression; rather, technically speaking, it is the trick by which art, as the heiress of the Sirens, achieves remembrance. Under the viewpoint of the culture of suffering [*Leidkultur*], this may be a blasphemous philistinism, but perhaps this is not the only viewpoint.

The following episode from the aptly named Ernsttal, a town near Amorbach in the Odenwald region, could be seen as an emblem of another viewpoint: "A person commanding respect appeared in a bright red summer dress, the wife of the railway-president Stapf. The tamed wild sow of the Ernsttal forgot her tameness, and sped away with the screaming woman on its back. If I had a model, it would be this animal."[14] *Quid pro quo*.

Of course, that is no way to close. Hence, I propose a double conclusion: the connection of mimesis and *quid pro quo* is central for aesthetic theory—for Adorno's, but perhaps not only Adorno's—because it allows for a functional dissolution: namely, of the questionability of similarities and differences between the abominable substitutability in the culture industry's "universal nexus of delusion" and the autonomous, singular work of art.

But there may also be other reasons for holding onto Adorno's privileging of mimetic behaviors and impulses, which are exceptional—if not unique—in the history of aesthetic theory since the eighteenth century. One could, for instance, investigate the possible significance of such a concept of mimesis for the much-incriminated formative projects of *Bildung* and *Erziehung*. Both are the co-evolutionary products of enlightenment and

---

14 Theodor W. Adorno, "Amorbach," in Theodor W. Adorno, *Gesammelte Schriften, vol. 10: Kulturkritik und Gesellschaft I: Prismen. Ohne Leitbild* (Frankfurt am Main: Suhrkamp, 1977), pp. 302–309, here p. 308.

aesthetics, which, since the eighteenth century, had to get by without models or examples to which one might have likened oneself, only to discover—for better or worse—that this is not possible.

*Translated by Sebastian Truskolaski*

Sami Khatib

# Marx, Real Abstraction, and the Question of Form

## I.
## The Form of the Commodity

In the first chapter of the first volume of *Capital*, originally published in 1867, Marx summarizes the research question of his ongoing project:

> Political economy has indeed analysed value and its magnitude, however incompletely, and has uncovered the content concealed within these *forms*. But it has never once asked the question why this content has assumed that particular *form*, that is to say, why labour is expressed in value, and why the measurement of labour by its duration is expressed in the magnitude of the value of the product.[1]

The project of the *Critique of Political Economy*, which is also the subtitle of *Capital* 1 and its preceding studies,[2] is thus the question of form. The *categorical* unfolding and presentation of form—the commodity form—is the main challenge of the first chapter of *Capital* 1, which otherwise might be mistaken for a merely linear account of how capitalism and its major social relations came

---

1   Karl Marx, *Capital: A Critique of Political Economy*, Volume 1, trans. Ben Fowkes (London: Penguin, 1990), pp. 173–174. Emphasis added.

2   See Karl Marx, *Grundrisse: Foundations of the Critique of Political Economy (Rough Draft)* (1857/58), trans. Martin Nicolaus (London: Penguin, 1993) and Karl Marx, *Contribution to the Critique of Political Economy* (1859), Karl Marx and Frederick Engels Collected Works (MECW), Vol. 29 (New York: International Publishers and Moscow: Progress Publishers, 1987).

*historically* into being. This mode of presentation cannot rely on the presupposition of an already given content, but needs to develop its historical object through a logical construction of form. The presentation [*Darstellung*] of the constitutive intertwinement of logic and history is central to Marx's critical project.[3] Here, form does not designate an ahistorical realm of pure logic; likewise, content is not related to the domain of a given history. This historico-logical intertwinement comes into perspective only by virtue of a critical practice of reading. The question of *how* to theoretically present the value form of the commodity (and particularly the commodity form of labor power) defines the scope and stakes of Marx's entire critical project. As Michael Heinrich rightly comments, "Marx is not predominantly criticizing the conclusions of political economy, but rather the manner in which it *poses questions* […]."[4] Changing the questions and research perspective, Marx does not only engage in an immanent critique of previous (classical liberal) theories of political economy; rather, his critique seeks "to break down the *theoretical field* (meaning the self-evident views and spontaneously arising notions) to which the categories of political economy owe their apparent plausibility."[5] Marx's "epistemological break"[6] with the categories, research questions, per-

---

3 A precise account of this intertwinement and its difference from Engels' understanding of "logical-historical method" can be found in Heinz-Dieter Kittsteiner, "'Logisch' und 'historisch'. Über Differenzen des Marxschen und Engelsschen Systems der Wissenschaft," *Internationale Wissenschaftliche Korrespondenz zur Geschichte der deutschen Arbeiterbewegung* 13 (1977), pp. 1–47.

4 Michael Heinrich, *An Introduction to the Three Volumes of Karl Marx's Capital* (New York: Monthly Review Press, 2012), p. 34. Emphasis in original.

5 Ibid., p. 35. Emphasis in original.

6 Louis Althusser, *For Marx* (London: Verso, 2005), p. 28. Althusser's formulation was aimed at Marx's theoretical development from his early critique of ideology, which still shared Feuerbachian motifs of critique, to his later dialectical materialism after the *Theses on Feuerbach* (1845/46). However, in the sense I use this phrase here it characterizes Marx's entire project of the critique of political economy in relation to its subject matter.

spectives and findings of traditional political economy, ranging from Adam Smith to David Ricardo, defines critique as a practice of transformative reading that changes the criticized content on the level of the constitution of its scientific objects. In other words, the object and subject matter of the critique of political economy is not simply "out there," but has to be produced by way of a critical method. By exposing the epistemic blind spots of the criticized theoretical field, Marx presents his own dialectical method and constitutes the scientific objects of his inquiry. But what, then, is the *subject matter* of the critique of political economy, if it is not only an immanent critique of given classical liberal theories of political economy? If the object of the critique of political economy is not given without its form, how can we construct this form and what could be a knowledge of this form? As we shall see, in the case of Marx form is *not* an intellectual product of the mind that could be opposed to empirical objects. The ontological status of form escapes epistemologies and ontologies, which operate by way of non-dialectical, binary doublets like appearance vs. essence, or imagination vs. existence.

Already the first sentence of *Capital* 1 contains the central problem and challenge of Marx's critical project: "The wealth of societies in which the capitalist mode of production prevails appears [*erscheint*] as an 'immense collection of commodities'; the individual commodity appears as its elementary form [*Elementarform*]."[7] How, then, are we to discriminate between the levels of appearance [*Erscheinung*] and essence [*Wesen*] without relegating Marx's critical project to a binary logic? What is the categorical and historical genesis of the commodity's essence and why can it only appear in this form? In fact, as Hans-Georg Backhaus put it, "[t]he

---

7    Marx, *Capital* 1, p. 125; compare Karl Marx, *Das Kapital. Kritik der politischen Ökonomie*, Erster Band, Marx-Engels-Werke (MEW), Vol. 23 (Berlin: Dietz, 1962), p. 49.

dialectical method cannot be restricted to leading the form of appearance back to the essence; it must show in addition why the essence assumes precisely this or that form of appearance."[8] The commodity as an abstract yet real category of societies in which the "capitalist mode of production prevails" appears, at first sight, as "an extremely obvious, trivial thing."[9] However, as Marx is quick to tell his readers:

> Its analysis brings out that it [the commodity] is a very strange thing, abounding in metaphysical subtleties and theological niceties. So far as it is a use-value, there is nothing mysterious about it, whether we consider it from the point of view that by its properties it satisfies human needs; or that it first takes on these properties as the product of human labour. [...]. But as soon as it emerges as a commodity, it changes into a sensuous supra-sensuous thing [*sinnlich übersinnliches Ding*].[10]

As a "sensuous supra-sensuous thing" the commodity assumes two contradictory characters: in the *sensuous* world, it appears as one thing among other things; at the same time, however, it has acquired *supra-sensuous*, metaphysical or even theological properties. These real yet supra-sensuous or non-empirical properties cannot appear as such: they pertain to the specific *social form* through which the commodity appears. Commodities acquire the capacity of being exchangeable due to "essential" value relations that only "appear" with these commodities in their mutual exchange relations. This mode of appearance does not pose a merely epistemological problem, but relates to the split character of

---

**8**    Hans-Georg Backhaus, "On the Dialectics of the Value-Form," *Thesis Eleven* 1 (1980): p. 102.
**9**    Marx, *Capital* 1, pp. 125 and 163.
**10**    Ibid., p. 163; translation changed, compare Karl Marx, *Das Kapital. Erster Band*, p. 85.

capitalist reality and the ontological status of its ruling social form, the commodity form.

Unpacking the intricacies of the value dimension of commodities, Marx, in the first edition of *Capital* 1 in 1867, provided his readers with an intriguing image:

> It is as if alongside and external to lions, tigers, rabbits, and all other actual animals, which form when grouped together the various kinds, species, subspecies, families etc. of the animal kingdom, there existed also in addition *the animal*, the individual incarnation of the entire animal kingdom.[11]

The problem of the value form of the commodity cannot be explained on the level of empiricist economy only, which simply counts and accounts for concrete "animals." The value of a commodity is expressed in money and as money the commodity redoubles itself into two seemingly independent existences: as a specific commodity (or, as in Marx's image, as "lions, tigers, rabbits" etc.) the commodity exists in the sensuous world; however, as value, expressed in money (or, as in Marx's image, as "the animal"), it also exists in a non- or supra-sensuous way along with and in addition to its sensuous mode of existence. The problem of form and the stakes of critique, hence, can be summarized as the challenge of presenting the mode of existence of these two dimensions of the commodity and the dialectical, that is, "sensuous supra-sensuous" *unity* of the commodity form. As we shall see, it would be too simple and utterly wrong to assume that one dimension of the commodity is concrete and really existing (as sensuous content), while the other is abstract and conceptual (as supra-sensuous

---

11  Karl Marx, *Das Kapital. Kritik der politischen Ökonomie . Erster Band*, Hamburg 1867, in *Marx–Engels–Gesamtausgabe* (MEGA), ed. Institut für Marxismus-Leninismus beim ZK der KPdSU und der SED, vol. II.5.1 (Berlin: Dietz, 1983), p. 37. Translation by Sami Khatib. Emphasis in original.

form). To complicate matters further, neither dimension is derived from the other in a deductive or inductive manner. How, then, to present the commodity form?

Marx's well-known entry point is the split or dual nature of the commodity: use-value and exchange-value.[12] Whereas the former seems unproblematic as long as it refers to an empirical thing, satisfying a determinate human need, exchange-value expresses an abstract social category: economic value. Exchange value is the form of appearance of value: it designates the merely quantitative value-relation of one commodity vis-à-vis another commodity as relational difference. From the presentation of the dual nature of the commodity Marx moves on to the next categorical level of redoubling. The labor that produces a commodity also has two sides: concrete and abstract labor. While use values are produced by concrete labor, measured by concrete labor time (chronometric time),[13] the very act of concrete production also produces value. Value is produced by "abstract human labour,"[14] which exceeds linear chronometric measurement. However, in real time, these two acts of production are the same: abstract labor or value designates a social relation between different expenditures of labor power materialized in the results of this expenditure. Put differently, the concrete use value dimension of labor does not come into being independently from its abstract value-producing dimension. However, on the market they appear as two independent (if not antagonistic) entities, endowed with a life of their own: the commodity exists as a commodity-thing and as money. (Here we recall Marx's earlier image: it is as if "tigers, rabbits, and all other actual animals" exist along with "the animal.")

---

12  Marx, *Capital* 1, pp. 125–131.
13  Ibid., p. 129.
14  Ibid., p. 137.

As has been mentioned by numerous Marx scholars,[15] Marx's distinction of concrete and abstract labor is ambiguous and invites misreadings. Marx defines abstract labor also as the expenditure of human labor power as such, instead of focusing solely on the fact that abstract labor expresses the totalizing exchange relation (mediated through and by money) of *all* expenditures of concrete labor in a given capitalist society, which is ultimately the world market. There are passages in *Capital* 1 where Marx seems to define abstract labor as "an expenditure of human labour power, in the physiological sense,"[16] as "essentially the expenditure of human brain, nerves, muscles and sense organs."[17] Against these formulations we are to insist on the purely social and differential-relational nature of value and its "substance,"[18] that is, abstract labor. For Marx, substance is not an empirical essence (in the sense of natural or physiological substratum) but a purely social relation, constantly moving and transforming itself. Marx couldn't be clearer when he writes:

> Not an atom of matter enters into the objectivity of commodities [*Wertgegenständlichkeit*] as values; in this it is the direct opposite of the coarsely sensuous objectivity of commodities as physical objects. We may twist and turn a single commodity as we wish; it remains impossible to grasp it as a thing possessing value. However, let us remember that commodities possess an objective character as values only in so far as they are all expressions of an identical social substance, human labour, that their objective character as values is therefore purely social. From this it follows

15 For example Michael Heinrich, Hans-Georg Backhaus, Moishe Postone, to name only a few.
16 Marx, *Capital* 1, p. 137
17 Ibid., p. 164.
18 Marx, *Capital* 1, p. 128.

self-evidently that it can only appear in the social relation between commodity and commodity.[19]

If value and its substance, abstract human labor, can only appear in a relation between things—between commodity and commodity—we have a further clue to the problem of presenting this *mode of appearance* in a merely empirical manner as it appears in concrete reality. Following such an empiricist approach, we would have always already missed the point as to why a specific appearance appears in *this* way: why *this* content (commodities, prices, exchange relations etc.) assumes *this* form.

## II.
## From Abstraction to Concretion

In the first chapter of *Capital* 1, Marx develops the problem of the value form of the commodity through a presentation of *abstract* yet *real* social relations. That is to say, in capitalism, *real* social relations are constituted in an *abstract* manner: abstract exchange relations between concrete commodities and concrete commodity owners weave a totalizing net of *really* existing asymmetric social relations. In other words, in capitalism relations between humans are social only in this sense: they pertain to a world of abstract exchange relations between commodities; they cannot be developed and analyzed from their inherent "thingly" properties. For instance, the social relation of workers to their colleagues or superiors is not defined by the material properties of their

---

**19**  Ibid., pp. 138–139. I have commented on Marx's oxymoronic German compound noun "Wertgegenständlichkeit" (literally: value-objectivity) in Sami Khatib, "'Sensuous Supra-Sensuous': The Aesthetics of Real Abstraction," in *Aesthetic Marx*, ed. Samir Gandesha and Johan F. Hartle (London: Bloomsbury, 2017), pp. 49–72, especially pp. 56–58.

tasks, performances, mental or emotional affinities or the nature of their activities. Social relations are mediated objectively—through and by objects in their abstract commodified relation as bearers of value. Commodities are things in their capacity as bearers and expressions of value. And the value of each commodity is the form of its social existence. However, this form does not present itself as such: value only appears *après coup* on the market as a relation between things after things-as-commodities have already acquired a price for which they can be bought. This is why Marx does not begin with the world of appearances, concretely existing things, agents on the market, persons and activities which can be seen, perceived or otherwise sensuously intuited. The method of "ascending" from the base level of abstract social relations to the concrete, "grown-together" (*concrescere*) level of experienced social reality is outlined in Marx's earlier draft *Grundrisse* (1857/58), in which he lays bare his own dialectical-materialist departure from Hegelian dialectics.

It seems to be correct to begin with the real and the concrete, with the real precondition, thus to begin, in economics, with e.g. the population, which is the foundation and the subject of the entire social act of production. However, on closer examination this proves false. The population is an abstraction if I leave out, for example, the classes of which it is composed. These classes in turn are an empty phrase if I am not familiar with the elements on which they rest. E.g. wage labour, capital, etc. These latter in turn presuppose exchange, division of labour, prices, etc. For example, capital is nothing without wage labour, without value, money, price etc. Thus, if I were to begin with the population, this would be a chaotic representation [*Vorstellung*] of the whole, and I would then, by means of further determination, move analytically towards ever more simple concepts [*Begriffe*], from the imagined concrete towards ever thinner abstractions until I had arrived at the simplest determinations. From there the journey would have to be retraced until I had finally arrived at the population again, but this time not as the chaotic conception of a whole, but as a rich totality of many determinations and relations. The former is the path historically followed by economics at the time of its origins. The economists of the seventeenth century, e.g., always begin with the living whole, with population, nation, state, several states, etc.; but they always conclude by discovering through analysis a small number of determinant, abstract, general relations such as division of labour, money, value, etc. As soon as these individual moments had been more or less firmly established and abstracted, there began the economic systems, which ascended [*aufstiegen*] from the simple relations, such as labour, division of labour, need, exchange value, to the level of the state, exchange between nations and the world market. The latter is obviously the scientifically correct method.[20]

In this dense passage Marx engages with the method of classical political economy, criticizing its empiricist commonsense approach. In Marx's view, we are precisely *not* to begin with the sensuously given world as it appears to us at first glance. This anti-intuitive move is based on Hegel's refutation of "abstract thinking."[21] By beginning our analysis with the given reality, knowingly or not, we include untheorized abstractions already present in the concepts we apply to reality in the first place: the rich totality of the concrete world, i.e. the population, is itself an abstraction. What has been abstracted from disappears in the epistemic blind spot of such an approach. Instead of examining those

20 Marx, *Grundrisse (Rough Draft)*, pp. 100–101. I have changed the existing translation; compare Karl Marx, "Einleitung [zu den 'Grundrissen der Kritik der politischen Okonomie']," Marx-Engels-Werke (MEW), Vol. 42 (Berlin: Dietz, 1983), pp. 34–35.
21 Compare Georg Wilhelm Friedrich Hegel, "Wer denkt abstrakt?," in *Jenaer Schriften*, Werke, Vol. 2, ed. Eva Moldenhauer and Karl Markus Michel (Frankfurt am Main: Suhrkamp, 1986), pp. 575–581.

abstractions already present and "at work" in the given concrete reality, we only ascend to ever thinner and less significant abstractions by way of analyzing, dissecting, breaking down. Such an approach can never come to terms with the real abstractions *present in reality*, for it can grasp abstraction only as a conceptual operation generated by the intellect. In strictly nominalist fashion, the really existing abstraction of the commodity form would remain a conceptual abstraction existing in the scholarly world of theory only. Marx's critical method, however, does not simply opt for the realist flipside of classical political economy's positivist nominalism but shifts the entire epistemic field in which these notions are rooted.

Let us consider the dense passage where Marx explains his "scientifically correct method" as ascending from the base level of simple abstract determinations and categories to the synthetic totality of concrete ("grown-together") reality:

The concrete is concrete because it is the concentration [*Zusammenfassung*, literally: gathering together] of many determinations, hence unity of the manifold [*Einheit des Mannigfaltigen*]. It appears [*erscheint*] in the process of thinking, therefore, as a process of concentration [*Zusammenfassung*], as a result, not as a point of departure, even though it is the point of departure in reality and hence also the point of departure for intuition [*Anschauung*] and representation [*Vorstellung*]. Along the first path the full representation was evaporated to yield an abstract determination; along the second, the abstract determinations lead towards a reproduction of the concrete by way of thought. In this way Hegel fell into the illusion of conceiving the real as the product of thought concentrating itself, probing its own depths, and unfolding itself out of itself, by itself, whereas the method of ascending from the abstract to the concrete is only the way in which thought appropriates the concrete, reproduces it as the concrete in the mind.

But this is by no means the process by which the concrete itself comes into being. For example, the simplest economic category, say e.g. exchange value, presupposes population, moreover a population producing in specific relations; as well as a certain kind of family, or commune, or state, etc. It can never exist other than as an abstract, one-sided relation within an already given, concrete, living whole. As a category, by contrast, exchange value leads an antediluvian existence. Therefore, to the kind of consciousness—and this is characteristic of the philosophical consciousness—for which conceptual thinking is the real human being, and for which the conceptual world as such is thus the only reality, the movement of the categories appears as the real act of production—which only, unfortunately, receives a jolt from the outside—whose product is the world; and—but this is again a tautology—this is correct in so far as the concrete totality is a totality of thoughts, concrete in thought, in fact a product of thinking and comprehending; but not in any way a product of the concept [*Begriff*] which thinks and generates itself outside or above intuition [*Anschauung*] and representation [*Vorstellung*]; a product, rather, of the working-up of intuition [*Anschauung*] and representation by concepts [*Vorstellung in Begriffe*]. The totality as it appears in the head, as a totality of thoughts, is a product of a thinking head, which appropriates the world in the only way it can, a way different from the artistic, religious, practical and mental appropriation of this world. The real subject retains its autonomous existence outside the head just as before; namely as long as the head's conduct is merely speculative, merely theoretical. Hence, in the theoretical method, too, the subject, society, must always be kept in mind as the presupposition.[22]

---

**22** Marx, *Grundrisse (Rough Draft)*, pp. 101–102. I have changed the existing translation; compare Marx, "Einleitung [zu den 'Grundrissen der Kritik der politischen Ökonomie']," pp. 35–36.

Marx seems to position himself here between a materialist Kant and an idealist Hegel: the appropriation of the real world by way of intuition and conceptual representation does not bring the world into being, does not cause its existence. A realist reading of Hegel, for which thinking and reality, concept and world, are ultimately the same, is ruled out. However, reality is not simply given outside the cognizing mind; abstractions already exist in the actual world in the form of social relations. Marx's dialectical materialism thus tries to salvage Hegel's critique of abstract thinking. While Hegel's dialectical mode of presentation remains valid as a method of the intellectual reproduction of the concrete world by means of intuition and (abstract) conceptual representation, this *re*production in theory is not the production of the concrete world itself. Unlike its appearance in the absolute idealism of the Hegelian mode, being is not ultimately thinking and vice versa. Of course, for Marx too the mediations and transformations of being and consciousness are dialectical; yet conceptual mediation is never a predicate of existence. Against the dual background of Kant and Hegel, Marx's dialectical materialism performs a kind of "original reproduction" of the concrete world, since his critical method does not succumb to the dualist empiricist, vulgar-materialist or neo-Kantian worldview of two unmediated worlds: the one external being "out there," the other internal "in the mind" (and, hence, compelled to simply copy, reflect, reproduce the former). Such a flat theory of reflection would remain within the worldview of unmediated categories of the mind and an independent uncritical world outside. Marx's point is that being and consciousness are *inherently* mediated; hence, his dialectical materialist method investigates the social forms, characters and embodiments this inherent mediation assumes.

For our problem of coming to terms with the real abstract nature of the commodity form a central insight can be extracted from the above-quoted passage from the *Grundrisse*. If the concrete is concrete because it is the "gathering together" [*Zusammenfassung*] of many determinations, hence unity of the manifold, we can conclude that this concrete is real in a specific sense: concrete reality is "glued" or "sewn" together out of abstract determinations already present and at work in reality. However, the materiality of these abstract determinations is not empirical sensuous like the sensuous concrete reality. Rather, they are "made" out of a supra-sensuous materiality that Marx defined as the abstract social relations addressed in the dimension of value. Value, as we know by now, only appears in the relation between commodities. It *is* the essence of value to appear in these objective commodity relations. Again, Marx does not invite us to read his critical method as a mapping of two different worlds: here the concrete world of sensuous appearance, there the non-sensuous world of abstract determinations (which theory would then seek to "unveil"). On the contrary, the commodity as existing presents the unity of both: a sensuous supra-sensuous thing. Form here means the differential disparity of appearance and essence without making a dualist claim on two worlds existing in parallel. We understand now why Marx in his earlier formulation from the first edition of *Capital* 1 carefully writes that the dimension of value ("the animal"), materialized in money, exists among and in addition to the commodities ("lions, tigers, rabbits" etc.) in a specific way: it is only *as if* this animal existed in such a real way. However, this as-if mode of existence is not an illusion.

The concrete world of capitalist appearances (commodities, workers, capitalists, population, classes etc.) designates a totalizing ensemble of social relations which is made out of abstractions, abstract determinations that really exist in a peculiar sensuous supra-sensuous manner. In order to grasp them we are to begin with abstract determinations in order to ascend [*aufsteigen*] to the concrete world as concentration, gathering-together of the manifold of capitalist relations of production. Marx's vertical topology of ascending from abstract base-level to concrete appearance-level provides us with a first clue about capitalist ontology: the abstract base-level of really existing abstractions exists *in the same world* as its mode of appearance. The surface of concrete reality is made of really existing abstractions. This concrete surface of commodity relations, however, is not accidental but essential in the precise sense of presenting an ensemble of "grown-together" abstract relations. In fact, the essence of essence is to appear, there is no epistemological problem here: the essence of the commodity form (real abstractions) appears as an "'immense collection of commodities'; the individual commodity appears as its elementary form."[23] The famous "secret"[24] of commodity fetishism only arises from the redoubling of the abstract base-level: it appears twice, as value-properties of sensuously existing commodities in their mutual relations and as money. These two modes of appearance act and function *as if* they existed next to each other in the same world. Again, there is no illusion involved here. The epistemological problem only emerges once I take the sensuously appearing commodity as the only really existing objectivity and treat its redoubling value-objectivity as merely derived, intellectually abstracted, secondary, illusionary, etc.

## III.
### Real Abstraction, or the Unconscious of the Commodity Form

Having established Marx's method, its departure from Hegel's dialectics and its critical distance and proxim-

---

23  Marx, *Capital* 1, p. 125.
24  See Marx's subchapter "The Fetishism of the commodity and its secret," ibid., pp. 163–173.

ity to a Kantian materialism, we can now flip over the vertical topology implied in the metaphor of "ascending" from simple, abstract determinations to the level of concrete reality. Following a horizontal topology, we can grasp the base level of abstract determinations as actually existing along with concrete reality. Earlier we said Marx was rightly cautious about not ascribing to the dimension of value ("the animal") a full existence of its own. However, now we can add a second complication to this peculiar as-if existence of the dimension of value, which brings our close reading back to the ontological and epistemological status of form in Marx.

The problem of form arises at the intersection of the historical genesis and logical validity of capitalist relations of production. Form thus does not designate a stable entity, bound to ahistorical logics or purely transcendental forms. "For Marx," as Alfred Sohn-Rethel reminds us, "form is time-bound. It originates, dies and changes within time."[25] Without going into the details of Sohn-Rethel's otherwise problematic reading of Marx with Kant and against Hegel, we can draw a crucial insight here: For Marx's dialectical materialism, form does not only change within time; time as form (i.e. as the form of spatial measurement) is also a historically produced form. Marx "understands the time governing the genesis and the mutation of forms as being, from the very first, historical time—the time of natural and of human history."[26] The interaction of the level of the "time of natural and human history" and the level of time as a historically-produced and changing form renders it impossible to give a linear account of how capitalism, its forms and categories came "once upon a time" into being.

---

**25**  Alfred Sohn-Rethel, *Intellectual and Manual Labour* (London: Macmillan, 1978), p. 17.

**26**  Ibid., p. 18.

If form is time-bound and, in this sense, also the historical expression of the social production of time-as-form, we can think of form as a changing social relation, which contains its own unhistoricizable historicity while producing historical time. This peculiar historicity is unhistoricizable because the standard of historicization (time as chronometric measurement, diachronic sequentiality etc.) is itself produced by and through it. Assuming an unhistoricizable historicity of socially valid forms does not imply their eternalization. However, this historicity cannot be told either in a linear way. So, what then is the epistemological and ontological status of an unhistoricizable historicity? If this unhistoricizable historicity is not simply something untold, forgotten or unaccounted for (which could be accounted for, at least in theory) but *repressed* in a structural sense, it always escapes the presentation of its historical (diachronic) genesis.

It is the wager of this reading of Marx and Sohn-Rethel that the peculiar historicity of the commodity form is *structurally repressed and real*; it does spring from the intellectual realm of syllogisms or Kantian antinomies of pure reason. Apparently, neither the discourse of political economy nor the one of philosophical epistemology can provide us here with a model. However, if we change the discursive terrain and turn to a different field of knowledge, we may find a structure of argument that could elucidate the logical temporality at work here. In Freudian psychoanalysis the ontological status of *Urverdrängung*, primal or originary repression, is precisely this: an "event" that is real but exists only in its status as repressed. Originary repression is real only insofar as it has real effects (it exists in its effects only); yet it comes "before" that which is being repressed. Put differently, it cannot be told or made conscious because the prefix *Ur-* or originary (primal) indicates the quasi-transcendental status of primariness—a primariness that comes logically *before* anything historical can be

**85**

repressed. Freud insists that "repression is not a defensive mechanism which is present from the very beginning, and that it cannot arise until a sharp cleavage [*Sonderung*] has occurred between conscious and unconscious mental activity—that *the essence of repression lies simply in turning something away, and keeping it at a distance, from the conscious.*"[27] In other words, originary repression is unconscious in a different way than particular repressed mental states, which could be symbolized in the process of the psychoanalytical cure and whose returning/recurring symptoms can be made conscious.

Repression already presupposes the unconscious, and its function does not consist so much in suppressing, inhibiting or hindering satisfaction but in keeping the drive away from consciousness. The paradox of repression lies in the fact that repression is secondary, despite being constitutive of the repressed. It can only emerge after the scission of the mental apparatus between consciousness and

---

27  Sigmund Freud, "Repression," in *The Standard Edition of the Complete Psychological Works of Sigmund Freud*, trans. James Strachey, Vol. 14 (London: Hogarth Press, 1957), p. 147. Emphasis in original. Compare Sigmund Freud, "Die Verdrängung," *Gesammelte Werke*, Vol. 10 (London: Imago, 1946), p. 249. For a detailed discussion of this passage in Freud, the temporality and ontological status of *Urverdrängung*, see Samo Tomšič, *The Capitalist Unconscious* (London: Verso, 2015), pp. 130–148. Tomšič's convincing argument places the homology of the discourses of Freud and Marx at the epistemo-ontological status of "Ur-" or "ursprünglich" (primal, originary). The Marxian counterpart to *Urverdrängung* is, of course, *ursprüngliche Akkumulation*, "primitive accumulation"—an "event" that cannot be historicized since it has to be restaged and repeated always anew to keep capitalist relations of production in power. As I have argued elsewhere, so-called primitive accumulation—the disruptive transformation from feudal to capitalist society, the violent separation of labor power from the means of production by way of expropriation, expulsion, enclosures and brutal force—is the repressed origin and primal scene of the capitalist world market without which the valorization of abstract labor as surplus value is not possible. In other words, the entire project of the critique of political economy is at stake when we try to theorize the historical and logical origin of capitalism's major social form and mode of production. See Sami Khatib, "No Future: The Space of Capital and the Time of Dying," in *Former West: Art and the Contemporary after 1989*, eds. Maria Hlavajova and Simon Sheikh (Cambridge MA: MIT Press, 2017), pp. 639–652, especially pp. 641–643.

the unconscious has been established, but it is also the necessary condition for this cleavage.[28]

If we distinguish between "constitutive repression" [*Urverdrängung*] (i.e. constitutive of repression) and "constituted repression" (i.e. repressed content and its mode of returning in the form of symptoms, which can be subject to the psychoanalytic cure),[29] we have found a homological model to come to terms with the onto-logical status of an unhistoricizable historicity, which is both secondary to and constitutive of the history of the commodity form, i.e. the historical formation of capi-talist relations of production. The unhistoricizable his-toricity of the commodity form can only emerge once we are already in capitalism; yet its ontological status of assuming an unhistoricizable historicity structurally conditions the split in capitalist reality that Marx theo-rized in terms of the dual character of the commodity, the dual character of labor, and the redoubling of the commodity as commodity ("animals") and money ("*the animal*").

Speaking of an unhistoricizable historicity of the com-modity form is nothing else than taking a real yet uncon-scious historicity of capitalist history into account, which has, in the "first place," produced these socially valid forms. In other words, we can allow for the pos-sibility of forms that are not generated by the conscious mind of conceptual thought. Instead, we are pointing to forms that exist in an abstract manner—forms that are not reducible to any empirical historical subject and his or her intellectual faculties, and the ontogenetic and phylogenetic history of these faculties. Accounting for an unaccountable, that is, unhistoricizable historicity of socially valid forms (i.e. the commodity form), we could

---

**28** Tomšič, *The Capitalist Unconscious*, p. 138.
**29** I take the instructive differentiation of "constitutive and constituted repression" from Tomšič, *The Capitalist Unconscious*, pp. 133–140.

speak of an unconscious of form, or, to be more precise, of the problem of the "unconscious of the commodity form"[30] as distinct from the unconscious content of
capitalist history, i.e. repressed events of counter-hege-
monic struggles.[31] The unconscious of the commodity form would then be another term for "constitutive
repression," whereas repressed events of history could
be read as "constituted repression."

With the notion of constitutive repression and the
unconscious of the commodity form we finally arrive
at the ontological status of the real-abstract character
of the value form of the commodity as distinct from
thought abstractions. "While the abstractions of natural science are thought abstractions, the economic concept of value is a real one. It exists nowhere other than
in the human mind but it does not spring from it."[32] As
paradoxical as this seems at first sight, the commodity
form assumes the form of thought, exists in thought, yet
does not originate or spring from thought. Sohn-Rethel's characterization of the value form of the commodity
gives us a possible definition of what the unconscious of
the commodity form could be.

Value, that is, a denaturalized, literally abstracted
(*abstrahere*) social relation, comes into being by virtue
of a *real* process of exchange—an actually performed
equation of things as commodities, which acquires at
the same time the form of *thought*, that is, abstraction.
"Wherever commodity exchange takes place, it does so
in effective 'abstraction' from use. This is an abstrac-

---

**30** Slavoj Žižek, *The Sublime Object of Ideology* (London: Verso, 1989),
p. 9–16.
**31** Those negative or unconscious events of history are addressed for
instance in Walter Benjamin's notion of the "tradition of the oppressed." See Walter Benjamin, "On the Concept of History," in Walter Benjamin, *Selected Writings: Volume 4, 1938–1940*, ed. Marcus
Bullock and Michael W. Jennings (Cambridge MA: Belknap Press of
Harvard University Press, 2003), p. 392.
**32** Sohn-Rethel, *Intellectual and Manual Labour*, p. 20.

tion not in mind but in fact."[33] Value can only appear in accordance with the conscious form of thought, i.e. intellectual abstraction; however, its "dark," unaccountable, unhistoricizable historicity points to a really performed abstraction outside of the conscious mind, which only retroactively conforms to the forms of the mind. From a linear historical perspective, this argument is easily to grasp since "[b]efore thought could arrive at pure *abstraction*, the abstraction was already at work in the social effectivity of the market."[34] The critical kernel of Sohn-Rethel's argument, however, goes beyond a disputable analysis of the historical genesis of abstract thought out of the first socially-valid coinage system and exchange economy, dating back to Ancient Greece and the Phoenicians. With Sohn-Rethel's reading of Marx, we are to ask what is the status of that form of thought *"whose ontological status is not that of thought."*[35] In the case of abstract labor, we can conclude that it has the form of thought but it owes its existence to an unconscious mode of social interaction, which becomes conscious only at a different site, namely, in the mind as intellectual abstraction.

In his reading of Marx, Freud and Sohn-Rethel, Slavoj Žižek thus proposes to take the formula *"the form of thought whose ontological status is not that of thought"* as one of the possible definitions of the unconscious.[36] In this way, real abstraction becomes the unconscious operator and mediator of the form of abstract thought logically prior to abstract thought-content. As a quasi-transcendental (and seemingly time-less, ahistorical) form of thought, real abstraction necessarily remains unconscious; it cannot acquire a conscious history without losing its quasi-transcendental status as originary repressed. In other words, the ontological status

33 Ibid., p. 25.
34 Žižek, *The Sublime Object of Ideology*, p. 10.
35 Ibid., p. 13. Emphasis in original.
36 Ibid.

of the real abstraction performed by commodity relations remains unconscious in a radical way: it points to the unconscious of the commodity form—to an unconscious form, which only appears in the mind as necessarily timeless and ahistorical, i.e. as the Kantian transcendental forms of pure thinking (quantity, quality, relation and modality) and pure intuition (time and space).[37] Of course, we cannot deny the fact that the concept of abstract labor, which stands in the center of Marx's presentation of the commodity form, conforms to the (logical and aesthetic) forms of the Kantian transcendental subject; however, this epistemological status of conformity does not tell us anything about its ontological status and the question of how abstract labor came into being.

With Marx, we can conclude that form in its radical sense as *changing in and with time* remains unconscious and constitutively repressed. Otherwise, the commodity form would relapse either to a historical form without epistemological consequences or to a purely ahistorical concept without historical determinations. Grasping real abstraction as the unconscious of the commodity form makes us understand that form is never reducible to conscious abstractions of the intellect only. If the commodity is a sensuous supra-sensuous thing, we can conclude that the commodity is the sensuously perceptible and intellectually conceivable object that owes its existence to an unconscious (supra- or, rather, *infra*-sensuous) dimension.

If the commodity form and its unconscious kernel, that is, real abstraction, contain an unaccountable, unhistoricizable historicity, whose ontological status and logical temporality can be understood as homological to originary repression (constitutive repression)

---

37  Immanuel Kant, *Critique of Pure Reason*, trans. Paul Guyer and Allen W. Wood (Cambridge: Cambridge University Press, 1998), B 36 and B 106.

in Freudian psychoanalysis, we can eventually ask the question about the constituted repression enacted and displaced by capitalist relations of production. The dimension of value and abstract labor symptomatically points to and, at the same time, occludes the repressed history of an unconscious subject. Labor power is the unconscious subject of value that keeps on bringing the commodity form into being. For the later Marx of *Capital*, this subject is not stable or always already existing, but produced as the bearer of labor power, that is, the proletariat. Whereas the commodity form is real-abstract and general, the proletariat is really universal and singular. "The proletariat is a particular type of the universal, a singular universal, which stands opposite to the abstract and false universalism of the general equivalent and the commodity form."[38] This opposition is asymmetric in the sense of the asymmetry implied in the exchange relation of the value of the commodity of labor power (wage) and the value produced by the application of labor power in the production process (surplus value, i.e. capital).[39]

The history of the proletariat is class struggle—yet this history is repressed. The repressed history of class struggle pertains to an ongoing history of constituted repression; it can only be "cured" in the labor of "working-through" the conditions of its repression, i.e. by symbolizing and displacing class antagonism in a series of revolutions and revolutionary defeats. Such struggles for revolutionary "cure," however, do not necessarily

---

38  Tomšič, *The Capitalist Unconscious*, p. 193.
39  The value of the commodity of labor power, as Marx defined it, finds its standard in the costs of its reproduction and, hence, also in unpaid reproductive labor. What appears as surplus value on the side of the capitalist (who employs labor power) appears as loss of living labor on the side of the owner and seller of labor power, historically the wage laborer. Surplus value thus implies the extraction of surplus labor time. However, while being equated, time and value are not equal but express a systemic asymmetry. See Marx, *Capital* 1, pp. 247–257 and 270–280.

abolish the level of constitutive repression enacted by and through the commodity form. Ultimately, we arrive at a seemingly circular conclusion: the unhistoricizable historicity of the commodity form structurally conditions and represses the negative history of an unconscious subject (the proletariat) without which the commodity form could have never come into being "in the first place." However, this seemingly circular conclusion is itself the effect of the primal separation, the originary cleavage of an unconscious historicity and a conscious history. It is the ontological inconsistency of this cleavage that is addressed in Marx's concept of the commodity form.

# Forms of Work / Forms of Life

**Birgit M. Kaiser and Kathrin Thiele**

# Forms of Critique,
# Modes of Combat

The humanities are currently adjusting to their task in the globally entangled world of the twenty-first century—a century that inherits the various deconstructions of humanism, colonialism, sexism, and racism, but also struggles with persisting structures of racial oppression, deepening social inequality, morphing nationalisms, militarized borders and anti-immigration policies. The practice of critique as the capacity to diagnose social power-formations, to eschew dogmatisms and to provide tools for emancipatory transformations seems more urgent than ever. In an economically, ecologically, culturally and politically co-dependent and entangled world—to which border controls and neoliberal nationalism are invalid responses—it is difficult, however, to sustain the traditional image of critique: the calm distancing by way of setting apart and judging. Given our awareness of multifaceted connectedness and global entanglements, our critical evaluations and assessments, as well as our actions, (must) come about from within the processes of on-going change and differentiation, in continuous feedback loops and multilateral negotiations. Since its foundation in 2012, the interdisciplinary research network *Terra Critica*[1], whose

1   For further information about this research network and its ongoing events and activities, see http://terracritica.net/. Given the overall collective character of this research network and its rhizomatic structuring, the following discussion is not meant as an objective presentation of *Terra Critica*'s work. Rather, we see our presentation here as a perspectival engagement with what we as founders and members of the initiative see as its critical potential.

work we have been invited to reflect on here, has asked about the transformations that critical methodologies might have to undergo *if* entanglement and systemic intra-connectedness are our onto-epistemological starting points. In that sense, the *forms* of critique have played a role for *Terra Critica* from the start, especially in its various verbal modalities such as to form, to transform, to reform, to inform or to perform. For *Terra Critica*, the stakes of form have been less about specific genre(s) of critique but rather about the *form(ations)* of critique itself. The network's engagements ask after the *potential transformations* of critical practice today.

In what follows, we want to reflect on the directions of such transformations, because our interest lies with transformations directed toward specific practices. Affirming the situated starting point of any critical intervention seems foundational. *Terra Critica* itself has been a situated endeavor, whereby situated means more than merely specifying a standpoint or claiming partiality; to be situated also always implies *implication* in the matters at stake. In terms of its own implicatedness, it is not unimportant that the initiative was started in the Netherlands in 2012, at a moment when the post-2008 neoliberal politics of austerity hit the Dutch institutions of higher education, and at a time when macro-economic decisions were said to be without alternative, so that the spaces for critical questioning—politically, but most immediately for us also academically, within the humanities—were transforming, i.e. disappearing. Asking critical questions seemed the least appreciated perspective, even in circles where critical scholarship had been practiced before, because, it was claimed, critique was too ideological a resistance strategy for the present situation and prevented participation by claiming critical distance. Provoked by that moment, the initiation of our network was thus not only an academic project, but an existential one *in that lived situation*. This reference to our starting point is not merely anecdotal, but speaks to an important point of critique: critique comes about not as a purified, contemplative or intellectual endeavor, but in response to something crossing its path. In that sense, our network's research into terran[2] modes of critique was *effected* by something with which we crossed paths contingently in 2012—a contingency that was, of course, an afterlife and after-effect of 2008 and so many earlier events, implicated within Western academia and its institutions. Or, to say it otherwise: as a theory-practice, *Terra Critica* emerged from the messiness of things, and in its conceptual and corporeal composition the project has tried to consider critique from the viewpoint of an immanent *effectivity/affectivity*, rather than from the perspective of transcendent or universal (capital T) Truth.

The problems that emerged there and then have not yet disappeared. Implicated within Western academia, and affirming critique as a crucial disposition and interventionist practice of the humanities, the question of how the conceptual registers of critique need to adjust and *transform* if they are to respond to today's planetary condition (in Gayatri Spivak's sense) still remains.[3] If what Félix Guattari's short but insightful *The Three Ecologies* (1989) called Integrated World Capitalism— the "post-industrial capitalism" that supersedes the production of goods by the production of signs and subjectivity—means that "we" are profoundly entangled with/in capital flows, how does the categorical distinction in the classical form of critique, of a subject of critique from an object of critique, become untenable? If critique instead happens as embodied and situated,

---

2   For the term "terran," as pointing to earthly and no longer human exceptionalist coexistence, see Donna Haraway, *Staying with the Trouble: Making Kin in the Chthulucene* (Durham NC: Duke University Press, 2016), chapter 2; Déborah Danowski and Eduardo Viveiros de Castro, *The Ends of the World*, trans. Rodrigo Nunes (Cambridge: Polity Press, 2017), especially pp. 88–98.

3   Gayatri Chakravorty Spivak, *Death of a Discipline* (New York: Columbia University Press, 2003).

how do practices of critical engagement, both intellectual and activist, *re-form* themselves (as in *form anew*)? Or, to speak with Sylvia Wynter: how to "overturn"[4] critique's Western, modern frames to make critique sharp enough again to tackle the planetary? Wynter's critical work has become increasingly significant to our project, most of all in view of her work on the question that Frantz Fanon posed in view of colonial European exclusivist humanism/s: "How do we extricate ourselves?"[5] In Fanon's case, this question means: How do we extricate ourselves from the exclusivist Western humanist conception of the human in order to free humankind? In light of the different ends of that humanist tradition and *its* (hegemonic) modes of critique, Fanon's question could perhaps be translated for critique itself into something like this: How do we extricate criticality from its Enlightenment legacy?[6] But also: How does this hege-

---

4  Sylvia Wynter, "The Ceremony Found: Towards the Autopoetic Turn/Overturn, its Autonomy of Human Agency and Extraterritoriality of (Self-)Cognition," in *Black Knowledges/Black Struggles: Essays in Critical Epistemology*, ed. Jason R. Ambroise and Sabine Broeck (Liverpool: Liverpool University Press, 2015), pp. 184–252, especially p. 207.

5  Frantz Fanon, *Black Skin, White Masks*, trans. Charles Markmann (London: Pluto Press, 1967), p. 12. Wynter cites from Markmann's translation. Richard Philcox renders this in his new translation of *Black Skin, White Masks* as "How can we break the cycle?" (New York: Grove Press, 2008), p. xiv.

6  We use critique and criticality interchangeably. While *Terra Critica* refuses to abandon critique as a term and legacy of thought, we also affirm the shifting ground upon which it must be revisioned. Irit Rogoff has described the differences between the two terms concisely in "From Criticism to Critique to Criticality" (2003), where she notes that classically critique has meant "finding fault, [...] examining the underlying assumptions that might allow something to appear as a convincing logic" and that "we have been able to move from" this to criticality as an engagement that "operat[es] from an uncertain ground" and in a mode "other than one of illuminating flaws, locating elisions, allocating blames." (https://transversal.at/transversal/0806/rogoff1/en [last accessed 12 October 2019]). The work of *Terra Critica* shares this analysis, but we are hesitant to envision criticality as a move away from or beyond older forms of critique. As this chapter hopefully makes evident, the effort is rather to avoid the imagination of temporal succession and to overturn critique with/through/as criticality.

monic European tradition (famously instantiated in Kant's three critiques) necessarily continue to *inform* critical gestures, the contemporary practices of critique? And how could practices of critique be *performed* if they are situated and entangled with/in planetary life, if they are immanent to it, so that the gesture of judging a situation from above or dissecting an object from an unquestioned distance becomes obsolete?

These are some of the main questions that *Terra Critica* revolves around and so far, perhaps for good reason, the form of the question has proven to be one key mode in the endeavor to transform critique. Transformation in that sense implies the persistent but constant attempt to arrive at adequate questions. The stress that we are putting on transformation implies, however, also a focus on critique *today*. We have already inferred that today a transformation of critique seems warranted. In view of the question as mode, it is less important to note the content of this specific "today"—i.e. what is the world of today like, what is specific to our present. Rather, the point is to stick with "today" as the horizon of critique, with "today" itself as a critical question.[7] "Today" in this sense is thus not simply a situated temporal vantage point, a given point in time, but it requires finding out "what the case is." An investment in "today" as such a non-presentist here/now (or *nowhere*) is very much part of the transformation of critical practice that interests us, striving to understand what "this time that is ours— *today*"[8] entails. For each today, it becomes necessary

---

7   See Jacques Derrida, *The Other Heading: Reflections on Today's Europe*, trans. Pascale-Anne Brault and Michael Naas (Bloomington: Indiana University Press, 1992). Derrida's text on the idea of capital and the metropole (Europe) stems from the same historical moment— the end of a bipolar northern hemisphere and its capitalist-communist confrontation, and the emerging "integration" of Schengen—as Guattari's *The Three Ecologies*.

8   See Derrida, *The Other Heading*, p. 79.

to "discern the *unprecedented* forms"[9] that a problem, a socio-political anxiety or a pathology might be taking, at a particular juncture. From this angle, "today" is less a temporal moment from which to look or measure, but a term for the need to bring into view and establish what the case is; an exploration and process that is part and parcel of the critical work itself. Thinking with Nietzsche, the assessment of such a "now" requires taking into account "who speaks?", "where from?", "with/for/ to whom?", as well as "at what juncture?" Critical work in this sense accounts for the discursive, material-semiotic field with which any critical practice co-emerges, which means acknowledging perspectival situatedness, but it also implies, as Guattari notes, "a reconstruction of the objectives and the methods of the whole of the social movement *under today's conditions.*"[10]

After having noted some of the underlying attitudes of *Terra Critica*'s work, we want in what follows to flesh out further what form a critical practice might entail "today," and we will do this by closely considering two texts, which—at the occasion of our second annual meeting in 2013—made these stakes of critique visible to us as a group: Virginia Woolf's *Three Guineas* (1938) and Guattari's *The Three Ecologies*. Despite coming from other times than our own, both texts became exemplary resources in our conversations around questions of critical transformations "today."[11] Along with their theoreti-

---

**9** Ibid., p. 80, emphasis added.
**10** Félix Guattari, *The Three Ecologies*, trans. Ian Pindar and Paul Sutton (London: Continuum, 2008), p. 29.
**11** The selection of Woolf and Guattari as readings for the second meeting of *Terra Critica* was partly tongue-in-cheek venturing to arrive at a response to Kant's three critiques and these two promised to take the figure *three* in new directions. But it was also to start from within the Western tradition, as we consider trans-forming critique as *unworking* its European Enlightenment, rather than delinking from it. While both authors clearly speak from a white European viewpoint, they also crucially do so from a feminist-poetic angle (Woolf) and an ecosophical perspective (Guattari), sharing therefore an unambivalent disapproval of hegemonic colonial-patriarchal capitalism.

cal propositions, they are both especially remarkable for the modes in which they intervened into their "todays." Woolf wrote *Three Guineas* at the height of nationalism and fascism and on the brink of world war, while Guattari's *The Three Ecologies* speaks from the European historical juncture of 1989 and its massive shifts in the world's order. While in what follows we will touch on these *objects* of their critical engagements (the problems of their todays, which are uncannily close to ours), we will specifically pursue the *gestures and moves* their arguments make, reading them primarily for the *methods and strategies* employed to delineate their critical points and to speak to/with their historical junctures. As the title of our contribution states, our primary interest lies with the modes of combat that critical gestures and strategies open up. The steps of this essay then are as follows: we will first attend to Guattari's delineation of the complications of critique under contemporary conditions of Integrated World Capitalism (IWC), as he presents them in *Three Ecologies*, which will secondly lead us to the notion of combat as a mode of negotiating forces within the matrix of IWC. Subsequently, we will move to Woolf, whose *Three Guineas* brilliantly performs a move of "indirection" that fleshes out what combat as a critical form could possibly mean: a situated, embodied, perspectival, and, therefore, *effective* critical intervention.

## IWC and the implications of critique

*The Three Ecologies*—written at the end of a (cold) war, the onset of a reordered Europe and the re-constellation of geopolitical landscapes and media ecologies— identifies two simultaneous shifts that gained momentum in the late 1980s. On the one hand, the "extreme complexification of social, economic and international contexts"[12] that resulted from the decline of the dualist confrontation between the USA and the USSR in the late 1980s and the rise of what Guattari calls "Integrated World Capitalism"[13]; and, on the other hand, the standardization and homogenizing of desire, largely promoted by the "mass-media,"[14] intimately linked to and at the service of the production of signs and subjectivity that Guattari perceives as the *modus operandi* of IWC. He writes:

> [C]apitalist power has become delocalized and deterritorialized, both in extension, by extending its influence over the whole social, economic and cultural life of the planet, and in "intension," by infiltrating the most unconscious subjective strata. In doing this it is no longer possible to claim to be opposed to capitalist power only from the outside, through trade unions and traditional politics.[15]

Given increasingly decentralized sites of power in IWC and the "introjection of repressive power by the oppressed"[16] that goes along with it, the question still arises in 2019 roughly in the same way in which Guattari asked it, namely: How to exercise critique? How to modify, refuse or bend the effects of a power whose force lies in integrating everything and thus makes an oppositional outside harder and harder to conceptualize or access? Or, as Guattari himself phrased it: How to

---

12 Guattari, *Three Ecologies*, p. 21.
13 Ibid., pp. 32; also pp. 32–35.
14 Guattari wrote at a time when television was the predominant visual medium. The proliferation of new media and the internet in the almost 30 years since *The Three Ecologies* was published (at which Guattari hints as possible future tools for undermining standardization), have made the claim regarding the simple anaesthetizing effects of television somewhat outdated, but the larger analysis still stands.
15 Guattari, *Three Ecologies*, p. 33.
16 Ibid., p. 32.

activate "catalysts of existential change"[17] from within? In part, Guattari responds to this question in *The Three Ecologies* with a microphysics of power. He very much relates the task ahead to questions of form, in the sense of "formation" and "cultivation." Since opposition from the outside is profoundly difficult (if not impossible), he notes that it is

equally imperative to confront capitalism's effects in the domain of mental ecology in everyday life: individual, domestic, material, neighbourly, creative or one's personal ethics. Rather than looking for a stupefying and infantilizing consensus, it will be a question in the future of cultivating a dissensus and the singular production of existence.[18]

Phrasing the mental, psychological, subjective domain as *ecological*—that is, placing it next to the social and environmental domains—is crucial here. Ecology, not so much as *Umwelt* or milieu that precedes and surrounds a subject, but as their co-emergent "environmentality,"[19] stresses the existential modes it names as "capable of bifurcating into stratified and deathly repetitions or of opening up processually from a praxis."[20] This means that the very production of existence is a domain which can close or open, it can de- and re-territorialize, be channeled into the narrow constraints of the law or become cancerous, but it can also be cultivated otherwise. Therefore,

17 Ibid., p. 30. In his later book *Chaosmosis*, Guattari notes that a "poetic-existential catalysis [...] is to recompose artificially rarefied, resingularised Universes of subjectification. For them, it's not a matter of transmitting messages, investing images as aids to identification, patterns of behaviours as props for modelisation procedures, but of catalysing existential operators capable of acquiring consistence and persistence." Félix Guattari, *Chaosmosis: an ethico-aesthetic paradigm*, trans. Paul Bains and Julian Pefanis (Bloomington: Indiana University Press, 1995), p. 19.
18 Guattari, *Three Ecologies*, p. 33.
19 See Erich Hörl, "The Environmentalitarian Situation: Reflections on the Becoming-Environmental of Thinking, Power, and Capital," *Cultural Politics* 14:2 (2018): pp. 153–173.
20 Guattari, *Three Ecologies*, p. 35.

critique also becomes a corporeal activity tied to the production of subjectivities, an activity that is presented here as a question of cultivation. When Guattari speaks of an "ecology of resingularization,"[21] and therefore of a "subjectivity of resingularization,"[22] a differentiation of desires (between, underneath and above the molar unit of the individual) from which transversal alliances for transformation can emerge, what is at stake for him is not liberal individualism. Rather, what is at stake in the emphasis on such a microphysics of power—and the micro-political critical strategies it permits—is letting unforeseen desires become effective, bringing into existence what was not imagined and lived before." [T]he essential thing here is the break-bifurcation, which it is impossible to represent as such, but which nevertheless exudes a phantasmatic of origins [...]."[23] Perhaps not surprisingly, given their long-standing collaboration, this stress on diversion and bringing into existence echoes with Gilles Deleuze's assertion in "To Have Done With Judgment" (a text on Antonin Artaud) that the trick— also of critique—might be "to bring into existence and not to judge."[24] And regarding the singularization of subjectivity, Deleuze also notes in the same essay that "[t]his is not subjectivism, since to pose the problem in terms of force, and not in other terms, already surpasses all subjectivity."[25]

If IWC is (among other things) a stratification and homogenization of existence for profit, then the de-stratification and differentiation of existence is a key move to "break-bifurcate" and re-route desires, as a form of critique *under these conditions*. Importantly, Guattari's

**21** Ibid., p. 42.
**22** Ibid., p. 44.
**23** Ibid., p. 37.
**24** Gilles Deleuze, "To Have Done with Judgment," in Gilles Deleuze, *Essays Critical and Clinical*, trans. Daniel W. Smith and Michael A. Greco (Minneapolis: University of Minnesota Press, 1997), p. 135.
**25** Ibid.

dissensus as cultivation and re-routing comes not in the name of already articulable alternatives or programs. Rather, it becomes the experimental means to re-singularize existence itself, a growing proliferation of difference without presupposing or proposing a new structure or a *telos*. Critical dissensus is phrased as the affirmation of cultivating new existential refrains to which the corporeal and affective are key. In Guattari's microphysics of power, then, critique comes as an embodied negotiation of these forces. Deleuze also follows this specific line of flight for critique when he defines critical negotiation in "To Have Done with Judgment" as a form of "combat." Here, Deleuze writes that for Artaud it is precisely combat that replaces judgment. In his works, Artaud revalues what Deleuze calls "the physical system of cruelty" (which is the system of affects) over the "theological doctrine of judgment."[26] And, as Deleuze continues to specify,

> [c]ombat is not war. War is only a combat-against, a will to destruction, a judgment of God that turns destruction into something "just." The judgment of God is on the side of war, not combat. [...] In war, the will to power merely means that the will wants strength [*puissance*] as a maximum of power [*pouvoir*] or domination. [...] Combat, by contrast, is a powerful, nonorganic vitality that supplements force with force, and enriches whatever it takes hold of.[27]

If IWC exerts power on the level of signs and subjectivities and *affective* dispositions, then an *effective* critique is one that mobilizes precisely these forces and (impersonal) affects otherwise. Even if combat might appear to be used here "*against* judgment," Deleuze notes that, much more profoundly than being *against*, combat is

26  Ibid., p. 130.
27  Ibid., p. 133.

*between* the combatant's "own parts, between the forces that either subjugate or are subjugated, and between the powers that express their relations of force. [...]."[28] Critical practice has now become an attempt to re-direct rather than to oppose the forces exerted by power, by IWC and/or by colonial-patriarchal capitalism. The last of these is also the terminological realm of Woolf's *Three Guineas*, the second text that guided us in the *Terra Critica* meeting in November 2013. Reading Woolf next to (and diffracting her text with) the questions that Guattari—with Deleuze's echoes—put forward, turned out to specify further the different *how to* that combat as critical form point toward. What we strive to show in the following is Woolf's specific move of *indirection*, which to us fleshes out what combat can mean as a situated, embodied, perspectival, *a/effective* critical intervention.

### Combat and the moves of indirection

Combat war then, in or for critical projects. The turn toward combat and the question of war resonated unexpectedly well in our discussion of Guattari with the key question of Woolf's text. At her very specific historical juncture in 1938, Woolf published *Three Guineas* in full view of the societal fascism ruling her time, when there seemed to be no time left, when an alternative to the horrors of Nazism and war lurking at the doorstep was desperately wished for. Yet, surprisingly, if we read *Three Guineas* closely, this text seems to be all about (taking) time: the time it takes to produce a meaningful answer to letters received; and the time it takes to think ("Think we must!"[29] is probably one of the text's most well-known exclamations). The narrator in *Three*

---

28  Ibid., p. 132.
29  Virginia Woolf, *Three Guineas* (San Diego and New York: Harcourt Inc., 1966), p. 62.

*Guineas* allows herself to take time in order to elaborate what actually is at stake when educated men ask the daughters of educated men "How in your opinion are we to prevent war?"[30] And, thus, Woolf presents an intricate problem for any critical endeavor: How to effectively intervene—critically—into "today," especially when a matter seems to have such urgency? Counter-intuitively perhaps to both effectiveness and urgency, instead of beginning directly with an answer, Woolf's text moves by deferral and raises other crucial questions first. Most of all she asks in the course of this text if the question addressed to her is actually one that each and every one of "us" (interpellated as those who consider themselves strong opponents of violence and fascism) can—or better: should—answer in the same manner? This is what "the educated man" (who asks the narrator the question) seems to take for granted. But, the narrator gives us to think, are we here not facing a question that must be differentiated according to many grammars, perspectives or intersections (sex/gender, race, class, geopolitical location, etc.), since who speaks, from where, and to whom, is of utmost significance to how meaningful the answer itself will be? *Three Guineas* pays close attention to these concerns. It takes the form of three letters, which all struggle with the question of *how* to respond—in a fashion that does not merely choose sides and/or lay the issue aside, but that expresses as adequately as possible the complexity of the matters at stake. It can therefore also be read as the question: "How to produce an *e/affective* critique?" Or: "How to be *e/affectively* critical?"[31] This is Woolf's *critical* situation, when her narrator is

30  Ibid., p. 3.
31  The superposition of effect and affect into *e/affective* will be addressed more extensively below with the help of François Jullien, although for us it is certainly linked mainly to a Deleuzian/Spinozian heritage of affectivity as the body's capacity to affect and be affected, which avoids both a too hasty humanist understanding of what a body is and also a too simple (post-)modern opposition of affect and ratio.

confronted with a letter that, as she says, has been lying around unanswered for "three years" already, and that has this immense question in it: "How in your opinion are we to prevent war?"[32] In response to this question, the narrator then writes three letters over the course of three years, which each give reasons for why she commits guineas to causes that might assist to prevent war: a woman's college, a fund for women's professions, and a society for the promotion of peace.

A closer engagement with *Three Guineas* is unfortunately beyond the scope of this essay, and we have to focus here on our main interest, namely Woolf's gestures and strategies of critique. By taking the time to stake her claim, taking time that is not given and taking time to detour to other issues first, Woolf's narrator turns precariously differentiated positionings into a critical matter, and by doing this she makes them matter to the very issue of war itself. The narrator does not answer the educated man's question straightforwardly, because what she is faced with is a question asked from within an exclusivist and colonial-patriarchal history. What *Three Guineas* insists on is space ("a room of one's own"[33]) in which, first of all, the very basic question can be asked as to whether or not "we" want to "join that [the educated man's] procession."[34] For any answer that truly wants to make a difference as an e/affective critical intervention, this must remain open *as a question*. As Woolf formulates so well: "We have to ask ourselves, here and now, do we wish to join that procession, or don't we? On what terms shall we join that procession? Above all, where is it leading us, the procession of educated men?"[35]

**32**  Woolf, *Three Guineas*, p. 3.
**33**  Virginia Woolf, *A Room of One's Own* (San Diego and New York: Harcourt Inc., 1981).
**34**  Woolf, *Three Guineas*, p. 62.
**35**  Ibid.

If it is with such powers of *indirection* that Woolf's literary critical engagement with both the addressee of her letter and the issues at stake becomes *e/affective*, then what we call indirection here—one of Woolf's critical strategies—can be differentiated once more. Indirection is used by Woolf as a *politics of location*, i.e. indirection does not hide, but instead highlights the historically specific distribution of speaking positions and silences within the terrain of the discussion at stake; and indirection is also used as a *diffractive maneuver*. By literally indirecting the discussion, Woolf "gains space" for the matters at hand. In her critical and analytically sharp answers we see new interference patterns emerge, whereby the terrain of discussion itself is opened in unprecedented ways. And finally, indirection is also presented by her as an *earthly practice*. Woolf—this is at least our generous feminist reading of her here—is fully aware of the necessary entanglements with/in the matters of educated men, however indirect they may be. In an echo of Guattari's point regarding the productive power of IWC, for Woolf also there is no secure "outside" from which one can judge and defy implicatedness. In *Three Guineas*, this plays out in various ways. For one, the fact that the narrator gives a *guinea* highlights the long entanglement of the forces she struggles with: patriarchal nationalism and its logic of warfare, which includes colonialism. The guinea was the English gold coin that preceded the British pound. It went out of use in 1814, more than a century before the time of writing *Three Guineas* and carried the name of the Gold Coast (present day Guinea), hub of the European transatlantic slave-trade, a region from which the gold was extracted that was minted into this English colonial coin, the guinea. So, donating this coin in 1938 is not about historical inaccuracy; rather, if listened to closely, it makes a point: that the narrator can give a guinea now for "emancipatory" causes is predicated upon the constitutional implication of the giver in the structures of injustice, which the donations are meant to help undo. The outdated coin, the guinea, keeps this implication visible—thus Woolf's is not a critique that distances itself fully from the state of affairs. And yet, the indirection which brings to light underlying questions and intersecting lines of in/exclusion, does make a difference. It introduces a different "logic" of critique than any either/or criticism; it shifts the field of questions that can be asked, and it gives room to diversify and differentiate, or (in Guattari's terms) to resingularize the field of problems.

In light of such shifting of the questions, we have continually stressed *e/affective* modes of critique. To specify why *e/affectivity* is important, we want to turn for a moment to François Jullien, who in his *Treatise on Efficacy: Between Western and Chinese Thinking* writes that reaching effectivity might not imply "a psychology of will," but rather "[a]ll that is needed is a phenomenology of effectivity—as in affectivity—that is to say, effectiveness."[36] With this in mind, what we aim to argue here in relation to criticality and *e/affective* forms of critique can be further specified. Reading Woolf—and also Guattari—with Jullien's argumentative move from effectiveness as efficacy (a purely willed effect) to effectiveness as efficiency (emergent and indirect), it is possible to argue that criticality's effectiveness "is not something that one 'seeks', steering towards it directly and deliberatively."[37] Instead, critique "is always a matter of how to impinge upon the process upstream (*en amont*), in such a way that an effect will then tend to 'come' of its own accord."[38] Such an emergent, processual effectiveness as form of critique does not confront head on,

---

36  François Jullien, *A Treatise on Efficacy: Between Western and Chinese Thinking*, trans. Janet Lloyd (Honolulu: University of Hawai'i Press, 2004), p. 120. While building on his arguments in terms of *e/affectivity*, we are also troubled by Jullien's treatise in how it so clearly distinguishes between what he calls "Western and Chinese Thinking."
37  Ibid., p. 121.
38  Ibid., p. 121.

but on first sight might sometimes even suggest indifference in respect to the desired result. In his *Treatise*, Jullien speaks in this context also of a thinking of efficiency "unconnected to the notion of a cause" which, when it does not get reconnected to a theological/transcendental absolute principle, "becomes *efficiency*, the processivity of which stems from the fund of immanence."[39] It seems possible to read Woolf's provocative quest of indirection in such an immanent manner. Her daring claim to "look elsewhere" (which is not the same as "looking away") in such a pressing situation as the eve of World War II can be read as Woolf's consequential expression of the fact that, as she also very famously writes in *Three Guineas*, "my country is the whole world."[40] In a daring, nearly indifferent indirection, by looking elsewhere, taking time and re-directing the question towards matters that seem unrelated, she critically impinges on the very colonial-patriarchal framework in which the question of how to prevent war has reached her. And if we also turn our attention again to Guattari, we see that both Woolf and Guattari insist on an immanent criticality with their difficult yet consequential in-difference and/as indirection. With it, they hope to make "us" *e/affected and e/affective* as critical voices in response to the situations they/we face—war (1938) and integrated global capitalism (1989).

## Critique and/as transformation

As exemplary *modes* of critique, Woolf's and Guattari's texts keep instructing the work we are doing in the *Terra Critica* network. Despite the different historical moments the texts tackle, their critical gestures of dissensus, singularization, transversality, indirection, stay-

39  Ibid., p. 133.
40  Woolf, *Three Guineas*, p. 109.

ing with and thickening the questions are, in our view, highly informative ways to transform and reform critical practice today. On the final pages of *Three Guineas*, Woolf once more phrases this revised critical "how to" in regard to what she calls "the society of outsiders." In relation to this secret society she states that part of a critical "how to" would be concretely "to cease all competition and to practise [our] profession experimentally, in the interest of research and for love of the work itself."[41] To this she later adds: "Elasticity is essential; and some degree of secrecy...we, remaining outside, will experiment not with public means in public but with private means in private. Those experiments will not be merely critical but creative."[42] In his own manner Guattari also emphasizes experimental and creative practice as the most useful critical strategy, when he describes his "new ecosophy" as "at once applied and theoretical, ethicopolitical and aesthetical," and not as "a discipline of refolding on interiority, or a simple renewal of earlier forms of 'militancy'."[43] Critical thinking, as a quest for critical worldly/earthly engagements, is a transformative practice in this micro/macropolitically-entangled sense. Criticality cannot but continue to be about transformative powers and it relies in its practice on an engagement with the world that allows (or even more so: strives) for change to happen—pushing boundaries, un-working what appears fixed and aiming to make a difference. Michel Foucault says as much in his reading of Kant in "What is Enlightenment?" The critical modus emerging from the Enlightenment might be best understood, Foucault suggests, as an *ethos* (attitude) that follows the continually transformative and demanding

---

41  Ibid., p. 112, emphasis added.
42  Ibid., p. 113. We would like to suggest Woolf's reference to "private" here as one in which she again tries to break open rather than confirm the opposition of the feminized private to the masculinist public realm.
43  Guattari, *Three Ecologies*, p. 44.

maxim of "[w]hat difference does today introduce in respect to yesterday?"[44] and thus produces "a mode of relating to contemporary reality."[45] *Thinking with* Kant, Foucault's affirmative critical stance enables him to grasp Kant's enlightenment imperative *sapere aude* (dare to know), not as the enlightenment fantasy of progress (and omnipotence), but as a strenuous exercise of theo-retico-practical engagements, "a task that requires work on our limits, that is, a patient labor giving form to our impatience for liberty."[46] In this light, Foucault refor-mulates critique as "limit-attitude"[47]: a form of critique that no longer looks for "formal structures with univer-sal value"[48] as transcendent(al) critique, but one that becomes a fully immanent, worldly endeavor. Rather than imagining a cathartic reversal, an elevation *out of this* situation, criticality today—Woolf and Guattari have proposed this in their own conceptual-existential ways—has to both conceptually come to terms with its primary implicatedness (i.e. it has to change its vocab-ulary into one of an *entangled* critical ontology) and learn to maneuver in—i.e. *negotiate*—this situation in which relationality rather than opposition is the more *a/effective* criterion. Under today's conditions of IWC, the Foucaultian critical potential "to give new impetus, as far and wide as possible, to the undefined work of freedom"[49] lies for us precisely in the seemingly weak criteria of "experimentation" and "partiality,"[50] which Woolf and Guattari practice in their texts. Critique as "limit attitude"—as working on and from the limits

44  Michel Foucault, "What is Enlightenment?," in *Ethics, Subjectivity and Truth: The Essential Works of Michel Foucault*, Volume 1, ed. Paul Rabinow (New York: The New Press, 1997), pp. 303–319, here p. 305.
45  Ibid., p. 309.
46  Ibid., p. 319.
47  Ibid., p. 315.
48  Ibid.
49  Ibid.
50  See ibid., p. 316.

of Woolf's outsider society or Guattari's resingularized existential refrains—is a practice that is "committed to making a difference."[51]

Saying this, we can however not quite end yet. Claiming critical thinking as committed to making a difference might be the very trap into which critical practice will always fall: the unavoidable slippage into seemingly knowing better, and assuming a critical *position* that imagines things differently into a future, with the stubborn incapacity to abandon the vision *that* (and implicitly also suggesting *how*) the world could be otherwise. A critical movement of thought and/as practicing (in) this world does not seem to be able to fully avoid the ethico-onto-epistemological dangers of progressivism, optimism, and over-generalizing truth claims. And yet, what seems to matter here is, perhaps, to approach the critical transformative powers of what Guattari calls the "production of human existence itself in new historical contexts"[52] in such a way that we do not *directly* fall into either the trap of progressivism (linear time) or a better vision (teleology). With Wynter, therefore, we wonder (in the affirmative) about the possibility of a way to envision transformation otherwise than overcoming—the Hegelian "relève" [*Aufhebung*]—or moving on. We wonder if "we" might not become (more) capable of negotiating ways of practicing transformation as an unworking of the logics of "beyond" and "after", without, however, ever giving up "being after" as a critical intervention. Pushing in this sense for an "after" that always doubles itself but does not get outside itself cannot be aligned so easily with simple linear-teleological narration or philosophizing, or with finally finding the accurate models of critique. Transformation, then, is no longer the process of either overcoming or simply letting

---

51  Donna Haraway, *Modest_Witness@Second_Millennium.FemaleMan©_ Meets_-OncoMouse™* (London and New York: Routledge, 1997), p. 273.
52  Guattari, *Three Ecologies*, p. 24.

go. Rather, it might be better characterized as the effects of a mode of combat "between the forces that either subjugate or are subjugated,"[53] as the effects of a form of critique that commits not to overcoming but to processes of "abandoning (to)"[54]—in the multidirectional and multidimensional sense of a "re-turning (to)"[55] the matters of care and concern for "today."

53  Deleuze, "To Have Done with Judgment," p. 132.
54  See Peta Hinton and Xin Liu, "The Im/Possibility of Abandonment in New Materialist Ontologies," *Australian Feminist Studies* 30 (2015): pp. 128–145.
55  See Karen Barad, "Diffracting Diffraction: Cutting Together-Apart," *Parallax* 20:3 (2014): pp. 168–187; Birgit M. Kaiser and Kathrin Thiele, eds., "The Ends of Being Human? Re-turning (to) the Question," Special Issue of *PhiloSOPHIA: A Journal of Continental Feminism* 8:1 (2018).

Oona Lochner

# "To Arlene on Wings of Love"

## Shared Forms of Life, Art, and Writing

The forms of my life and work changed radically, and
literally overnight, when eight weeks ago my son was
born. I write now when he is asleep, interrupted by
every waking or squirming or sound. Because he sleeps
best when he is close to me or in motion, I mostly work
standing up, the computer on an emptied bookshelf, the
baby bound to my constantly rocking body. I know the
many hours of standing and walking don't exactly help
my body's recovery from pregnancy and birth. Many
nights I feel worn out and my hip hurts. Having a child
and writing are two, often conflicting forces forming
my days. Both pulling at me, competing for my attention, making me feel guilty for never having enough
time, focus, devotion, love for either of them. Still, I like
the simultaneous presence of these two, body and mind,
you might think. And more often now I value even their
unnervingly rubbing against each other, because one
alters my view of the other. To acknowledge or, in fact,
to spell out how the ways you live are always entangled
with the ways you write holds the promise of rethinking both.

My doctoral thesis revolves around the work of three
women who in the late 1960s and 1970s wrote about art
and earned a reputation as feminists. Each of them, at
a time when the personal was turning political, made
her writing about art the place where she also reflected
her life: all three rejecting the roles offered to them as

critics and as women.[1] Jill Johnston (1929–2010) wrote an infamous dance column for the weekly New York newspaper *The Village Voice*, where her writing slowly shifted from dance to herself. Lucy Lippard (\*1937), prominent curator and critic of conceptual art, reinvented herself as a feminist in 1970, flipping back and forth then between an emphatically subjective writing and a more conventional, almost formalist style. Lastly, Arlene Raven (1944–2006) created her texts out of the all-women community of feminist Los Angeles, having her writing reflect the relationships that formed her work and life. Much could be said about Johnston and Lippard being mothers and writers and how this speaks to me. But in fact, it is Arlene Raven who teaches me most about how changing forms of life and work can bring forth new aesthetic forms.[2]

***

An art historian and later critic, Raven moved to Los Angeles in 1972 to join its evolving feminist art scene. She began to teach at the CalArts Feminist Art Program that had been established by artists Miriam Schapiro and Judy Chicago, but soon felt the need to educate women artists apart from the patriarchal structures of art schools. She founded, together with Chicago and designer Sheila de Bretteville, the education program

---

1    "Women" in the 1970s, especially in separatist all-women groups like the ones mentioned in this text, have often been understood in terms that have since been criticized as essentialist and exclusionary. I mostly refer to this as a historical position here. Where I talk about *women* from my own perspective, I'm closer to Sara Ahmed's phrasing: "referring to all those who travel under the sign women." Sara Ahmed, *Living a Feminist Life* (Durham NC and London: Duke University Press, 2017), p. 14.

2    Raven had a stepdaughter. For biographical details and a chronology of the events recounted in the following see Anne Swartz, "She Is Who She Wants To Be: A Critical Biographical Essay on Arlene Raven," *Critical Matrix: The Princeton Journal of Women, Gender and Culture* 17 (Arlene Raven's Legacy) (2008): pp. 48–65.

Feminist Studio Workshop (FSW), opening doors in September 1973, and its location, the Woman's Building, which was to become a hub of L.A.'s feminist community. In the mostly male post-1945 art world, abstraction had triumphed over narrative content, and women's lives and experiences, in particular, were frowned upon as too trivial to be used as material for art.[3] The FSW countered this by conflating education and community among women. In "an atmosphere that encourages caring and non-competitive exploration of personal experience and women's consciousness," students should break free from male institutions and from identifying chiefly in relation to men (be it as their wife, mother, daughter or, more generally, their counterpart, their Other). They were challenged to create art out of their lives lived as women.[4]

Consequently, being enrolled in the FSW meant not only working but spending time together. Designed as a two-year program, it offered several elective "projects," dedicated to visual arts, writing, graphics or performance. These complemented the so-called "Core Process, which include[d] consciousness raising, the formation and experience of community, and an examination of historical and personal issues in the light of a feminist perspective."[5] Far beyond creating and presenting art, students were expected to take part in discussion groups and consciousness-raising, to fix up studio space,

---

3   This, according to Raven, was the case even at progressive CalArts. See Terry Wolverton, "Looking Through A New Lens: An Interview with Arlene Raven," in *From Site to Vision: The Woman's Building in Contemporary Culture*, ed. Sondra Hale and Terry Wolverton (Los Angeles: Otis College of Art and Design, 2011), pp. 119–138, here pp. 130–131.
4   Citations are taken from an untitled FSW description (c. summer 1978), *Woman's Building records, 1970–1992*, Archives of American Art, Smithsonian Institution, Washington DC, Box 11, Folder 35. All Woman's Building documents cited here are also available online: https://www.aaa.si.edu/collections/womans-building-records-6347 (last accessed October 12, 2019).
5   FSW description, *Woman's Building records*, n. p.

to offer support and criticism to each other.[6] Their art evolved out of sharing and collectively reflecting their lives as women—and so did Arlene Raven's writing.

From the late 1960s on, artists and scholars had been challenging the dominant tales of art history by unrolling the narratives and structures that had served to keep women out. They unveiled how the figure of the Genius had been used to naturalize artistic talent as male and how the rules and traditions of art education had guarded its institutions against women entering.[7] At the same time, writers and artists discussed the notion of a specific *female sensibility* or *imagery* that might distinguish women's art from that of their male colleagues.[8] Tapping into these debates, Raven asked what kind of art is produced when female artists work outside of the male-dominated institutions and instead build a community between women. If culture until then had reflected mainly a male perspective, what could a *women's culture* look like that would be based on female experience? And unlike most writers, Raven raised these questions by openly reflecting on her personal life, her relationships at the FSW, and the Woman's Building, realizing in her

---

**6**  Wolverton, "Interview with Arlene Raven," p. 126. See also "Curriculum Description FSW, 1976–77," *Woman's Building records, 1970–1992*, Archives of American Art, Smithsonian Institution, Washington DC, Box 11, Folder 49. Many of these principles were prefigured in the Feminist Art Project founded by Judy Chicago, first in Fresno, then CalArts. Compare Betty Ann Brown, "Feminist Art Education at the Los Angeles Woman's Building," in Hale and Wolverton, *From Site to Vision*, pp. 141–159.

**7**  Most prominently, Linda Nochlin, "Why Have There Been No Great Women Artists?," *ArtNews* 69:9 (January 1971): pp. 22–39.

**8**  Notorious in this debate was Judy Chicago arguing that women artists frequently used a "central core image" in their painting and interpreting this as unconscious reference to female genitalia. See Judy Chicago and Miriam Schapiro, "Female Imagery," *Womanspace Journal* 1:3 (Summer 1973): pp. 11–14, reprinted in Amelia Jones, ed., *The Feminism and Visual Cultures Reader* (London and New York: Routledge, 2002), pp. 53–56. Others were more skeptical. See the discussion "What Is Female Imagery?," in *Ms.* 3:11 (May 1975), reprinted in Lucy Lippard, *From the Center: feminist essays on women's art* (New York: Dutton, 1976), pp. 80–89.

writing her theoretical claims as to the formative potential of women's experience and collectivity.

In the academic year 1976/77, Raven took a sabbatical from the FSW to focus on her art historical work on
lesbian artists such as 1920s painter Romaine Brooks.
(Another reason for her leaving, rumor has it, might
have been that her romance with a student created rip-
ples among FSW faculty).[9] In the spring of 1977, she
returned for two workshops, presenting her research
and inviting students to participate in a project of lesbian art history at the FSW. Six women joined her and
named themselves the Natalie Barney Collective (after
the expatriate writer and Romaine Brooks' lover, known
for her literary salon in Paris).[10] Together they launched
the Lesbian Art Project (LAP), committing to weekly
meetings and consciousness-raising sessions, planning
work-sharing events, workshops, and exhibitions to
carry a lesbian perspective into the FSW curriculum.[11]
And in fact, before long, the LAP was listed as one of the
FSW electives along with Visual Arts, the Women Writing Program or Women's Graphics Center.[12] What Raven

9   While the Curriculum for 1976/77 still lists Raven as teacher, poet
    Terry Wolverton, in her autobiography, recalls her absence. In fact,
    Wolverton, who was a student at the FSW, Raven's collaborator at
    the Lesbian Art Project (LAP), and later executive director at the
    Woman's Building, is one of the main sources when writing about
    the FSW and, particularly, the LAP. Based on her personal memories,
    her account is naturally biased and fragmentary, often unverifiable,
    at times contradictory, yet highly valuable and, in the context of
    this text, a perfect example of how knowledge production is entan-
    gled with the personal and unconscious. See Terry Wolverton, *Insur-
    gent Muse: Life and Art at the Woman's Building* (San Francisco: City
    Lights Publishers, 2002), here p. 49; "Curriculum Description FSW,
    1976–77," pp. 4, 7.
10  The Natalie Barney Collective consisted of Kathleen Berg, Nancy
    Fried, Sharon Immergluck, Arlene Raven, Donna Reyna, Maya Ster-
    ling and Terry Wolverton. My account of the LAP follows Wolverton,
    Insurgent Muse, pp. 57–90, 107–111, and Terry Wolverton, "The Art
    of Lesbian Relationship: Arlene Raven and the Lesbian Art Project,"
    *Critical Matrix: The Princeton Journal of Women, Gender and Culture*
    17 (Arlene Raven's Legacy) (2008): pp. 66–71.
11  Jennie Klein, "The Lesbian Art Project," *Journal of Lesbian Studies*
    14:2–3 (2010): pp. 238–259, here p. 239.
12  FSW description, *Woman's Building records*, n. p.

had initially envisioned as a joint art historical research, according to fellow collective member Terry Wolverton, turned into an "exploration of the meaning(s) of 'lesbian,' […] and the manifestation of a *culture* in which those meanings can be expressed and amplified."[13] In finding artistic and quotidian forms for lesbian life, the LAP members shifted focus from the oppression of lesbian experience to its celebration, while building a community "in which research and life would become inseparable."[14] Just how successful they were in merging life and work came to light when in early 1978, nine months after the LAP was formed, the relationships across the group had grown so complicated (romances ended and were resumed, creating jealousy and conflicts of loyalty) that the Collective fell apart.

Arlene Raven and Terry Wolverton, both still committed to the LAP, decided to start over and began a dialogue about lesbian education and, from there, about the quality and dynamics of relationships between women. They "defined these relationships as 'lesbian' in that they excluded men, whether or not they included sexual expression."[15] They discussed the different roles and power balances between women and, specifically, in their own difficult relationship. They tried to build a non-hierarchical collaboration with mutual "mentoring and 'peership'."[16] Nevertheless, Raven, ten years older and co-founder of the FSW where Wolverton was a student, could hardly escape the role of a teacher. Working together was further complicated by Raven and Wolverton sharing a passion not only for the LAP but (at different times) also for artist Cheryl Swannack. She had been with Raven previous to her sabbatical, was then Wolverton's lover and was now living again with Raven. This made things difficult for Wolverton who, by work-

---

13  Wolverton, *Insurgent Muse*, p. 59, my emphasis.
14  Wolverton, "Art of Lesbian Relationship," p. 67.
15  Ibid., p. 70.
16  Wolverton, *Insurgent Muse*, pp. 70–71.

ing with Raven, had to involuntarily interact with her ex-partner.

To re-establish the LAP, they developed a new education program, started workshops, art and social events and continued Raven's art historical research, but they also kept to weekly meetings of discussing and dealing with their personal relationship. A work relation on the surface, it was in fact messy. Their matter-of-fact talk about concepts and organizational tasks was deeply entangled in affects like jealousy, guilt, desire, anxiety and shame that, only with great effort, were dug up in their meetings. Declaring mutuality in the face of an imbalance of power (Arlene being the more mature, the teacher, the prominent feminist, the one who was not permanently confronted with her ex-girlfriend) runs the risk of not dissolving but glossing over hierarchies. Entering into a romantic triangle between teacher and students takes chances with the sexiness of authority and with the more powerful, however unconsciously, taking advantage of their position. Raven would have known that. She had married her master's thesis advisor at George Washington College, then got divorced after she found out he had an affair with a student.[17]

By the beginning of 1979, tensions between Raven and Wolverton had escalated, and in July of that year they eventually ended their collaboration.

\*\*\*

Two years before, just when the LAP was founded in the spring and summer of 1977, Raven and art historian Ruth Iskin wrote the dialogical text "Through the Peephole: Toward a Lesbian Sensibility in Art" for the feminist

---

**17** Carey Lovelace, "Arlene Raven and the Foresight of the Advocate Critic," *Critical Matrix: The Princeton Journal of Women, Gender and Culture* 17 (Arlene Raven's Legacy) (2008): pp. 96–104, here p. 98.

magazine *Chrysalis*.[18] Again, the relationship between the two women was complicated. Both were among the founding editors of *Chrysalis*; both were teaching at the FSW, where they started The Center for Feminist Art Historical Studies.[19] In early 1977, when they co-authored the essay, they also shared a home (just before Raven took things up again with Cheryl Swannack).[20] Maybe surprisingly, it is precisely this *messiness* of Raven's collaborative relationships, their affective overload and precariousness, which yields the potential to rethink writing. Raven not only sheds light on how thinking is always entangled in relations and the affects they cause, but rather, she makes use of it. Feeling your skin tingle or your stomach turn becomes part of her thinking about art and women in art. It creates new thoughts while, in passing, also offering a critique of authorship and knowledge production as they comply with a dualism of mind/rational/male versus body/feeling/female.

Far beyond Raven and Iskin, "Through the Peephole" mirrors the personal bonds underlying the FSW program. The text's main body is a dialogue over six pages between "Arlene" and "Ruth," discussing an art production that would be based on women's lives and relations. Embedded in and supported by an all-female community, they argue, women artists could value their specific experience as relevant for humankind—as for a

**18** Ruth Iskin and Arlene Raven, "Through the Peephole: Toward a Lesbian Sensibility in Art," *Chrysalis: A Magazine of Women's Culture* 4 (1977): pp. 19–31.

**19** Swartz, "Biographical Essay," pp. 50, 54.

**20** Klein, "Lesbian Art Project," pp. 245, 248. Several writers who met Raven and Iskin around that time remember them to be lovers as well. See, besides Klein, Joanna Frueh, "All Queer," *Critical Matrix: The Princeton Journal of Women, Gender and Culture* 17 (Arlene Raven's Legacy) (2008): pp. 114–124, here p. 115. Their relationship is also remembered by Raven's partner Nancy Grossman, personal conversation in Brooklyn, October 9, 2018. However, according to Terry Wolverton, Iskin never acknowledged this romance nor being lesbian within the community of the Woman's Building. Instead, Iskin states today that the rumors are not accurate. Personal emails by Wolverton, November 30, 2019, and by Iskin, November 29, 2019.

long time had been the universalized male perspective. They would start creating art from "a woman-centered world view" or, as the community envisioned by Raven and Iskin was "de facto homosexual in the sense that it is exclusively female," from a lesbian perspective.[21]

Traditionally, Iskin expands, artmaking is seen as corresponding to the heterosexual relationship between male artist and female muse or matter, visualized in portrayals of artists and their mistresses.[22] Rejecting this "longstanding dichotomy between the active creator and the passive model/artwork that is acted upon," she proposes instead a female-female relationship of mutual inspiration and creation.[23] The figure of the lesbian, now in Raven's words, is "an exemplary symbol—the woman who takes risks, who dares to be a creator in a new territory, who does not follow rules, who *declares herself the source of her artistic creation.*"[24] A metaphor and model for all women, the lesbian no longer makes sense of herself in relation to men, is no longer oriented towards men, but in more than one way is "woman-identified": by drawing upon her personal experience of being a woman as well as upon her kinship and relations to other women.[25] Conceptually as

---

**21** Iskin and Raven, "Through the Peephole," p. 21.

**22** Giving the example of Jean-Auguste-Dominique Ingres' "Raphael and La Fornarina." Ibid., p. 24.

**23** Ibid. As early as February 1973, Iskin was interested in women relating to each other, giving a slide lecture about this idea as part of a Lesbian Week at Womanspace gallery. Raven, on this occasion, talked about Romaine Brooks. See *Womanspace Journal*, 1:1 (1973): pp. 26–27.

**24** Iskin and Raven, "Through the Peephole," p. 21, my emphasis.

**25** Using this term seven times, Raven and Iskin align their text with the radical lesbian feminist group Lavender Menace (later: Radicalesbians) and their "Woman-Identified Woman" manifesto (1970), demanding the inclusion of lesbians in the women's movement. The manifesto, too, sees the lesbian as model for women's liberation, calling women to break free from relating to men. Also see, in this respect, Sara Ahmed, who argues that sexual "orientation" has everything to do with patrilinearity and the spaces bodies can or cannot occupy. Sara Ahmed, *Queer Phenomenology: Orientations, Objects, Others* (Durham NC and London: Duke University Press, 2006).

well as linguistically, the text converges being lesbian and being feminist. Both terms alternate in rapid succession or are conflated into "lesbian/feminist," hovering indecisively between its possible readings of lesbian and/or/as feminist.[26] Consequently, being lesbian in their dialogue, like in Raven's discussions with Wolverton, does not necessarily include sexuality or romance. Rather it alludes to women caring for and relating to each other in creating their work and their selves. Such a community, Raven and Iskin argue, can be the source of a new artistic production.

This is realized also by their writing. Raven and Iskin point out that they developed their thoughts "based on the artwork created at the Feminist Studio Workshop […] and on our experience in that community."[27] This relationality is translated into the form of their text. On each spread, their dialogue is framed by images of artworks by their friends and students (fig. 1); the last five pages are reserved completely to them. However, the images are not mere illustrations of the discussion, but reflect back on it. They are accompanied by short commentaries that are part description, part association. Some are written by Raven or Iskin, others include the artists' voices. Together, images and captions form independent miniatures about lesbian desire and its potential for creating art that speaks to everyone. Some of their key terms or ideas return in the main dialogue. Thus, "Through the Peephole" does not follow a linear and unitary argument but creates meaning in the intersection between main text, images and captions, in having the reader's eye and mind jump across the page and across media, in giving sound to different voices, in drawing lines between artmaking and writing,

---

26  "Woman-identified" as well as "lesbian-feminist" become in the 1970s self-descriptions of "women who often made a deliberate political choice to embrace lesbianism." Klein, "Lesbian Art Project," pp. 244–245.
27  Iskin and Raven, "Through the Peephole," p. 20.

Allyn describes the irrationality and disruption of romantic passion, portraying a lesbian experience to express a human dilemma.
**A.R.**

*A Play on Passion in Four Movements:*
Passion is a crush which has nothing to do with the other person, aside from a tingling sensation throughout, a pounding heart, speechless voice, and general paralysis whenever you see them.
Passion is dropping animals, friends, and a lifetime's worth of work in a matter of hours to be with that "certain someone," day and night.
Passion is knowing nothing about the person and claiming to be in love.
Passion is surprise in discovering as you get to know the person, you have nothing in common.

**Arlene:** The important difference between the private and public contexts is that the private context you described would not spawn a lesbian sensibility which could enter the public domain intact. Sanction is also significant, however, because the context for our work is always patriarchy, and our expressions are prey to gross misinterpretation by all but the few who can choose to interpret them through lesbian history and culture. "Deviant" individuals are often crushed by an alien culture: We increase our control and power when we form communities and express our point of view through the institution of the community.

Lesbian sensibility reflects a new process, form, and content because it expresses the transformational process that takes place in a feminist community. Personal relationships –which might form the private context–happen within the community, but the important factor for work is that there is enough immediate support so that one can turn to the interface between the community and the public. Lesbian sensibility is a positive woman-identified sensibility. It communicates publicly that woman-identified lesbian images and social relations transformed in a feminist community provide a world-view free of sexism–a way of life and consciousness in an environment free of patriarchy. It is true that economically privileged women like Rosa Bonheur were also able to live their lives in relative freedom; but unlike Rosa Bonheur–who, though habitually wearing pants, kept a closet full of frilly dresses as a concession to "femininity"–women today don't have to make those kinds of compromises.

Jerri Allyn, *A Play on Passion in Four Movements*

**Fig. 1:** Arlene Raven / Ruth Iskin, "Through the Peephole: Toward a Lesbian Sensibility in Art," *Chrysalis: A Magazine of Women's Culture* 4 (1977): p. 22.

teachers and students, friends and lovers. Raven and Iskin perform a process of writing in which knowledge is extracted from being enmeshed in personal bonds with artists and their work—be it as their teacher, a participant in their performances,[28] or as muse: the article features three of Nancy Fried's bread dough reliefs that show women together in domestic scenes (fig. 2). One, depicting a naked woman sprawled over a couch, is titled *To Arlene On Wings of Love*.

It is these relations, shared forms of life and work, that literally give form to the text. Raven and Iskin reject, verbally as well as by the form of their writing, the naturalizing tale of the male Genius-Creator brooding in his studio. They counter it with ideas of community, polyvocality and relation, of giving in to and drawing upon the interdependencies that shape all our lives. As Raven wrote later:

I think of my work as "writing alongside of" the visual or performative efforts of other people. The dialogue, and even collaboration, of my work and theirs "shows" visually in some of my written commentaries. Because I want artists to be seen and heard, I often use more than one voice in my prose. Even when others are not physically represented by varying typefaces or areas on the page, they are written into the text.[29]

This *relational authorship* is the bright side of *messy relationships*. It goes further than collaborative or collective writing in that it is, in fact, enabled only by the affective tissue of personal bonds. Creating new thoughts out of emotions and visceral sensations, it is a way to fight back against concepts of writing that restrict art and the writer to the intellect—as argued by Susan Sontag

28  Raven took part in several of her friends' and students' performances. Cf. Swartz, "Biographical Essay."
29  Arlene Raven, "Word of Honor," in *Mapping the Terrain: New Genre Public Art*, ed. Suzanne Lacy (Seattle: Bay Press, 1995), pp. 159–169, here p. 160. This has been pointed out for Raven's exhibition catalogue "At Home" (1983). See Swartz, "Biographical Essay," pp. 57, 60; Lovelace, "Advocate Critic," p. 101.

Nancy Fried *Woman Bathing*, dough, watercolor, acrylic

Nancy Fried gives the lesbian experience and everyday scenes in the feminist community a lovely, real setting. The beauty of these works lies in their wholesomeness – a tollhouse cookie! – and in the level of caring in color, design and detail. The accessibility of her style and her material – bread dough – present this radically new content in gentle, agreeable ways. Her highly detailed bread dough reliefs *are* like cookies, or other things we make for our friends. They are creations both in and outside of the art category, because they assert their legitimacy as art and have a real function – of giving and storytelling – in the community.
**A.R.**

Nancy Fried *To Arlene On Wings of Love*, dough, watercolor, acrylic

**Fig. 2:** Arlene Raven / Ruth Iskin, "Through the Peephole: Toward a Lesbian Sensibility in Art," *Chrysalis: A Magazine of Women's Culture 4* (1977): p. 30.

**Fig. 3:** Arlene Raven / Mary Beth Edelson, "Happy Birthday America,"
*Chrysalis: A Magazine of Women's Culture 4* (1977): pp. 52–53.

ppy    Birthday    America

**131**

as early as 1961, when she demanded we "recover our senses" when writing about art.[30]

*Chrysalis: A Magazine of Women's Culture*, where "Through the Peephole" was published, was in itself a collective endeavor. Co-founded and co-edited by Raven, Iskin, Susan Rennie, Kirsten Grimstad, and Sheila de Bretteville, it was fueled by the community of the Woman's Building. In its inaugural issue, early in 1977, appeared "Happy Birthday America," a programmatic text-image contribution calling for a new kind of culture, one "that honors women's experience," where women "are speaking brilliantly, sensuously, intimately, gleefully together."[31] The text is a "[c]ollage in letters, poems, and conversations between Arlene Raven and [artist] Mary Beth Edelson," taking the form of two double-spaced columns interlocked in the middle (fig. 3).[32] One introduces Edelson's work and its references to Goddess feminism while speaking of woman artists' contribution to overcome patriarchy. The second has Edelson speak about her artistic process. Mentions of life-giving are scattered across the text and its title, referring to the re-birth of the individual feminist as well as to her "vital contribution" to the birth of a women's culture that dissolves "the traditional art/life [...] dichotomy." Taking up most of each page, the text-columns are bordered by a row of small images, strung like beads or frames of a filmstrip: first photographs of Edelson's performances, then portraits of 86 women artists and writers, mostly from in and around the Woman's Building. The last page carries an adaptation of Jean-Auguste-Dominique Ingres' *Turkish Bath* that sub-

---

30  Susan Sontag, "Against Interpretation," in Susan Sontag, *Against Interpretation and Other Essays* (London: Penguin Books, 2009), pp. 3–14, here p. 14.
31  Mary Beth Edelson and Arlene Raven, "Happy Birthday America," *Chrysalis: A Magazine of Women's Culture* 1 (January 1977): pp. 49–53, here pp. 51–52.
32  Ibid., p. 52.

stitutes the faces of the harem nudes with the heads of 1970s feminists.

In its use of text and images this collaboration, too, counters the linearity of writing and reading by staging relational authorship. Constantly, you are thrown off from following one column by the other one taking up the thread. When Edelson is likening art to birth ("The art process"), Raven jumps in ("A feminist artist is a new artist") before Edelson can finish ("is like the birth process"). The images, too, join into this alternation. Edelson's "ritual photography" shows her naked body performing, creating symbols of lesbian or Goddess feminism like the circle, spiral, or triangle. This answers to Edelson calling her work process circular or spiral and to the portrayed feminists "encircling" not only the dialogue but also Ingres' "lascivious images of our century-old harem sisters."[33]

Thoughts, it is made clear, evolve in circles, in exchange with others. Authorship becomes malleable. In "Through the Peephole," most statements were marked with first names or initials. Here, the collaborators' voices merge into a collage and authorship dissolves or, rather, is deliberately obscured: the heading frames the text as Raven's "introduction" to a collage poster Edelson created for *Chrysalis* and which today is part of the collection of the Museum of Modern Art in New York.[34] In contrast to this, the issue's table of contents has them both as co-authors while the poster is captioned as "collaboratory." Raven's introduction is part of the artwork it supposedly introduces; the feminists summoned by Edelson's poster are collaborators of their own image. All their voices dissolve and merge, creating precisely the consonance of women speaking that the texts call for, giving birth to a new American

---

**33** Ibid.
**34** See online: http://www.moma.org/collection/works/117245 (last accessed October 12, 2019).

culture. In gathering women who have contributed to culture, "Happy Birthday America" evokes Judy Chicago's installation *Dinner Party*, which she was working on at the time (1974–1979). However, while the latter brings together mainly historical and mythical women, Raven in both texts depends on her real-life community of collaborators, students, friends and lovers.[35]

\*\*\*

With the work on my PhD came my own collaborative relationship. Together with my colleagues Laura Kowalewski and Isabel Mehl, I founded "From Where I Stand" (FWIS) in 2016. At first a workshop series dedicated to feminist writing about art, FWIS has by now expanded into a practice of collaborative writing, speaking, and thinking between Isabel and me (fig. 4). Both researching feminist writing practices and interested in strategies of collectivity and polyvocality, we are trying out different forms of writing together. What difference does it make whether we mark our individual contributions or blur them into collectivity? If we lay bare the detours and inconsistencies in our thinking together, could this prove productive for breaking with expectations of authorship or academic writing? Writing together changes the way we write and the way we look at writing as object of our research.

Like Raven's, my work relationships are messy, tainted by affects such as desire, fear, relief or envy creeping under my skin. I have overestimated closeness, have been disappointed by a sudden professional distance, have been surprised by unexpected friendship and care. When, this past September, Isabel and I were sitting on a

---

**35** Sometimes even without knowing. Number 8 of the honored feminists in "Happy Birthday America" is sculptor Nancy Grossman, Raven's future partner whom she met only five years later, in 1982. Nancy in turn was reminded of having a part in Arlene's text only by me writing this text in 2019. Personal email, August 11, 2019.

oonalochner
Katzen Arts Center - American University

♡ ◯ ▽                                    🔖

👥 Liked by **higashinoy** and **19 others**

oonalochner From Where I Stand on tour! Isabel Mehl and I
presenting at Feminist Art History Conference at American
University today: "The Voices Within: Splitting Subjectivity in
the Art Criticism of Jill Johnston and Lynne Tillman".
#fromwhereistand #femarthistory #femalesubjectivity
#dialogue #collaboration #jilljohnston #lynnetillman
@tillman_glossitis

⌂    🔍    ⊕    ♡    👤

**Fig. 4:** *From Where I Stand on Tour*, Washington D.C., September 2018.

plane travelling to a conference where we were to speak together, we wondered: are we still just collaborators or are we turning into friends? Taking long walks through the hills of Washington D.C., we carefully began to share more private things, talking about family, relationships, anxiety. Flying back three weeks later, the issue seemed settled. But then, does this really change that much? Feminist relationships, also the professional ones, are relations of care. They make us choose collaboration over competition, make us feel responsible and look out for each other. Thus, working together as feminists reaches into our lives and vice versa.

For Raven, relational authorship opened a way to reject a male-dominated culture, its mind-body dualism and its concepts of the Genius creator or the supposedly distanced art critic. She could stress, through the form of her texts, the structures of desire underlying the process of writing. For Isabel and me, writing together offers

**Fig. 5:** *Arlene Raven's Study, Bookshelf,* Brooklyn, October 2018.

ways to think anew how we want to write, within and against the grain of our academic environments. It helps us challenge the imperative of academic writing keeping its distance: from its object and from the writer's life. It helps us save ourselves, at least temporarily, from the rationale of contemporary academia that, often at the expense of personal life and relationships, demands long publication lists, rewards individual achievements and competition and sees collaboration mostly as clever networking. It helps us reintegrate writing and living.

My writing is entangled in a number of relations. Not only with Isabel, but writing about three writers, I live with them, too. Last year, I somewhat accidently stumbled into the late Arlene Raven's life (fig. 5). I spent hours reading in her study and equally as much time talking and having dinner with her partner Nancy. I was urged to eat more (mostly, but not only because I was pregnant at the time), was given books and copies for my studies. I felt cared for while I was caring more and more for Arlene. I can feel how the way she deals with life through writing about art is rubbing off on me.

With children, there are even more relationships at work in writing. Between desk and baby's crib, thoughts are taken up, turned and twisted. The forms and rhythms of work change. With my son bound to my body, I'm slow and often unreliable. Much as I'm tempted to make things look effortless, and hard as it is to fight back against feeling "Everymother's guilt" (Adrienne Rich) of never being enough, I insist on my relationships' potential for my writing. I don't want to assign them separate spheres and have them pull me in different directions, but to bear with their entanglement, as they are both full of body, full of mind. Having these and other relations come forward in writing takes a step toward liberation as, in Arlene's times, poet Adrienne Rich put it:

> Truly to liberate women, then, means to change thinking itself: to integrate what has been named the unconscious, the subjective, the emotional with the structural, the rational, the intellectual; to "connect the prose and the passion" in E.M. Forster's phrase; and finally to annihilate those dichotomies.[36]

---

36  Adrienne Rich, *Of Woman Born: Motherhood as Experience and Institution* (London: Virago, 1977), p. 81.

**Beate Söntgen**

# Decorating Charleston Farmhouse

## Bloomsbury's Experiments in Forms of Life, Work, and Art[1]

Charleston is an unusual home. In this small ex-farm-house in Sussex, southern England, a form of life materializes that was peculiar in the early twentieth century, when the group of artists and writers known as the Bloomsbury Group made it their own, but that still remains unusual today. (Fig. 1, fig. 2: the house, outside and inside). This form of life, offering an alternative to the norms of the Victorian bourgeois family, emphasizes the entanglement of autonomy and community, both socially and artistically. The Bloomsburies' form of life is shaped by a number of practices which concern artists' ways of working, their forms of expression, their interpersonal relationships, and their habitation of the house, particularly the house's furnishing and decoration. The Charleston Farmhouse is a concise expression and framework of these practices in that it is a product of collectivity, influenced by modernist ideas of the autonomy of art and of life, as well as by forms of collaboration, entanglement, and appropriation and dedication. Bloomsbury embodies an "aesthetics of existence" in the sense of an experimental form of resistance, as Elke Bippus, Jörg Huber, and Roberto Nigro described it, in reference to Foucault. In the following, I will outline how

1   This text is a first tentative attempt to sketch out a topic that is new to me. Thus, numerous aspects related to this complex of forms of life, work and representation only remain hinted at. I would like to thank Isabelle Graw, Anna Kipke, Holger Kuhn, and Mimmi Woisnitza for their support, advice and proofreading.

**Fig. 1:** *Exterior view*, Charleston.

Bloomsbury actualizes this form of resistance through "practices for creating new subjects and forms of life."[2]

The Bloomsbury Group was named after the London neighborhood where the Stephen siblings began their unconventional lives.[3] After the death of their parents, Virginia, Vanessa, Adrian, and Thoby Stephen moved from middle-class Kensington to Bloomsbury, where they established an intellectually and sexually liberal

2   Elke Bippus, Jörg Huber and Roberto Nigro, eds., *Ästhetik der Existenz. Lebensformen im Widerspruch* (Zurich: Edition Voldemeer, 2013), p. 9.
3   Out of the wealth of literature on the life and work of the Bloomsbury Group, the two most important sources for me are Quentin Bell, *Virginia Woolf. Eine Biographie* (Frankfurt am Main: Suhrkamp, 1982) and Christopher Reed, *Bloomsbury Rooms: Modernity, Subculture, and Domesticity* (New Haven and London: Yale University Press, 2004).

**Fig. 2:** *Interior view*, Charleston.

circle. Rarely enough, it was the women among the siblings who would become famous, namely, the writer Virginia Woolf and the painter Vanessa Bell. The circle was comprised largely of Thoby's university friends from Cambridge, including the sisters' future husbands, the politically active author Leonard Woolf and the art critic Clive Bell, as well as the writer and biographer Lytton Strachey and the economist John Maynard Keynes. The group was later joined by the art critic and curator Roger Fry and the painter Duncan Grant, who were influential for the furnishing of Charleston. Countless others were loosely associated with the group over longer periods of time.

Initially, the group met weekly at the Stephens' house in Bloomsbury and then at various members' homes, to discuss art, literature and politics in a setting that transgressed societal conventions and Victorian norms. Women were involved on an unprecedented scale, which was intentional, if not programmatic. Also, sexuality was a central topic. The circle was very much shaped by homo- and bisexual, as well as polygamous relationships,[4] which led to a constantly changing configuration of friends and lovers. The group documented their form of life in various ways and in different media and they did so to an astonishing extent. They collectively furnished, inhabited and animated spaces, and depicted these spaces and their occupants in texts and images. They also wrote with and about each other, in letters and biographies, as well as in critiques.[5]

One of the most significant constellations for the establishment of Charleston was the relationship between Vanessa Bell and Duncan Grant, a former lover of Keynes—a relationship that began as a love affair and ended as a long-term living and working partnership. This relationship also included Grant's lover, David Garnett, in a ménage à trois, as well as Clive Bell, Vanessa Bell's husband, who himself had numerous love affairs, including a passionate flirtation with his sister-in-law Virginia, which Clive and Vanessa Bell's son Quentin Bell wrote about in his aunt's biography with the sober air of a historian. Duncan Grant and Vanessa Bell's daughter, Angelica, later married her father's former lover, David Garnett. The curator and critic Roger Fry is also significant in this context. When his wife developed an incurable psychological illness and moved to a clinic, he began an intense love affair with Vanessa

---

4   See Christopher Reed, "Bloomsbury as Queer Subculture," in *The Cambridge Companion to the Bloomsbury Group*, ed. Victoria Rosner (Cambridge: Cambridge University Press, 2014), pp. 71–89.
5   Unfortunately, I am unable to elaborate on this important aspect in the context of this article.

Bell, which turned into a lifelong friendship as well. Fry was a frequent resident and co-creator of Charleston, and the theoretical advocate of the entanglement of life and work.[6] Despite the importance of sexuality for the Bloomsburies, as both a subject and a norm-breaking practice, sexual liberation was not the main objective of their form of life. Rather, to cite Foucault, it was about "[reopening] affective and relational virtualities," (as well, I would add, as the associated forms of artistic expression and work), through "diagonal lines" that can be traced "in the social fabric" which "make these virtualities visible."[7]

The fact that Charleston was used as the site and expression of such "transversity" or "queerness" was unusual considering the fact that in England at that time, modernism was understood in terms of heroic masculinity, technicity, toughness and urbanity. As Christopher Reed has pointed out, domesticity, and particularly a domesticity that was oriented towards intimacy rather than functionality, could be understood as the antithesis to modernity.[8] Taking Charleston as an example, I

6  The most significant texts, many of which were published in magazines, journals, or catalogues, were compiled by Fry in 1920 in a volume entitled *Vision and Design* (Warsaw: Amazon Fulfillment, 2017—unedited e-book reprint). For a selection, see Christopher Reed, ed., *A Roger Fry Reader* (Chicago and London: The University of Chicago Press, 1996).

7  Michel Foucault, "Freundschaft als Lebensform," (1981), in Michel Foucault, *Ästhetik der Existenz. Schriften zur Lebenskunst* (Frankfurt am Main: Suhrkamp, 2007), p. 72. In English: "Friendship as a Way of Life," in *Foucault Live: Michel Foucault Collected Interviews, 1961–1984*, ed. Sylvère Lotringer (New York: Semiotext(e), 1989, 1996), p. 311.

8  See Christopher Reed, ed., *Not at Home: The Suppression of Domesticity in Modern Art and Architecture* (London: Thames and Hudson, 1996). In England, the painter Wyndham Lewis and the poet Ezra Pound were among the promoters of this narrative, which was also articulated in a wholly different visual language. Reed has pointed out that domesticity, as a product of a capitalist economy and technological innovations, was a specifically modern phenomena, to which the avant-garde responded with another concept of modernity, namely "away from home, marching towards glory on the battlefields of culture." Reed, "Introduction," *Not at Home*, p. 7.

seek to illustrate how the relation between modernity and domesticity within the Bloomsbury Group can be understood as an implicit form of critique, directed equally against Victorian norms and an avant-garde constriction of modernity.

## The Art of Furnishing

The group's relocation from Bloomsbury to Charleston in 1916 was an effect of World War I and can be attributed to their pacifism. The men took on work as farmhands to avoid conscription. While Clive Bell stayed with friends in a comfortable country house (for which he was laughed at by the group), Duncan Grant and Vanessa Bell moved into the cold, run-down house with the Bells' sons, Julian and Quentin. With Roger Fry's help, their art of furnishing quickly transformed the house into a peculiar home. Virginia and Leonard were the ones who had found the house. Because of Virginia Woolf's unstable psychological condition, they had moved to the countryside and lived nearby. Angelica was born here in 1918, and, after the war, Charleston became the summer residence where the Bloomsburies met in various constellations. The group was privileged in that all members had access to familial wealth, yet most of them were still obliged to earn additional income. During World War II, Roger Fry moved in along with his library. This was not the first instance that changed the occupancy of rooms, which the inhabitants had furnished and decorated for and with each other.[9]

Without going into the—indeed quite beautiful—details, the pictures of the rooms (fig. 3, fig. 4) give a first impression of the interconnectedness of the walls,

9    Members of the group lived here until the 1980s. Today the house is a museum, managed by a foundation established by their descendants.

**Fig. 3:** *Interior view*, Charleston.

furniture, fabrics and things, both amongst themselves and with the inhabitants who designed, produced or painted them, either for the community or for individual members. Paintings and ornaments reminiscent of Post-Impressionism can be found on cupboards, tables, and wall panels, in window niches and on fabrics, many of which were collaborative designs, like some of the furniture pieces from the Omega Workshops. Remodeling work, such as the fireplace that was converted into a sitting area, was also done collectively.

**Fig. 4:** *Interior view*, Charleston.

The interior design is both a testimony to the community and a reference to art, with which it should be
given equal status. On the one hand, the style and ico-
nography of the decoration reflect the designs of the
Omega Workshops, founded by Fry, for which some
of the Bloomsbury Group worked, and which, like the
furnishing of Charleston, was inspired by Post-Impressionist painting.[10] On the other hand, the Bloomsburies repeated or quoted their own works, or incorporated
other members' particular modes of representation and
integrated them into the design of the rooms as a gesture of friendship or love. This entanglement between

---

**10**  Isabelle Anscombe, *Omega and After: Bloomsbury and the Decorative
Arts* (London: Thames & Hudson, 1981).

**Fig. 5:** Duncan Grant, *Interior*, 1918, oil on canvas, 163 x 174.8 cm, National Museums Northern Ireland.

the home and its inhabitants is reinforced by the paintings, which bring the rooms of Charleston to life and fill the walls there. They depict everyday rituals in the house, portraying the group at work (fig. 5) or in care of the children (fig. 6). Other paintings portray collaboratively-realized art projects. For example, Angelica appears in costume for her role in Virginia Woolf's comedy "Freshwater," which was only performed for a private audience (fig. 7). In the studios, which also often changed occupants, this play of quotations, dedications, and the appropriation of subjects and forms intensifies, in an individual's own paintings and in those they appropriated, on textiles and on furniture (see fig. 2).

The Charleston house manifests the ways in which its inhabitants lived community and, at the same time,

**Fig. 6:** Duncan Grant, *Lessons in the Orchard*, 1917, oil on canvas, 18 x 20 cm, The Charleston Trust.

continuously recreated it in acts of collaboration: from collective processes of producing and decorating the furniture, the mutual adornment and exchange of rooms, to the gifting of paintings and the reciprocal quoting of subjects and modes of representation. Such acts of dedication and appropriation can be understood in the sense of Marcel Mauss's "gift exchange," a notion that, with its commitment to reciprocity, constitutes a binding and visible sign of belonging and community.[11] At the same time, however, the visibility of the forms of dedi-

11  Marcel Mauss, *The Gift: Forms and Functions of Exchange in Archaic Societies* (London: Cohen & West, 1970). Barbara Wittmann adapted Mauss's reflections to nineteenth century artistic practices. Barbara Wittmann, *Gesichter geben. Édouard Manet und die Poetik des Portraits* (Munich: Fink, 2004).

**Fig. 7:** *Interior view*, Charleston.

cation and appropriation that manifests in the home's furnishing reactivates an entanglement of the inhabitants and their working methods. This entanglement thwarts artistic authorship just as the act of decorating defies the notion of artistic autonomy, which the reference to Post-Impressionist painting inevitably invokes. As I will discuss below, it was Roger Fry who not only coined this painting style but also associated it with the notion and practice of furnishing.

## Images of Living

Vanessa Bell and Duncan Grant, who were both trained in painting, learned to decorate rooms at the suggestion of Roger Fry.[12] A curator, critic, and painter himself, Fry, who was a generation older, had lost his post at the Metropolitan Museum in New York and was trying to re-establish himself in England. He had curated the controversial exhibition "Manet and Post-Impressionism" at the Grafton Gallery in 1910, which aimed to establish Gauguin, Cézanne, van Gogh, and Matisse as Manet's legitimate successors, and thus as foundational figures of modern painting. Inspired by the Post-Impressionists, Fry developed a concept of painting that relied on a strict pictorial organization and the structure and harmony of the visual elements; on formal criteria, in other words, that avoided any kind of representationality without renouncing the figurative.

Considering his view of art as generating meaning from form alone, it is particularly interesting that Fry, a painter himself, was committed to arts and crafts, and interior design (fig. 8, fig. 9). In 1913, he founded the Omega Workshops, which were albeit short-lived. The project provided a livelihood for a number of young artists and, at the same time, aimed to promote a new understanding of art directed toward vivid expression. Different artists worked on projects and designs together and signed them, at least that was the idea, not with their names but with the Greek letter Omega. Although there were commonalities with the Arts and Crafts movement, like the resistance to industrial products, unlike William Morris, Omega was not interested in social reform.[13] Omega was more concerned with

**12** Richard Shone provides valuable insight in *The Art of Bloomsbury: Roger Fry, Vanessa Bell and Duncan Grant* (Princeton: Princeton University Press, 2000).
**13** Roger Fry, "Prospectus for the Omega Workshops" (circulated in 1913), in Reed, *Fry Reader*, pp. 198–200.

**Fig. 8:** Vanessa Bell, *Omega Workshops. Model for a Nursery*, 1913.

the recuperation of spiritual life in modernity by integrating Post-Impressionist painting, with its emphasis on form and spirituality,[14] into interior design. To Fry, design is a fully realized form of abstract art which is brought to life not least through the "vital beauty of artistic handling."[15]

The role of art, as Fry wrote in "Art and Life,"[16] is to be a motor for spirituality, through its vitality and as an expression of the inner self, just like the Byzantine mosaics that Fry admired and the Italian paintings of

---

14  How exactly this term should be interpreted is not clear in Fry's writings either. His notion of a spirituality conveyed through painting was presumably nourished by his prolonged preoccupation with Byzantium and the early Italian Renaissance, as well as with the roots of Post-Impressionism in Gauguin's painting, Gauguin being celebrated by the Nabis as the prophet who liberated painting from illusionism towards a new spirituality. Later in his life, Fry remarked that he did not want to explain his ideas in more detail, as he would otherwise soon be accused of mysticism.

15  Fry, "Prospectus," p. 200.

16  Roger Fry, "Art and Life," lecture given to the Fabian Society, 1917, reprinted in Fry, *Vision and Design*, pp. 5–20.

**Fig. 9:** Roger Fry, *Still Life with Omega Flowers*, 1919, oil on canvas, 59.9 x 44.2 cm, Tatham Art Gallery.

the early Renaissance. Since then, "rational law in what seems to earlier rationalists the chaotic fancies and caprice of the human imagination" had been discovered. Humans, too, are "like other animals, mainly instinctive," and thus art's fantasies are "inevitable responses to fundamental instinctive needs."[17] The nineteenth

17   Ibid., p. 18.

century banned art from its conception of life as something "noxious," or simply as "useless frivolity," in part
because it activated religion, sensuality, and desires:

> To Herbert Spencer[18] religion was a primitive fear of the
> unknown and art was sexual attraction—he must have con-
> templated with perfect equanimity, almost with satisfac-
> tion, a world in which both these functions disappear. I sup-
> pose that the scientific man of today would be much more
> ready to admit not only the necessity but the great impor-
> tance of aesthetic feeling for the spiritual existence of man.[19]

Like the rationalist sciences of his day, Fry saw art finally
reorienting itself towards needs, instincts, and the inner
self. This, he says, is what Post-Impressionist painting
expresses perfectly. Far from any illusionism, its "design
and formal co-ordination"[20] leads to the "aesthetic unity
of the work of art."[21] As Fry wrote in an article accompa-
nying his exhibition, published in *The Nation* in 1910,
it was a matter of regaining the "power to express emotional ideas."[22] It was the "distortions and ruthless sim-
plifications ... of natural form, which allowed the fundamental elements of design—the echo of human need—to
reappear" in representation. In place of "facts of observation," what was needed was "re-creation," much like
what the Post-Impressionists achieved in their "purely
decorative quality of painting," which expressed itself
"harmoniously and beautifully." Like the works of the
early primitives and of the Orient, the paintings of the
Post-Impressionists did not produce "holes in the wall,
through which another vision is made evident. They
form a part of the surface which they decorate, and

---

**18**  Spencer (1820–1903) was an English philosopher and sociologist
      who applied the theory of evolution to social developments.
**19**  Fry, "Art and Life," pp. 18–19.
**20**  Ibid., p. 14.
**21**  Ibid., p. 16.
**22**  Roger Fry, "The Grafton Gallery – I," in Reed, *Fry Reader*, pp. 86–89.

suggest visions to the imagination, rather than impose them upon the senses." When furnished in accordance with these principles formulated for painting, the interior becomes a space of resonance, enveloped in expressive, vivid scenes.[23] Life in the interior should resemble the visions materialized in the art employed there: joyous, spiritual, and inspirational for creative production.

Matisse, whom Fry called upon as a key witness in "Art and Life," followed very similar ideas in his paintings and writings. Matisse also haunts the decoration of Charleston in the form of appropriated adaptations and translations of his subjects and representational styles. And it was Matisse, after all, who had associated modernity, in the sense of painting based on abstraction and autonomy, and domesticity equally with both the interior and the concept of the decorative—albeit with a somewhat different understanding to that of the Bloomsburies.

(Fig. 10) In his programmatic "Notes of a Painter" from 1908, Matisse defines "expression" as the highest goal of his artistic work.[24] "Expression" does not refer to the representation of something, however. It is bound first and foremost to the means of painterly realization and is best captured by the term "decoration," which foregrounds form. "Expression" therefore does not manifest in the physiognomic, but rather in the composition of the painting as a whole. Composition must adhere to the strict rule of necessity in order to guarantee the coherence of the pictorial structure. It is about the weaving of all pictorial elements into an ornamental-linear structure, in which all instruments of expression, in particular lines and color, are equally important and in relation to each other.

---

23 For more on the liveliness of painting, see Isabelle Graw, *The Love of Painting. Genealogy of a Success Medium* (Berlin: Sternberg Press, 2018).

24 Henri Matisse, "Notes of a Painter" [1908], in *Matisse on Art*, revised edition, ed. Jack Flam (New York: E. P. Dutton, 1978), pp. 35–40.

**Fig. 10:** Henri Matisse, *Red Room (Harmony in Red)*, 1908, oil on canvas, 180 x 220 cm, Hermitage, St. Petersburg.

This emphasis on interwovenness and relationality, which according to Yve-Alain Bois is the structural element of Matisse's painting,[25] is interesting for this context in two respects. Relationality concerns both the depicted pictorial elements and their correlation, as well as the relation between this depiction and its surrounding environment. As attested to by *The Red Room (Harmony in Red)* (1908), the interior serves as an ideal foil for the portrayal of a harmony that results from the reciprocal relations between forms and colors and that is only possible in art. The triad of primary colors, the rich complementary contrast between interior and exterior, and the corresponding lines create the balance that Matisse described as his ultimate goal of painting. What is realized in the painted interior is the reconciliation of

**25** Yve-Alain Bois, "On Matisse: The Blinding," *October* 68 (Winter 1994): pp. 61–121.

inside and outside, of nature and culture and, implicitly, of femininity and masculinity, and the forms of productivity and regulatory power ascribed to them. It is the structuring hand of the female figure that cultivates the interior for the painter, as "a kind of matchmaker of objects."[26] Thus the interior, in this case the painted one, is the place where Matisse manifests his vision of decorative art, an art of precise arrangement, of interwovenness and harmonious relationality. Matisse also assigned a social function to his painting, albeit in a passively contemplative way that did not activate the observer. To him, painting serves as a kind of "armchair" in which the stressed-out modern individual can rest,[27] a metaphor that reinforces the repeated reproaches brought against Matisse for his serene, hedonistic formalism.[28]

If one considers Roger Fry's recourse to the early Italian Renaissance and the historical context of the Futurist-oriented Vorticism, whose exponents also ridiculed the Bloomsburies for their Victorian "pretty-ness,"[29] Fry's emphasis on form might initially read like a *rappel à l'ordre avant la lettre*. Later critics such as Benjamin Buchloh vehemently dismissed the notion of such a return as a deluded, politically oblivious stance, reactionary in its artistic form and in denial of social, historical, and artistic ruptures, in favor of a transcendental notion of harmony that exceeds that which is depicted, along with the materiality and structure of the image.[30]

26  Matisse, quoted in Pierre Schneider, *Matisse* (New York: Rizzoli, 1984), p. 310.

27  Matisse, "Notes of a Painter," p. 34.

28  See Pia Müller-Tamm, "Henri Matisse: Figur, Farbe, Raum," in *Henri Matisse: Figur, Farbe, Raum*, exhibition catalogue, ed. Pia Müller-Tamm (Ostfildern-Ruit: Hatje Cantz, 2005), pp. 17–46.

29  See Sam Rose, *Art and Form: From Roger Fry to Global Modernism* (University Park PA: Pennsylvania State University Press, 2019), p. 94.

30  Benjamin Buchloh, "Figures of Authority, Ciphers of Regression: Notes on the Return of Representation in European Painting," *October* 16 (Spring 1981): pp. 39–68. Matisse himself speaks of a quasi-religious stance in his painting: "What interests me most is neither still life nor landscape, but the human figure. It is that which best

Nevertheless, Fry's ambitions for reform and his open stance towards production processes and questions of economy[31] do not amount to a merely transcendental, idealistic interpretation of his understanding of art. His call for a re-spiritualization of modernity by way of form is rather a vehicle for his concept of socially operative art. Fry is not concerned with a "simple formalism"[32] that defends art for art's sake, that denies other references, significations, and questions of intention, and that at best reflects itself, as Clement Greenberg claimed.[33] Instead, Fry's conception of form explicitly relates to his era and its specific issues and concerns. It is associated with an emphatic notion of experience that turns an idealistic understanding of art on its head. A work of art exhibits "human organization" by displaying the set of actions "that made it up and through with the artist's vision, emotions, or experiences." These find resonance in a "suitably informed and receptive viewer" through the work's particular form.[34]

From this perspective, which Sam Rose unfolds in his recent book *Art and Form*, form is a medium of communication. It is form, in a complex engagement with the world, that constitutes a community of artists, spectators and critics—an aspect that is more relevant for the relationship between life, work, and representation than Roger Fry's undeniably problematic psychologization and idealization of artistic work, or his imprecise aesthetics of expression. In Fry's opinion, form opens up an active and activating access to creativity

permits me to express my almost religious awe towards life." Henri Matisse, "Notes of a Painter," p. 38.

31   See Fry's article "A Possible Domestic Architecture," which he published in *British Vogue in 1918*, reprinted in Fry, *Vision and Design*, pp. 290–296.

32   See the chapter "Roger Fry's Formalism," in Rose, *Art and Form*, pp. 32–39.

33   Clement Greenberg, "Modernist Painting (1960)," in *Art and Literature*, 4. 1965, pp. 193–201.

34   This kind of communicative take on form was popular in the period after 1920. See Rose, *Art and Form*, pp. 39–47.

for both creators and spectators. It does so by way of a unique experience that derives from the form's respective medium and its materiality, as well as from a set of actions. Fry rejects the kind of passive, aestheticized viewing Matisse implies with his concept of the decorative, in favor of an act of seeing that produces an imaginary re-creation with a social dimension; namely, the awakening of empathy and the creation of community.[35] Sam Rose echoes Fry's essay on Cézanne, drawing the following conclusion:

> But in its [i.e. Cézanne's work] concern for contact with the inner lives of others, its desire to come to terms as honestly as possible with one's own experience, and the longing for a description of that personal experience that grounds communal enterprise, Fry's criticism, in its own way, attempted to be as open to the world of human concerns as it thought it possible to be.[36]

Here, in particular, a major distinction emerges in relation to Fry's revered Post-Impressionists, who focused on the individual and on high art. In spite of their differing stances, however, their artistic practices still played a significant role in Fry's conception of decoration and in the furnishing of Charleston.

As was mentioned before, Matisse haunts Charleston. He can be found most frequently in Duncan Grant's representational style. Grant's paintings often hybridize Matisse with his rival Picasso, such as, for instance, on a wooden box, on which Grant painted angels playing music and dancing (fig. 11). Like in Matisse's work, the figures are tightly captured within the pictorial space, almost incarcerated by the edges, which they, at the same time, threaten to burst open (fig. 12). This

---

35  Rose fails to acknowledge the fact that this notion of seeing ignores the situatedness of perception and presupposes a kind of universal subjectivity.
36  Rose, *Art and Form*, p. 61.

**Fig. 11:** *Interior view*, Charleston.

frame-bursting effect, one of Matisse's trademarks, can also be found in Duncan Grant's later works, such as the acrobats (fig. 13, fig. 14) who seem to fall out of a door panel.[37] The door of a bookcase containing Clive Bell's books on art history is adorned with a mandolin player, reminiscent of Matisse's odalisques (fig. 15). Vanessa Bell also quotes Matisse on a bed frame that she decorated with a painting for her husband (fig. 16, fig. 17). Quentin Bell's copy of a Picasso still life hangs above the bed; a painting that Clive Bell acquired from Daniel

---

**37** The figure itself more evokes Picasso. Consequently, two important references are amalgamated in this painting.

**159**

**Fig. 12:** Henri Matisse, *La Danse I*, 1909, oil on canvas, 259.7 x 390.1 cm, Museum of Modern Art, New York.

Kahnweiler in 1911 and that was sold again in 1957 for financial reasons.

For the occupants of Charleston, painting was an act of appropriation, particularly of modernist, Post-Impressionist painting styles, and also of former possessions as, in the case above, an important painting. It was also a way of dedicating images, subjects, and styles to those with whom they shared a form of life and expression. The art and process of painting served them as a kind of gift exchange that intensified the commitments of the communal working and living situation, in that it rendered its bonding visible beyond the gift itself. It is the distinctive mode of representation derived from Post-Impressionism that, based on its form, self-referentiality, and entanglement of all elements, constitutes a model for social cohesion. Post-Impressionism furnishes a visual language that communicates this sense of communal bonding, in that it shows the interrelatedness of all elements, which "work" towards a harmonious, autonomous whole.

**Fig. 13:** *Interior view*, Charleston.

Post-Impressionist painting, and particularly that of Matisse, represented an emphatic understanding of the picture as an autonomously placed canvas, framed and thus lifted out of its surroundings. In the works of the Bloomsburies, on the other hand, paintings as expressive forms wander into their surroundings, onto furniture, textiles and other objects. This migration of forms makes the paintings lose some of the strictness of the pictorial order. Yet in return, they emphasize the interwovenness with their surroundings, with other objects and with the inhabitants, as an expression of their relations to one another. The house stands for a picture frame that makes this wholeness visible as such. In the

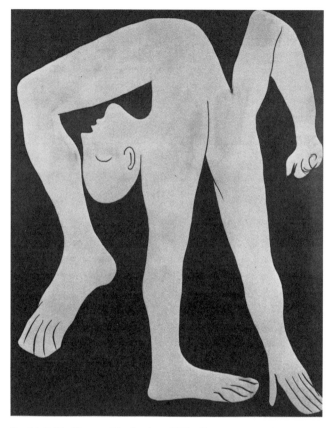

**Fig. 14:** Pablo Picasso, *The Acrobat*, 1930, oil on canvas, 162 x 130 cm, Musée Picasso, Paris.

house's decoration, a form of life materializes, which, due to its mutual referentiality and interwovenness, enables the autonomy of the whole. In our case, this wholeness represents Charleston's unconventional community as a counter-image of the Victorian form of life and its bourgeois concept of the family.

**Fig. 15:** *Interior view*, Charleston.

## Patterns of Relationship

How can forms of life as such be understood? As Rahel Jaeggi has shown, forms of life always precede concrete life, they are carved out in order to be recognizable as forms of life at all.[38] At the same time, they are only created based on specific clusters of practices, whose relatedness identifies them as forms of life. Forms of life are exercised, and, at the same time, they are understood

---

38  Rahel Jaeggi, *Kritik von Lebensformen*, second edition (Berlin: Suhrkamp, 2014). In English: Rahel Jaeggi, *Critique of Forms of Life* (Cambridge MA: Belknap Press of Harvard University Press, 2018).

**Fig. 16:** Henri Matisse, *The Painting Lesson*, 1918/1919, oil on canvas, 74 x 93 cm, The Scottish National Gallery of Modern Art, Edinburgh.

"as something." That is, they often assume meanings that derive from their functions. Forms of life are material and intellectual constructions that find both their expression and their regulatory frame in architecture and in houses.[39]

The example of Charleston brings to the fore precisely such an interplay between the carved-out paths of forms of life and the practices that realize them. The rooms bear witness to a practice of dedication and appropriation that traverses the patriarchal and monogamous notions of Victorian marriage and family. The future husband, for instance, needed to ensure that the Victorian house was ready for occupancy by the time of the marriage. A handbook for young men published at the

---

39  Jaeggi, "1.2. Duration, Depth, Scope," in *Critique of Forms of Life*, pp. 42–49.

**Fig. 17:** *Interior view*, Charleston.

time states: "...with care, prudence and forethought, first prepare your home. For 'tis not manly to allure a girl from peace and comfort, and sufficiency, to a sad cheerless hearth and stinted board."[40] In other words, the wife was expected merely to maintain a home that the husband had already furnished and decorated as testimony to his status. In contrast, Bloomsbury's art of furnishing can be understood as a collaborative community project that draws inspiration from a traditional practice cultivated by the Georgians in England between the eighteenth and

---

**40** S.W. Partridge, *Upward and Onward: A Thought Book for the Threshold of Active Life* (1851), cited in Judith Flanders, *The Victorian House: Domestic Life from Childbirth to Deathbed* (London: HarperCollins Publishers, 2003), p. 192.

early nineteenth centuries. As Amanda Vickery points out, at that time, furnishing a home was not regarded as a task of the husband prior to the marriage, but was undertaken jointly by the couple, as an expression and consolidation of the marriage covenant.[41]

The libidinal, erotic and emotional energies that materialize in Charleston's furnishing were not directed exclusively at spouses, who at that time were solely of the opposite sex. Nor were they directed at random love objects in a bohemian fashion. Rather, they circulated within the group, with an almost unconditional loyalty to the multiple friendships and love relationships, regardless of any implicit or explicit conflicts. Even though the Bloomsbury Group burst open the normative and legal structure of the bourgeois nuclear family, what remained unscathed were the underlying notions of morality, freedom and autonomy, which Hegel so efficaciously attributed to the Victorian concept of familiarity.[42] Yet Bloomsbury realizes and represents a form of life that deviates from Victorian norms through "rituals, procedures and technologies."[43] The group does not simply reject the concepts that underlie these norms, but seizes upon them and situates them in a new framework.

Hegel described the functional ideal of the bourgeois nuclear family not as natural, but rather as the very form that "fully realizes the concept of the family."[44]

---

**41** Amanda Vickery, *Behind Closed Doors: At Home in Georgian England* (New Haven and London: Yale University Press, 2009), in particular Chapter 3, "Setting up Home", pp. 83–105. See also the three-part television production "At Home with the Georgians" https://www. youtube.com/watch?v=gr0dQ_75ezQ , produced by Amanda Vickery based on her book.

**42** G.W.F. Hegel, *Elements of the Philosophy of Right*, ed. Allen W. Wood (Cambridge: Cambridge University Press, 1991), in particular Part 3, "Ethical Life," Section 1, "The Family," pp. 199–219.

**43** This is how Bippus, Huber and Nigro define the shaping of forms of life. See *Ästhetik der Existenz*, p. 7.

**44** Eva Bockenheimer, *Hegels Familien- und Geschlechtertheorie im Überblick*, Hegel-Studien, ed. Walter Jaeschke and Ludwig Siep, Supplement 59 (Hamburg: Felix Meiner, 2013), p. 20.

The bourgeois family is the precondition and framework for individual freedom, which realizes itself as social.[45] In England, it was the political philosopher and Hegelian T.H. Green, the founder of British Idealism, who advocated and propagated this notion. Individuality and collectivity were not understood as opposites in this perspective. Instead, liberalist tendencies and ethical socialisms of various political color advocated an organic view of society that regarded the individual as an integral part of a well-functioning community[46]—an understanding that found its own particular expression in the Bloomsbury Group, which was nevertheless at odds with Hegel's concept. In reference to George Moore's 1903 book *Principia Ethica*, Bloomsbury foregrounded the individual, but not as a functional part of a community regulated by norms.[47] Rather, the individual emerges as a formative element of a fluid and simultaneously cohesive community, which constitutes itself with an ambivalent stance that oscillates between the "repudiation, accommodation, and celebration" of Victorian forms of life.[48]

Hegel describes the covenant of modern marriage as a moral relationship, that is, as a social, spiritual, man-made institution that maintains its right to singularity,[49] because it is desired for its own sake. Such a covenant neither overvalues the erotic aspect nor regards marriage as purely contractual.[50] Nonetheless, sexuality plays a major role in Hegel's conception, bringing together gender relations and reproduction [*Gattungsprozess*]. He

---

45  Hegel, "Einleitung," Grundlinien der Philosophie des Rechts, §32. See also Jaeggi, "Problemlösungsversuche: Hegels Theorie der Familie," in *Kritik von Lebensformen*, II.4.3, pp. 216–227, and Bockenheimer, *Hegels Familien- und Geschlechtertheorie*, especially pp. 20–30.

46  See Rose, *Art and Form*, p. 9.

47  On the significance of George Moore see Bell, *Virginia Woolf*, p. 216.

48  See Katherine Mullin, "Victorian Bloomsbury," in Rosner, *Cambridge Companion to the Bloomsbury Group*, pp. 19–32.

49  Hegel, *Grundlinien der Philosophie des Rechts*, §§142–157, as well as Bockenheimer, *Hegels Familien- und Geschlechtertheorie*, p. 21.

50  Hegel, *Grundlinien der Philosophie des Rechts*, §§161–169.

regards sexuality as the most significant expression of the idea of life, of reason in nature. By insisting on the independence of the new community in relation to the family of origin and—contrary to patriarchal demands—on the autonomy of its members, individual freedom realizes itself as social freedom within an intimate emotional community.[51] It is in shared projects and interests, and through living a life together, that feelings of affection manifest themselves.[52]

The two elements that are particularly significant for our context are, on the one hand, the emphasis on autonomy and freedom as a form of morality, and, on the other hand, the latter's dependence on realization through practice. The Bloomsbury Group asserts autonomy and freedom, including from patriarchal structures and, at least to some extent, from the biological family, which in the case of the sisters was associated with intellectual encouragement as well as with emotional and sexual abuse. The group achieves this connectedness, which is oriented towards freedom and autonomy—one's own freedom as social freedom, as Hegel would say—through various practices, through collaborative artistic projects and shared intellectual interests, as well as through mutual representation in image and text, through the appropriation and transference of representational forms and the collective furnishing of the interior of Charleston.

The Bloomsbury Group achieves such a form of social autonomy outside of the marital framework, however, a framework that is of great importance to Hegel, par-

---

51  Bockenheimer, *Hegels Familien- und Geschlechtertheorie*, p. 58.
52  See Jaeggi, *Kritik von Lebensformen*, pp. 216–226. I cannot detail the problematic appropriation of reproductive labor power in Hegel's conception, primarily that of women, in this text. For this, see Silvia Federici, *Caliban and the Witch: Women, the Body and Primitive Accumulation* (Brooklyn: Autonomedia, 2004), as well as Carla Lonzi's 1970 manifesto "Let's spit on Hegel" http://blogue.nt2.uqam.ca/hit/files/2012/12/Lets-Spit-on-Hegel-Carla-Lonzi.pdf (last accessed on 1 December 2019).

ticularly in its consolidating and symbolic function and in its monogamous orientation, which grants full rights to both partners.[53] According to Hegel, marriage has a cultivating effect, because it transforms natural gender relations, determined by raw biology, into culturally molded and positively normative relationships. For the Bloomsburies, this cultivating effect did not derive out of the framework of marriage, but rather from the framework of modern art. Collectively shaped, domesticity here emerges as a visible sign of interconnectedness.[54] The home's furnishing reflects a form of art that is committed to a sense of order; a conception of rationally grounded, harmonious order that is nourished by sensuality and spirituality and profoundly reflects the desires of modernity.

To be sure, the Bloomsburies' key point of reference, Post-Impressionism, and in particular Matisse, asserts the autonomy of art as absolute purposelessness beyond the realm of art. Even though Matisse's metaphorical likening of painting to an armchair seems to functionalize the effects of his art, the implied mode of consumption still remains passive and contemplative and thus confirms the picture as an emphatically delineated entity in its own right. The Bloomsbury Group, on the other hand, allowed its members to escape the confines of high art. They established a demonstratively interwoven form of decoration that incorporates everyday objects and can be applied in a multitude of ways. Framed and ornamental images served as means of communication to articulate and encourage a new form of life as artistic form, in that they inspired the inhabitants to continuous artistic production of text and image.

While, in modern times, the house no longer served as a place of production, but only of reproduction, the

---

53  See Bockenheimer, *Hegels Familien- und Geschlechtertheorie*, pp. 38–39.
54  The written works containing mutual references and dedications, be they letters, biographies or critiques, have a comparable function.

Bloomsburies reactivated it as a place of production. Charleston includes studios, libraries and desks, in the constant repurposing of spaces, going entirely against the Victorian spirit, which demanded the clear assignment of a specific function to each room. The house of Virginia and Leonard Woolf in the neighboring village, for example, was home to the Hogarth Press, operated by Leonard as a small family business.

Whereas Hegel considered children born out of marriage to be an expression or indeed a sensual reification of love,[55] for the Bloomsbury Group, art takes this position. Angelica Bell symbolized the joining of both, art and reproduction. Her mother Vanessa Bell, as Angelica noted with a certain bitterness, wanted to have a child by Duncan Grant out of wedlock, perhaps to bring together her flesh with his genius and reproduce this union. In return, Vanessa had to forego her sexual relationship with Grant after the birth, despite staying together until her death.[56] Angelica did not become an artist herself, but she devotedly restored the collectively produced imagery that had wandered onto the furniture, textiles and walls of Charleston, a testimony to and sign of a new form of life.

How can this form of life be understood as a form of critique? Rosi Braidotti has attempted to redefine critique in relation to creativity.[57] The rejection of a given situation should not be limited to reactions that remain dependent on the conditions of that situation. Rather, critique should be about projecting alternatives that, in conjunction with new conceptions of subjectivity, affect and desire, can be used productively to affirm one's own

---

55  See Bockenheimer, *Hegels Familien- und Geschlechtertheorie*, p. 60, as well as Jaeggi, *Kritik von Lebensformen*, pp. 201–207.
56  Angelica Garnett, *Freundliche Täuschungen. Eine Kindheit in Blooms-bury* (Berlin: Wagenbach, 1990), pp. 166–167.
57  Rosi Braidotti, *Nomadic Subjects: Embodiment and Sexual Difference in Contemporary Feminist Theory* (New York: Columbia University Press, 2012), especially chapter 10, "Powers of Affirmation," pp. 267–298.

experience. Relationships are the place where affects and desire materialize. Braidotti emphasizes forms of community that she, in reference to Deleuze, understands in their process of becoming. It is not a coincidence that she uses the character Orlando as a paradigm for the relationship between Virginia Woolf and Vita Sackville-West.[58] As Braidotti describes it with the paradoxical phrasing of collective subjectivity, Orlando is an amalgam of both a model (Sackville-West) and an authorial force (Woolf), and had an equal impact on the lives, thoughts and feelings of both women.

With this in mind, Charleston can also be understood as the materialization of a collective subjectivity, as a collectively furnished space, fluid in its design and use. This is the expression and the framework of a new form of life, a framework that in turn influences the inhabitants and their form of community. The extent to which even this community internalizes and reproduces governmental techniques of controlling life, body, and soul,[59] as well as gender-determined notions of production and reproduction—be it through the work ethic in creative production, or through the juxtaposition of the intellectually productive, childless Virginia Woolf and the sensual, reproductive, but less discursive Vanessa Bell—merits further investigation. In her memoir, Angelica thanks her mother for the paradise that she created in Charleston. The title of this memoir, in which Angelica sheds light on both the rewards and the price of these experiments in forms of life and work, is *Deceived with Kindness*.[60] Nonetheless, new possibilities

58   Rosi Braidotti, "Intensives Genre und das Verschwinden von Ge-schlecht," in Rosi Braidotti, *Politik der Affirmation* (Berlin: Merve, 2018), pp. 69–104.

59   Rose, *Art and Form*, p. 149. Here Rose refers to a different, colonial context, but the question of self-governance is relevant for the Bloomsbury Group as well, precisely because of their insistence on freedom and autonomy.

60   See in particular the postscript, which emphasizes the ambivalence of this form of life. Garnett, *Freundliche Täuschungen*, pp. 174–175.

of relationships and articulation, which Braidotti describes as an "affirmative" form of critique, materialize in the Charleston Farmhouse "[diagonal to] the social fabric". They reveal not only alternative forms of life, but also new forms of collectivity in artistic practices. Thus, I interpret the Bloomsbury Group's diversity and multiplicity of mutual portrayals, which continue to shape culture to this day, less as a narcissism,[61] but rather as a "passion for articulation" that "permeates" this new form of life "as energy,"[62] giving it both expression and framework.

*Translated by Angela Anderson*

**61** See Vesna Goldsworth, "The Bloomsbury Narcissus," in Rosner, *Cambridge Companion to the Bloomsbury Group*, pp. 183–197.
**62** Bippus, Huber and Nigro, *Ästhetik der Existenz*, p. 13.

# Writing Differently /
# Writing the Self

**Isabel Mehl**

# Feedback Systems

## Artwriting as Critique?

Often there's a ghost of emotion when talking about things, about things in the culture. Emotion is never absent from life, the mind runs in spirals.
Given these facts, it's always struck me as strange when people approvingly describe my art writing as "honest" and "personal." What else can it be? Writing narrates experience.[1]

\*

When I studied at the New School in New York in 2013, I went to a reading on the occasion of the re-launch of Chris Kraus's *Aliens & Anorexia*. When listening to writers and poets Ariana Reines[2], Masha Tupitsyn[3], Kate Zambreno[4] and others reading Kraus's book, a whole new world opened up to me, one I had been missing. Until then I had been confronted with an academic

1  Chris Kraus, "Stick to the Facts," p. 131–133, *Texte zur Kunst* 70 (June 2008): p. 131.
2  Ariana Reines is an American poet, playwright, performance artist, and translator. In 2016 a conversation between Kraus and Reines was published under the title "The feelings I fail to capitalize, I fail: on Auto-Fiction and Biography," in the "Poetry" edition of *Texte zur Kunst* 103 (September 2016); https://www.textezurkunst.de/103/den-gefuhlen-die-ich-nicht-kapitalisiere/; (accessed on 02.03.2020).
3  Masha Tupitsyn is a writer, critic, and multi-media artist. Her new book *Picture Cycle* (2019) is published by Semiotext(e)'s Active Agents.
4  Kate Zambreno is an American writer and novelist. Her "critical memoir" *Heroines*, partially incubated on her blog "Frances Farmer is My Sister," centers on the women of modernism, and was edited by Chris Kraus and published in Semiotext(e)'s Active Agents in 2012.

system, and one could even say a cultural world in general, that often excluded women's voices. I was mostly educated in a school and university system that values the knowledge of (white, affluent) men. In her 1988 text "White Privilege and Male Privilege: A Personal Account of Coming to See Correspondences Through Work in Women's Studies," US-American feminist, anti-racism activist and scholar Peggy McIntosh reflected: "[T]hose few who will acknowledge that male privilege systems have over-empowered them usually end up doubting that we could dismantle these privilege systems. [...] In curricular terms, this is the point at which they say that they regret they cannot use any of the interesting new scholarship on women because the syllabus is full."[5] I heard sentiments and excuses like these frequently when in 2012 I was the co-founder of the feminist working collective (FAK) at Karlsruhe University of Arts and Design (where I studied at the time), which was formed in reaction to the lack of representation of women in the professorship and in the syllabi.

After Kraus's reading, and for the first time, I asked to have one of my books signed by its author. Besides being a writer, critic and former filmmaker Chris Kraus is the editor of the Native Agents Series at the publishing house Semiotext(e), "introduced in 1990 as an 'antidote' to the male-dominated, primarily French Foreign Agents series to explore American, primarily female, voices and issues of subjectivity."[6] Reading the books from her series— Eileen Myles's *Not Me*, Ann Rower's *If You're A Girl*—I encountered other women drifting in the city, like I was at the time, in all different states of mind, finding their voices and starting to speak. Reading their texts on my

---

**5**  Peggy McIntosh, "White Privilege and Male Privilege: A Personal Account of Coming to See Correspondences Through Work in Women's Studies," http://www.collegeart.org/pdf/diversity/white-privilege-and-male-privilege.pdf; (accessed on 02.03.2020).
**6**  Quote taken from their website: https://mitpress.mit.edu/books/series/semiotexte-native-agents (accessed on 02.03.2020).

daily subway rides from Brooklyn to Manhattan I slowly became less afraid of failure and more determined to find my own voice. In summer 2013 I also began to read another Native Agents book, *The Madame Realism Complex* (1992) by Lynne Tillman. It acted as the catalyst for my PhD project in 2016, which addresses the fictional art critic Madame Realism. In it, I deal with a type of criticism that works through and with the imagination, thus allowing the ambivalence we feel in experiencing the world to also be present when criticizing it. My interest for the involvement of the critic—her emotions and her situatedness—with its object/subject of research has been on my mind ever since.

**

Recently I came across a passage by Kraus in her book *Where Art Belongs* (2007), published shortly before she won the Frank Jewett Mather Award for Art Criticism in 2008 for her "hybrid art criticism." In one of the essays, which deals with artist collective Bernadette Corporation, Kraus addresses the relationship between artwriting[7] and artistic practice in the context of the art market: "Our job is to write about art; to give it a language that translates into value. Perhaps the only paid, non-teaching job now for poets and nonmainstream American writers is churning out art reviews and catalogue essays for high-profile art museum and gallery shows."[8] In 2011, Kraus describes a shift in artwriting from the catalogue to the book, "with writers being asked to 'write something' that isn't art critical."[9] Kraus understands this as a "trick" that compels writers to think

---

7   For a contextualization of the term, see also the Introduction to this
    publication.
8   Chris Kraus, *Where Art Belongs* (Los Angeles: Semiotext(e), 2011), p. 54.
9   Chris Kraus in conversation with Anna-Sophie Springer, pp. 21–33;
    in *Traversals*, ed. Anna-Sophie Springer (Berlin: K. Verlag, 2011), here
    p. 28.

about the artworks even more obsessively, because they find themselves in kind of a vacuum without the framework of an art catalogue. This way the discursive machine working "for" the arts keeps moving, one that increasingly relies on the intellectual/mental effort of the writer. When writing a text about a famous photographer for his gallery catalogue, Kraus reports, the passages that showed ambivalence in reflecting his work were simply cut out. Here, artwriting is understood as a practice that contextualizes the artwork and isn't critical of the work of art as such. It understands art primarily as an act of communication that gets "translated" by the writer. The job of the artwriter here is mediating the experience of art. Even though it is important to take the economic aspects of the shift described by Kraus into account to get a grip on the term artwriting, I find it just as necessary to differentiate between writing practices which pursue critical concerns, and those which don't; which also includes examining what these texts are critical of.

In a roundtable discussion organized by the art theory magazine *October* under the title "The Present Conditions of Art Criticism" (2002), literary writing on the occasion of art is under attack. In a conversation between art historians George Baker, Rosalind Krauss, Benjamin Buchloh, David Joselit, Robert Storr and Hal Foster; curator Helen Molesworth; artists Andrea Fraser, James Meyer and John Miller, the panelists discuss the relation between "Artwriting" (the term "Poetic Art Writing" is used synonymously) and "art criticism." These terms are often used as catchwords, but it is not clear what exactly is understood by these terms. The concerns articulated with regards to artwriting range from the danger of art criticism being degraded to an advertising text (James Meyer), the loss of interdisciplinary relevance and the use of criticism (George Baker) to the accusation of the author's personality pushing itself and her/his feelings to the fore (James Meyer). The problem of these assessments is the generalization of the accusation, without naming specific characteristics of the writing practices mentioned, including those by Dave Hickey and Frank O'Hara.

Reading this against the backdrop of Kraus's own, arguably critical writing, the question remains: is there any way that artwriting can function as critique?

Whereas art criticism critically examines an artwork/ an artistic practice, artwriting rather focusses on the context of the artwork/the artistic practice and is an examination of the perspective presented in and through the artwork. Art criticism is closer to a review that also includes a judgment, whereas artwriting is closer to literature, doesn't offer a direct judgment and focusses on the experience of the artwork. Still, artwriting can function as critique, namely, when it is a situated critical and creative practice, often from a feminist perspective, that actively questions a pseudo-objective approach in thinking about art. Such practices I'll refer to as art writing—trying to differentiate them from the rather entertaining artwriting, even though both tend to frequently overlap and blur.

Often the object of critique in art writing isn't the art as such, but its institutional contextualization. Here, it runs close to artwriting, likewise addressing art's sociocultural and institutional contexts, and its promotional function. However, as art writing renders the writer's subjectivity productive for exposing, questioning, or rejecting institutions' workings, it starkly differs from artwriting. And yet, art writing remains inherently ambivalent, as it doesn't assume the possibility of speaking from a distance/from outside, but rather works through proximity towards a critical stance that holds. Often art writers are poets or writers turned into art writers on occasion, often repeatedly. Like Kraus, Kathy Acker, Eileen Myles and Lynne Tillman also arrived at art writing via experimental writing, poetry, and literature.

Writing about art,
I look for the biography of the work itself, which may
or may not include the life of the artist. Discussing the
work of Eadweard Muybridge, Hollis Frampton paused to
reflect:
"As I write these words, a beautiful April afternoon is
passing outside my window."
Writing, like art, takes place in time.
Stick to the facts, draw no conclusions.[10]

Kraus's concept of critique, which shows through in
the passage quoted above, assumes a situated critic, a
critic who observes closely, aware of her surroundings,
her mood and the distractions of the mind. Kraus can
be seen as one of the pioneers of this specific form of
art writing—she is certainly the most visible one—that
functions as critique combining criticism, autobiography, social analysis, and feminist practice.[11] What I
want to deal with is art writing as an explicitly critical and creative practice that represents a break with
the previously dominant model of art criticism. In this
respect, I agree with the assessment of art historian
Susannah Thompson that art writing is a critical redefi-
nition of critique itself—and hence it is important to
distinguish it from current forms of artwriting, which
are primarily aimed at entertainment, or as mentioned
above are employed to create value by mediating art.[12]
These forms of artwriting tend to be published in catalogues by galleries and function as promotion for art-

10  Chris Kraus, "Stick to the Facts," p. 133.
11  In the recent "Literatur" edition of *Texte zur Kunst* the importance
    of recent literary productions "for a critical praxis, for radical reflec-
    tion on the present, distinct from more materially based works of
    art" is pointed out and might describe yet another shift concerning
    the (role of) writing in the art context. *Texte zur Kunst* 115 (Septem-
    ber 2019): p. 4.
12  Susannah Thompson, "The Dress of Thought: Form and style in con-
    temporary art writing," p. 95–115; *Journal of Writing in Creative
    Practice* (2017), Volume 10, Number 1: p. 107.

ists and their artwork. Critical reflections, as well as the ambivalence often present in art writing published in art magazines, are seldom present in these contexts.

Kraus herself offers some hints in her text "Artwriting" (2018)[13]. In contrast to art criticism, art writing can create greater autonomy, narrate the work of art, reflect it indirectly, but can also become a work of art itself. Kraus locates the beginnings of art writing as distinct from art criticism in texts by the dance and later art critic of the *Village Voice*, Jill Johnston: "[...] Johnston famously pushed herself to the absolute limit of physical/mental exertion, writing her way towards and into an art-work. This was a very literary project, of the modernist kind—jill as Artaud as an American lesbian—and one she would later renounce and retreat from." The art writings of Eileen Myles, Masha Tupitsyn and Dodie Bellamy are in Kraus's opinion related to each other, and to Johnston: they all identify themselves as writers or poets and came to art through writing: "[They] have used a similarly immediate, sometimes empathic, and always literary approach to their writings about art." Using Bruce Hainley as an example, Kraus describes it more concretely:

In "Store As Cunt," Bruce Hainley evokes and revises Elaine Sturtevant's early work by mixing the extraordinarily sexist reviews of her early exhibitions with archival material, the artist's own statements and conversations with her contemporaries. Hainley's objective—of forcing a new, long-overdue reading of Sturtevant's work through the lens of the appropriationists who would succeed her—is achieved through purely literary means of opposition, contrast and humor.

13 I'm quoting from Kraus's unpublished manuscript of that text. Different versions of it appeared on E-Flux and in her *Lost Properties* monograph, on the occasion of the Whitney Biennale (Los Angeles: Semiotext(e), 2014).

Like Kraus, Thompson locates the origins of art writing in the 1970s and 1980s. By "Artwriting"[14] she understands a writing that deviates from the then dominant model of academic art criticism—as practiced, for example, in the art magazine *October*—and reaches beyond established forms of the "standard" of art criticism.[15] From the mid-1980s, an increase in art publications could be observed, including non-academic art publications, exhibition catalogues and art magazines produced by artists. This development is also reflected in the increasing diversity of art-critical practices, as there are simply more and more different publication possibilities.[16] One of the consequences of the interdisciplinary of writing on the occasion of art is the variety of references used, which extends beyond the discourse of art and feeds on everyday life and pop culture. In this sense, art writing criticizes the established canon, the distinction between high and low culture, and embeds the art experience into the everyday experience: after all, the subject who experiences art is also the one who suddenly craves a snack and wants to leave the exhibition for this reason. Art writing thus emerged as a form of critical thinking that takes the arts as its starting point, but which, based on it, deals with social questions, a criticism of the canon and of dominant forms of knowledge, and the question of the critical subject and its situatedness. Art writing does not presuppose an autonomous, self-sufficient ego, but often deconstructs it. So, whereas at first this practice might seem highly subjective, art writing often deconstructs the notion of an individual subjectivity by exhibiting its constructedness, its preconditions and the unconscious aspects that play into art perception and the notion of self. Art writing inhabits potential in thinking about the way in which our sub-

14  Here she references David Carrier, *Artwriting* (Amherst: University of Massachusetts Press, 1987).
15  Thompson, "The Dress of Thought," p. 97.
16  Ibid., p. 108.

jectivity plays into perceiving art/the world, by tricking the reader into her/his narrative by employing the subjectivity exhibited. Art writing described this way differs from the current excrescences of artwriting, which often tries to appear "entertaining," but threatens to become banal. Art writing as critique is a specific way of reacting and writing in response to art, that starts with the subject and its interactions, and its reflections with and on the artwork. As art writers are often poets and writers turned into art writers, this shift is also rooted in their interdisciplinary background, and their occupation and education often not being "art" first hand. Asked in early 2019 if she sees a future for art writing, Kraus states: "I think visual artists still welcome parallel texts—writings or stories that are prompted by looking at art—but they don't necessarily explicate it in an art-historical or critical way. Adulatory adjectives and comparisons to critical theory can be really tiresome."[17]

---

**17** Maeve Hanna interviews Chris Kraus, *Los Angeles Review of Books*, 23.02.2019: https://lareviewofbooks.org/article/social-practices-an-interview-with-chris-kraus/; (accessed on 02.03.2020).

# On Slowing Down and
# Not Being Shy

## A Conversation Between
## Chris Kraus and Isabel Mehl

On the book tour to launch her German edition of *I Love Dick* in summer 2017, I met Chris Kraus for the second time. In Weimar we were both guests on a panel discussion about *I Love Dick*. Touching upon her newest publication *Social Practices* (2018) and wondering what a current mode of critique could be, we continued our conversation via email in early 2019.

[Henry] Taylor, whose recent New York show at Daniel Reich in Chelsea sold out before the opening, has lived in Chinatown for fifteen months. Before that, he was "kind of floating" between Culver City, Santa Cruz, and Thousand Oaks, making paintings on the backs of cigarette packs when his studio was a kitchen table. Like all of his larger works, they're sharp and sweet, blatant, simple narrative images that conjure more complex histories.

While Taylor talks a mile a minute, my eyes are wandering through the forty to fifty finished works around his studio. Like the painter R. B. Kitaj, many of his paintings are compositionally disjunctive narratives, but Taylor packs a more aggressive visual punch. Painted in deep colors, his people practically burst through the frame. The first one that sucks me in is a painting of a young black man in a T-shirt standing in front of a long, low Walmart building. Underneath the figure, a soldier crouches in a tunnel. It's any urban neighborhood, USA.[1]

---

1   Chris Kraus, *Social Practices* (Los Angeles: Semiotext(e), 2018), p. 58.

**Isabel Mehl:** In a conversation with artist Annette Weisser[2] in 2014 you stated:

> To me, critique is a twentieth century concept; it doesn't make the same sense anymore. I mean, what would we be critiquing? To mount a "critique" implies a fixed, mono-lithic structure that one can oppose, and it isn't really like that. The things most threatening to us are much more amorphous. More than critique, I think the most vital thing now is for artists and writers to describe the present situation as accurately as possible, and theory can give us a sense of how the present has arrived. The erasure of cau-sality is one of the triumphs of totalitarian capitalism. If everything just "is," all action becomes pointless. But cri-tique is too binary.[3]

What mode of critique do you suggest?

**Chris Kraus:** I think description is one of the most effec-tive forms of critique. Description encourages us to pause, and look hard at the world as it is. The cause-and-effect analysis that characterized twentieth-century left wing politics seems much too simple, but to just sigh that "it's complicated" doesn't help. It really seems important to focus on things that are finite, and graspable.

**IM:** What does "description" mean for you here?

**CK:** Something really simple. To say what you see. It's surprisingly difficult to render an image in words, but things are revealed when you slow down enough to observe what's actually there.

---

**2**  Annette Weisser was associate professor at ArtCenter College of Design, Pasadena (2006–2019), and now teaches at Kunsthochschule Kassel.
**3**  Chris Kraus interviewed by Annette Weisser, "For Every Theory There Is A Novel," in *In the Canyon, Revise the Canyon*, ed. Geraldine Gourbe (Shelter Press: 2015).

**IM:** Slowing down, this seems quite crucial for the critical endeavor in times of digital/virtual speeding communication. It takes time to take a critical stance and to reflect its preconditions. What role does the subjectivity of the critic play in that mode of critique?

**CK:** I think what the writer turns towards is always personal and singular. A description is always a synthesis of the thing being described, and the speaker. I also love close readings, and encourage students to do them when I teach writing. It's how to think like a writer, to get underneath the skin of a text. A close reading of something doesn't preclude placing it in a context and showing the bigger picture, as well.

**IM:** Is the addressee for these writing practices—art criticism and art writing—becoming more and more the same, are they both becoming more and more niche activities?

**CK:** I think art criticism is more of a trade magazine practice, read only within the profession, whereas art writing has a little more reach beyond the art world.

**IM:** One very interesting example of these combined audiences is the London-based magazine The White Review that brings together art writing, creative writing, fiction, essay and interviews. In a way a lot of art writing can be read without the reader actually knowing the artwork, it is a work on its own. Related to this: Is there any difference in the role the visual plays in art writing in contrast or in relation to art criticism?

**CK:** I think "art writing" takes more license to approach artworks indirectly, often laterally, and through different channels than "art criticism." How do we translate visual experience? Old-fashioned traditional art criticism used to very carefully describe the artwork in a material way—this isn't necessarily done any more. I don't think either of those approaches necessarily adheres more closely to the visual experience as such.

**IM:** I recently listened to a presentation by Eva Illouz[4] where in a sidenote she said, I paraphrase, that definitions often don't help: "I don't usually pay much attention to definition. You have to define with regards to what you want to do. Definitions are good but most often reality is more messy, trying to define is what one should do, understand why it's difficult."

But still I find it important to set the terms: What do we mean when we say art writing, in difference to art criticism? Referring to your own art writing, you state in the Introduction to *Social Practices*: "The only difference between these pieces and traditional art criticism was that they were written more to the work than about it. And so names, events, places, and ideas recur across this book."[5]

**CK:** As someone who came to the visual art world via writing, with no particular training in art or art history, I've never thought much about whether my writing about art was called "art writing" or "art criticism." Still, "art criticism" adheres more to a discursive description and analysis of an artwork, whereas "art writing" seems to allow for a more lateral approach … sometimes writing a text that responds to the artwork, rather than describes or analyzes it.

**IM:** Thinking about the relationship between the visual and the verbal I remember a statement of yours from a

---

4    Eva Illouz is a Professor of Sociology at the Hebrew University in Jerusalem. Her most recent book, with Edgar Cabanas, is *Manufacturing Happy Citizens: How the Science and Industry of Happiness Control our Lives* (Cambridge: Polity Press, 2019), which she also discussed on the occasion mentioned here.
5    Kraus, *Social Practices*, p. 9.

conversation between you and Mark von Schlegell in which you stated: "[T]he aesthetic values of the art and poetry worlds are more closely aligned [than with the literary world]. What's taught now as literary fiction rings false to artists."[6] Could you maybe elaborate on that statement a little, what are these "aesthetic values" and what "rings false" to artists?

**CK:** Writing programs, at least in the US, tend to be very industry-oriented and formulaic. There's a value of "well-written" literary fiction and non-fiction, that usually follows a pretty predictable narrative arc, that is completely alienating to me, and most people I know in the art world. The programs are very industry-oriented, geared towards producing the solipsistic American coming-of-age family novel … So, you know, yeck.

Annette Weisser and I are co-teaching a writing class with MFA Studio Art students at ArtCenter College of Design in Pasadena this semester, and the work of these students is far more interesting to me than writing produced in MFA writing programs. The students we work with tend to be better read and have a much broader understanding of culture. They're more willing to engage with larger existential, political and formal questions than most MFA writing students.

**IM:** What are you reading in that course?

**CK:** Annette chose a couple of books for the class to read—Annie Ernaux's *The Years*, and Didier Eribon's *Returning to Reims*—and I chose Colette's short novel *Vagabond*. All these books have to do with work experiences, and approaching the cultural center from the outside. We were both interested in that, so that's what we assigned. And then in class, we often write together,

6    https://obieg.u-jazdowski.pl/en/numery/art-and-literature/beyond-fictocriticism (accessed on 02.03.2020).

around various themes that come up in our conversations. Reading and writing together in a group can be so powerful. At the best times, the class feels like a coven.

**IM:** How do you read—physical books, e-reader, on your computer?

**CK:** Always physical books—with embarrassing underlinings and even notes in the margins, so I can return to them.

**IM:** In France, intellectuals like Ernaux, Eribon and Édouard Louis[7] support the protests of the *gilets jaunes*. The issue of "class," a topic that is central to their texts, is very much discussed in Germany right now, also in the art world: In 2017 there was an exhibition called "Klassensprachen" [Class talk] in Berlin, and in 2018 the show "Klassenverhältnisse" [Class relations] opened at Hamburger Kunstverein. But then the "class" visiting these events is so homogenous. And that actually is no surprise because first of all the language often is elitist, very exclusive in a way. Language often seems to be more of a distinctive feature than a means of communication.

**CK:** I think about this all the time. The art and cultural worlds are increasingly closed to anyone outside the upper/upper middle class. Semiotext(e) has always championed work that comes from slightly outside, whether by culture or class. I find the exclusionary nature of the high culture world totally alienating. Additionally, the competition for non-precarious academic employment has become so fierce that only those who've been preparing for this career since age five will

---

7    Édouard Louis is the author of two novels and the editor of a book on the social scientist Pierre Bourdieu. His debut *The End of Eddy* (London: Harvill Secker, 2017) is a portrayal of the French working class and the racism and homophobia that Louis grew up surrounded by.

succeed. Anyone who has deviated, hesitated or paused is automatically excluded. And these are the people who are always most interesting to me.

**IM:** Your interest in dialogue often results in professional collaborations: in teaching, in writing in response to artworks, or editing for Semiotext(e) with Sylvère Lotringer and Hedi El Kholti. Is this a way to counter the loneliness of writing?

**CK:** Writing is solitary, for sure, and I wouldn't want to escape that by writing collaboratively. Annette and I co-teaching is a special, unusual thing—we've been in touch as colleagues and friends for a while, and it just seemed like a cool thing to do, especially since she'll soon be returning to Germany. But the intellectual contact and stimulation of working with Semiotext(e) is so rewarding and valuable. Especially in the years since Hedi has joined us (2004–the present), Semiotext(e) has created an international community of readers and writers. We did an event this week at the Edendale Library in Echo Park with the German writer Heike Geissler[8] that turned into a kind of town hall meeting. The library director remarked afterwards that she loves hosting Semiotext(e) events because they're so intimate.

**IM:** When you started editing Native Agents for Semiotext(e) you were reacting to the absence of women in the program of the publishing house. The focus of that series has expanded since then...

**CK:** Yes. By the time Hedi joined us in 2004, I'd pretty much finished what I set out to do with Native Agents in the 1990s. This left the door open to something else.

---

8   Heike Geissler is a German writer based in Leipzig. Her novel *Seasonal Associate*, which is based on her own experiences, describes what happened when she took a seasonal job at an Amazon Order Fulfillment center. It was published by Native Agents in 2018.

It's hard to say what it is, exactly—except that it's a very international list, and all of the works are strongly narrative, but at the same time, formal. That is: they're more readable than purely "experimental" work, but more formally conscious than most reader-friendly literary fiction. And of course, the subject matter is never purely domestic drama—all of the books have a strong sense of reflecting the larger world and the present.

**IM:** Considering what Native Agents set out to do: Certainly, there has been a change regarding the equality of the genders, but still there is much more to do. This also holds true for a true multiplicity of voices in cultural discourse that includes black writers, writers who have not had the privilege of higher education and other marginalized groups that are excluded for different reasons, but united in being understood as working in some kind of niche and not in the same "universal" realm as (affluent) white men. When *I Love Dick* came out in Germany and the mainstream press discovered this "new genre" of "Autofiction,"[9] oddly enough, it seemed necessary for it to be verified by a man, namely Karl Ove Knausgård and his autobiographical series of novels *Min Kamp*. Even though there were other female writers working in that "non-genre" as well, for example Sheila Heti,[10] Maggie Nelson[11] or Annie Ernaux. And hence I wondered if the

---

9   "Autofiction" is a term used to refer to a form of fictionalized autobiography. The use of the term "autofiction," as well as the specific way in which female writers put the first person to strategic use, I discussed in the article "Die Ich-Funktion," in *Texte zur Kunst*, 11 September 2019: https://www.textezurkunst.de/articles/die-ich-funktion/ (accessed on 02.03.2020).

10  Sheila Heti is the author of eight books of fiction and non-fiction, including *How Should a Person Be?* (Toronto: House of Anansi Press, 2010) and *Motherhood* (London: Harvill Secker, 2018). In this latter book she traces the social contexts of the wish to become, or not to become, mother, and questions its individual validity.

11  Maggie Nelson is an American writer who has been described as genre-busting and defying classification, working in autobiography, art criticism, theory, scholarship, and poetry. Her most recent book is *The Argonauts* (Minneapolis: Graywolf Press, 2015).

idea you evolved in *I Love Dick*, to universalize the personal, can only finally arrive in the literary mainstream when realized by a man.

**CK:** Yeah, I think that's about right. The female writers you mention are widely appreciated, but I don't think the experiences they describe are considered to be universal, even now.

**IM:** You once said that when you write, you are always ghosting someone, for instance in *I Love Dick* you were writing in the tracks of Henry James[12]. Was there also someone in your mind when writing *Social Practices*, or certain parts of it?

**CK:** Yes—but since it's an anthology, there were different models to copy, different influences. The first piece, "Trick," about working in the New York City hustle bars in the late 1970s and early 1980s, I remember consciously trying to adopt a "flinty" voice, kind of a cross between the mid-twentieth century *New Yorker* writer Janet Flanner[13], and William S. Burroughs[14]. The pieces about artist Lucie Stahl, I was aiming for a kind of delirium.

**IM:** What is the last artwork / museum visit that stuck with you?

**CK:** Last night I co-hosted an event at Scripps College in the Clark Humanities Center, where there was an exhibition of photos by the American artist Larry Fink: very sharp, crisp black and white images of society people at parties in New York City in the mid-1970s. They were

---

12  Henry James was an American-British author regarded as a transitional figure between literary realism and literary modernism.

13  Janet Flanner was an American writer and journalist who served as the Paris correspondent of *The New Yorker magazine* from 1925 until she retired in 1975.

14  William S. Burroughs was an American writer of experimental novels. He is part of the Beat Generation.

beautiful, in the way they showed this very restrained aggression and tension, manifesting only in a facial expression or gesture. This was combined with an exhibition of drawings and prints from nineteenth-century Japan, and I found that really interesting. With very limited resources, the curator juxtaposed these two disparate but equally distinct forms of cultural code.

**IM:** Speaking about the combination of two artistic practices: It has become obligatory for artists working today to somehow render their practice into verbal or written language. But if that's a result of writing migrating into the art world, as you examined, isn't there also something lost? Certain kinds of artists can no longer succeed since they don't (want to) speak that language. I find that this migration is also leading to a certain kind of theory-informed art that excludes artists who are less concerned with art theory and philosophy. In *Social Practices* you're directly referring to the alienation artists like Henry Taylor, Julie Becker or Andrea Bowers experienced towards the theory-centric reading lists at CalArts.[15] On a very basic level someone with no high school degree has much less of an opportunity to apply successfully for scholarships that rely on the artist giving a well-informed discursive statement about her/his art. It's kind of a "discursive dictate" that also links back to the capitalization of the art market. But how could one deal critically with these standards, or why is that done so little? At least I'm not aware of practices attacking that apart from those coming out of the International Art English debate[16]?

---

15  Kraus, *Social Practices*, p. 59.
16  Alix Rule and David Levine, *International Art English* (New York: Triple Canopy, 2019). On the rise—and the space—of the art-world press release, see: https://www.canopycanopycanopy.com/contents/international_art_english (accessed on 02.03.2020).

**CK:** I agree with you. There are exceptions, but the artist needs to be in the right place to break through these rules. I watched Marion Scemama's beautiful documentary recently about the American artist David Wojnarowicz (1954–1992). Wojnarowicz was a total artist ... always making something, whether in collage, painting, video, writing or installation. Watching the film, I wondered if this kind of work would even be possible now. Wojnarowicz sold work and had gallery representation during his lifetime, but the engagement with his work went well beyond the artworld. I wonder if anyone would have the confidence to do this, to be an artist, rather than a pursuing a "practice."

**IM:** As you explain in the foreword of your new publication, its title *Social Practices* addresses the diversity of art-informed practices when leaving the cocoon of the art scene. Could you give me a little bit more context for that concept?

**CK:** There's the genre now known as "social practice," that I guess succeeded "relational aesthetics" and has established itself in the last decade or so ... but that interests me less than the strange, anomalous and idiosyncratic projects that I discover by chance. And that kind of activity isn't so anchored to decades—it always exists, you just need to find it. Hedi El Kholti, Lauren Mackler and I have recently collaborated on a book of Reynaldo Rivera's extraordinary photographs of LA's Latino drag bars and Echo Park house parties from the early 1990s. Rivera is an artist who's worked consistently in LA for several decades alongside, but just outside, the mainstream art world. His work feels really timeless to me.

**IM:** You don't have Facebook, Twitter or Instagram. Is that a political choice of yours?

**CK:** I have a very dormant Facebook page, otherwise nothing, you're right. Social media posts are just as geared to an audience as published writing, and it just seems like too much work. I don't think it's political, necessarily—although I do have a horror of being data-mined, tracked and surveilled. Social media is a lot like capitalist exceptionalism: incredibly hegemonic, but we stay tuned for the rare chance that something new and worthwhile will slip through the cracks.

**IM:** Yesterday I was at a conversation between philosopher Jacques Rancière and philosopher Peter Engelmann[17]. In the subsequent discussion one woman stood up and asked Rancière why in his opinion no woman had asked something until now in the discussion. He didn't really reply but I was left wondering why this situation is always the same—women silent, men often doing monologue-like statements. Is that something you have any thoughts about?

**CK:** Yes! I'm really shy, too, when I'm in an audience, and hardly ever ask questions. But when I do events, the balance is different—usually it's women who speak more, making statements as well as asking questions. A conversation between two male philosophers, well—it's not surprising that the discussion afterwards would be more male than female, more statement than question. Silence is a sign not just that people are shy, perhaps, but that they feel alienated from the terms of the discussion.

---

**17** In 1985 Peter Engelmann founded the publishing house Passagen Verlag in Vienna that published numerous works by Rancière.

**Lynne Tillman**

# The Horse's Eye

**Fig. 1:** Carroll Dunham, *Study for Horse and Rider (My X) (44)*, 2014, Graphite on paper, 13.3 x 9.2 cm, Gladstone Gallery, New York and Brussels.

# I.

Writing and reading happen incrementally, one word, another; the speed of a reader, or writer, doesn't count, really. A writer might draw a line through a word or phrase; she might keep the first word visible under the new one, like a palimpsest or background reading. In writing, a superimposition doesn't fuse layers the way it does in films and photographs. A painting's surface compares better, when, say, its first or second layer shows through it.

In writing, shapes or structures for a composition build while the writer works. Paragraphs suggest idea shifts; line breaks and punctuation, breath, pauses, full stops, and starts. Gertrude Stein resorted to periods, though she didn't like them much: she knew their necessity—things always come to an end. But that first written word might be, in the end, at the end. A writer begins somewhere, there's an unavoidable linearity.

Visual compositions are different. In painting, the frame, or the scale of the canvas or other surface, comes first. Drawings may have preceded the painting—they often do in Carroll Dunham's work. The size or scale of a painting will usually be considerably larger than a drawing for it. So, the paint-composition begins as a shape, with its limits and characteristics—square, rectangle, hexagon etc. A painting could exceed its perimeters by dripping onto the floor or onto a wall beside it, but rarely does.

Painters address various parts of the surface, at different times. Every element unsettles or resolves a composition—work in one corner affects the entirety. Painters think variously, spatially, for one, and spatial order has its own exigencies, which compel adjustments and responses, painting over, over-painting, erasures.

Carroll Dunham visualizes ideas, thoughts, feelings. His approach to composition has shapes. In the "Now and Around Here" series, for instance, he chose recognizable forms—people, animals, birds, leaves, trees. He worked on linen with mixed media, and used vivid colors. Dunham covered the entire canvas. He drew and painted, because in his paintings line matters. His surfaces might show under-painting or pencil lines, like a writer's first thoughts.

## II.

"Don't explain, only describe."
Ludwig Wittgenstein

Close readings aren't popular, but I like doing them. In film, counting seconds between shots; in photography, noticing what the frame excludes, where it sits; in sculpture, measuring negative space, and the eye's movement through shapes, front, sides, back, if a piece has them; in dance, counting time between movements, and, in music, beats, rhythms, noting a singer's range, what sounds are amplified. Noticing musical stops. What's left out in writing is key.

I don't usually think about what's outside a painting's frame. I might think, this space is art, the empty space beside it is not. I ask myself what that inference about art's impact means. I notice where I look—first, second, third. I pull the painting apart, mentally: colors, textures, thickness or flatness of paint. There's a sense of the visceral, of feel, a hand might or might not be involved. I note the presence or absence of representational forms, look at the sides of a painting, because sometimes they're painted, sometimes left alone. I always wonder about that decision. And even though material might bleed off its sides, nothing has been excluded from a painting, or everything has been.

With a close reading, even by "only describing," artworks are interpreted. The language chosen by a critic characterizes the elements she sees, because words have their own specificity, and, as important, associations and connotations. A synonym, close to a chosen word's meaning, inflects meanings with difference.

Interpretations are parenthetical to a work. I mean, an interpretation is not the work. An interpretation can be a simile or metaphor, say. In writing, anything parenthetical can be removed from a sentence, not disturbing the sense of a sentence. It can be lifted out, without change. In fiction, I hardly ever use them, because of that. One day, I hope to use many, in a story.

I wonder whether a description is an interpretation is an explanation. I prefer not to explain, but contend with inevitable and annoying slippages.

### III.
### Descriptions of Carroll Dunham's Paintings

*Horse and Rider (My X)*
Two naked asses—horse's and woman's—occupy center stage. (They make me want to laugh.) The dark-haired woman's (which resembles a pair of melons) is poised on the brown horse's broad one, while his genitals hang down (like over-ripe fruit).

The woman rider looks away from the center, toward a yellow sun above her head, rounder than her ass. Her gray-white arms, lightly outlined in black, are thrown up and out. (In abandon, or maybe as V for victory. If she is victorious, I wonder what her victory might be.)

The horse's head, poised below the woman rider's outstretched arm, faces out, and looks at me or any viewer. His eyes peer (steadily, unnervingly) from the painting at the space before it. (The horse is reminiscent of Velazques' painter, who looks out from the court scene in Las Meninas: both figures situate the viewer. Both are seeing and also being seen.)

He stares ahead, his brown pupils dot the middle of the whites. (I fall into the horse's eyes, where there is such benignity. Or, unblinking surprise, maybe compassion.) Painted like that, the eyes appear to follow a viewer wherever she might go. (I keep looking back, to check.)

The long-haired rider, her back straight, arms open, is going forward. Her pose looks exuberant. (Her exuberance defies sadness, for one, and she might be experiencing joy, in life. There's so little joy to feel, and yet here it is.)

A tree rises from the ground on the other side of the rider, parallel to the horse's face. It's a tree but it also isn't, though green leaves sprout, seemingly, from it; they're drawn with a light, gay hand (as Matisse might).

Tree, telephone pole, fence post, the brown shape complicates Dunham's picture. Its branches, if they are, have been chopped off; they haven't fallen off. The "trunk" is literally truncated, a visual pun that unsettles the "fate" of the horse and woman. (It suggests other doubled readings, such as, is this a tragedy or comedy?)

The rods appear to enter the woman's body, but stop short of impaling her, only to emerge on the other side of her, piercing the horse's neck. That might have just occurred, since time in a painting is always, in a sense, in the present tense.

(And, just now the horse's eyes register shock, or hurt and pain.)

The broken tree or pole has sawed-off parts, boughs. It is just not a tree. (Maybe a fence whose planks police the space.) Horse, woman, the ambiguous structure—here a bough, there a rod— break up the space. (Or break it down.)

At the bottom of the picture, a fallen bough presents an obstacle to the horse, who has a lifted hoof. (Otherwise, the horse would trip, bolt, or rise up in fear. Then the woman would fall to the ground.)

## *Game*

A naked woman swings (like a circus performer) from the top branch of a faux tree. (Sawed-off branches or rods is a trope in Dunham's "Here and Now" series, appearing in all of them.) This woman, maybe "My X" (X marks the spot; X as in ex), is powerful, has great upper body strength. She is parallel to the ground, her legs thrust forward, and her nipples and vulva colored a deep, bright red. (The nipples extrude, erect; the vulva and labia are a heart-shape. A valentine or V, for victory?)

A large black bird, a crow, sits on the same bough as the one from which she swings. Three others fly or are suspended near her; they might be looking in her direction or at the other crow. Again, the yellow sun rests above the woman's head, off center. If Game has a center it is a line running across it horizontally; the space might be divided in quadrants. The lowest crow's head is on a line with the woman's vulva.

(Disorienting, this game, if it is one, and if it is, what is the game? There's a chance of losing, a sense of winning, or at least trying is important in these paintings. Survival is winning. Must be. Or, maybe its title is not a noun but a verb: "I am game for this." Or, is he gaming me? The painter may be playing a game. Later, Carroll Dunham tells me, there's a third sense. They're game for each other, crow and the woman, they're both prey. That hadn't occurred to me at all.)

The woman is swinging forward, her body parallel to the ground; the birds flightless, or stuck in motion; a turquoise blue sky envelopes them all. It is impossible to know where in space this painting is: There is no definite ground. (I wonder if the faux trunk shoots into the sky, if it has a connection to the earth, or is entirely disconnected. The earth may have been deserted.)

### Now and Around Here 1, 2, 3

This is a group of three paintings.

In #1, a man's gray-white body, like the X-woman's, outlined lightly in black, is at the base of each. Headless, erect red nipples, his legs spread, his penis rests between his thighs. He is lying on his back. (And not playing an active "male" role; he is an observer in and of the landscape/scene.) Squiggly black lines, drawn gaily, represent his chest hair.

Red flowers, yellow leaves, green grass, a round yellow sun, all are within his purview. The brown boughs pierce the purple sky, two boughs entering from both sides of him, at the level of his knees. (This curious, possibly dangerous, and endangered "tree" behaves differently in each painting, though always in position to cause a threat to the other bodies. If this is meant to be Nature, Nature isn't behaving neutrally; and, a sense of "the natural" is under scrutiny. While primary colors usually signal exuberance and presence, and they also do in these paintings, the colors are blunted or leavened by damaged Nature or its threats. The colors spell "unnaturalness.")

In #2, central again, the dark-haired woman's round ass. She is a full figure, naked, back to the viewer, one of her arms reaching out (beseechingly?), the other hanging by her side (no exultation). She looks into the distance; above her and off-center, a very large, round, bright yellow sun. She is standing in a field of blue (water, pool, lake, ocean); the blue rises above her knees. A lime-kelly green is background to her and the sun. (No sky here, or it's green from pollution. Or, it's a painting not at all about a natural setting.)

The man is supine, though his legs appear to be spread apart farther than in #1. He is looking at her, seeing her, who stands, in the distance, and from his point of view, as if between his legs. A purplish-blue flower seems to be sprouting under him, emerging from him, and it is near or touching his genitals. (Or it is taking over.)

The faux-tree's boughs hang in or protrude into the green "sky," separately. (Like cut ups, or as in a collage, seemingly glued on.) There are three purplish-blue flowers and six leaves, four the same type, green ovals; two, a lighter green, whose tops are straight edged. (Maybe they are dead, or from a different kind of tree.)

In #3, except for the yellow sun and dark-brown boughs or logs, the colors in this painting have changed (dramatically. I feel I'm looking at rust). The sun may be setting (impossible to ascertain, except that it seems to be). The man is again supine, but his nipples are dusky pink, and near his genitals, three yellow-brown objects rise (plants, fingers, growths, sprouts, other penises?). There are many of these, four rows of them; the boughs or logs enter the space from every side, except where the man lies. Some are crossed, thick rods; some narrow, and some are sticks. Brownish-pink flowers (maybe daisies, dried and dead) hang from the top of the painting. (One looks like a badminton shuttlecock.)

A brown dog, with eyes painted like the horse's, sits off center, as if between the man's legs. The sun is directly above the dog, off center also. The background or sky is tangerine orange (it might be sunset). The dog is just sitting, looking out of the painting to any viewer or space. (Or, might be waiting for its "master" to arise and play, go for a walk. But maybe the man is lifeless, sunset of his life, his nipples so pale. Has the blood left him, is his body cold?)

Three variations on a theme: a naked man lies or rests at the bottom of the three paintings. The picturing is from his point of view.

(I see what he is seeing. Or, imagining.)

The male and female figures do not see themselves. The man sees her. She does not see him or look at him. They are objects in different picture planes.

The horse's and dog's eyes matter, because the humans don't have eyes. The man doesn't have a head. The woman's eyes are indicated not articulated. Eyeless human beings, somehow they seem to be looking at something. The dog and the horse are looking out of the painting, at the viewer, and the dog may be looking also at the male figure.

A headless, male body, with arms, legs, feet, penis, nipples. Does he have a mind? He is a match to a Dunham female, though no female is headless. Does she have a mind? If so, what are they both thinking about? Or, rather, they are not thinking, or I can never know their thoughts. What do the paintings make a viewer, me, think about? The ubiquitous binaries, nature/culture; artificial/organic; male/female; life/death. Adam/Eve: banished from paradise into a living hell.

And, also they raise a persistent, devilish issue: is the female in art always, or merely, an object of male desire? Is she an object in ways a male nude could not be? Painting nudes in a time of easy-access porn—does it effect the practice or product? Does the sex, or sexuality, of the artist who paints or draws— nudes—matter? Some of Dunham's contemporaries: Lydia Yuskavage, Nicole Eisenman, John Currin, Jeff Koons. Or, earlier artists Picasso, Bonnard. Or, in another register, Robert Crumb and Aline Kominsky-Crumb.

In Dunham's paintings, these Eves and Adams play other parts, rebel against traditional roles. His nudes— overblown, comic, ironic, unrealistic—may be metaphors, in an allegorical setting, that refer to newer realities, about gender, for one. His female is active, the male, passive, antithetical to stereotypes of femininity and masculinity. The figures exist inside bright colors, but the scenes are disturbing. They are in disrupted spaces. The female—arms outstretched, swinging from a fake tree: Triumphant, capable, strong? The male—subdued, maybe defeated, or resigned, only there to observe this new world? Dunham may be portraying a female world in which males have been redefined and relocated.

I wander into Dunham's field of inquiry, don't settle my thoughts, and pursue the pleasures of possibility.

I can't explain Dunham's paintings.

Interpretation is not explanation.

The reader of any art is a second responder. The maker, the first responder, is the thing's first intended and dedicated audience.

I recall Churchill's famous phrase "victory in our time." During World War II and the Battle of Britain, Churchill spoke over the radio and gave the British, still fighting the Nazis alone, hope. The woman's V is different. In Dunham's settings and in these times, if the female is triumphant over, say, patriarchy, her victory has many shadings. Some think women have gained what has been lost—I mean, that she triumphs over scorched earth, to succeed during permanent wars, and to witness nature in peril or destroyed. She might be restorative or also destructive. A pessimistic reading, this, and, I'm being literal, which can, in part, result from close readings.

To paraphrase Freud, sometimes a cigar is just a cigar; sometimes it's a penis. Now I rejig and consider: a supine male figure may also be an artist who created this—who "takes" this lying down. From this position, he observes the state of things, imperturbable, upset, resigned, or content.

### Culture as a Verb

People, bodies, are gone. The palette is three colors: rosy red, pale tan-pink, and brown. The tree is facing out, its cut-off branches shooting toward the viewer. The thirteen leaves are a deep red: It could be fall. (It could be the aftermath of the Fall, when Adam and Eve were banished. It's hard for me to avoid the allegory of the Garden of Eden.)

Culture as a Verb is a leading title, like a leading question. (I can't stay away from its implications.) "To culture" is to cultivate, bring into being, to educate. It is an active, ongoing process. To cultivate may entail mixtures and choices, determinations about ways to produce what kind of cultures. Culture then is not a process, but a product of many determinations. (Is the painting addressing the process of making "culture"? Maybe.)

A mass of swirling rosy red covers or entangles the bottom half of the painting. The mass surrounds nine, brown, sawed-off branches or rods that point at the viewer. This (confrontational) pose or stance is unique in this series of paintings. In the background, behind the rosy red mass, Dunham's trope: a faux tree, with cut-off branches, hovers. Swirling, the mass is dynamic, an object in movement.

(The red mass threatens to advance. It looks like an armored vehicle—a tank. The brown rods are the main guns. Now the tree might be the turret of a tank, with more main guns or cannons. What is being cultured might explode or shoot to kill, what is being cultured is active and destructive, and intimates future human-made disasters.)

### Big Bang 1, 2, 3

A group of paintings—three variations on its eponymous title. All bright orange and golden yellow, with some black, abstract and loosely figurative, a roundish shape is central. Its perimeter changes, the roundness expands as if pulled like taffy at its sides, but still keeps its globe-like shape, cosmos, world, universe. (The orange might be flames or represent internal explosive events that affect the look and shape of things—the order of things.)

The universe began, physicists say, because of the Big Bang. In Dunham's paintings, he pictures the wildness, the bizarre reality of everything beginning—true for each of us, a beginning, in life. Multitudes of relation-ships, of nations, religions, identities, wars, the natural order, everything begins.

Before the Big Bang, scientists say there was nothing. I want to be able to see nothing. I try, often, and find it impossible: "what" is nothing, a vastness of nothing, forever: if nothing is there, I can't see nothing, which can't be "there." An infinity resides in this tautology, or any tautology. A belief in God seems convenient and comforting, because a transcendent, omniscient God is always, and was always, and so there never was nothing. Even a few physicists believe that God, or a first or prime mover, caused the Big Bang, and "created" the universe. So, maybe rocket scientists also find "Nothing" impossible.

The Big Bang is a fact. In 1964, the sound of it was accidentally discovered by a horn antenna developed and built, by two scientists, for Bell Labs in New Jersey. The first photons released after the Big Bang, its afterglow, exist in the cosmos as radio waves. The horn antenna captured this sound, similar to a hissing noise, and recordings of it have been made. This seems as if it shouldn't be actual, but it is: the beginning of the universe is still around, in the atmosphere, as sound. It can be heard. I find this entirely startling.

## IV.

People live with abstract ideas, absorb (or reject) complex concepts, often referred to, with amusement, as "not rocket science." Which means even a non-scientist should understand.

A painting is not considered rocket science, but can be difficult, because it might refer to or represent what isn't immediately accessible or understood, and needs a viewer to see it, to complete it. This requires projections, identifications, and a feeling of necessity—to understand it or understand what one is looking for. Looking, I am not just looking at something but also "for" something. Then I see it a certain way. I might be drawn or repulsed, and wonder: What is it I am apprehending? I doubt my perceptions, which aren't "natural," but educated. What is it addressing? What is it making or "seeing," what is it about, that I may not "see"? I often ask myself what I believe are the hardest questions, about necessity: Why is it there? Why do I look at it? These often can't be answered.

Paintings are fictions, human-designed constructions. Even when referring to actual events, like the Big Bang—fiction. This seems obvious: art is made, not born. Some fictions seem truer than others: that is, some speak less indirectly to conditions and feelings, or present a greater verisimilitude—an awareness of the relationship to what is outside it.

Dunham's paintings, abstract and figurative compositions, conjure everyday realities as both more and less than real; the so-called "ordinary" is unfamiliar, new terrain, politically, sexually, environmentally. Fictional portraits of the known moving into an unknown, they show vivacity, even about the incapacity to know the future. I mean, they have vitality, these frank, beautiful misfits, or funny, smart, bold disturbances. Not stories but wordless pictures, the paintings ask a viewer, like me, to draw or write her own conclusions.

Human beings are devouring machines, Dunham's paintings suggest, competing with the natural world and carelessly upending it. Human beings don't perceive the damage they do, as it happens; they will turn a blind eye, adapt, go on, and live in peril. People will themselves to survive; they will do whatever it takes to survive. People don't get the big picture, because they are in it.

Inevitably it's said: Artists address the human condition. But the human condition is unstable, in flux—human-made. Art also represents—and has always—the inhuman condition, inhuman acts, wishes, circumstances, commissions of horror, of terror, all in the name of humanity. But then humans named it humanity.

I look at Carroll Dunham's paintings, and think about being alive. I'm alive now, and then I won't be, but I don't know when. Life is always endangered, by death, for one. In Dunham's paintings, there are no condemnations, there's no shame. Jeremiads would lose me. I think about Samuel Beckett: "Dance first. Think later. It's the natural order." The paintings may be cautionary tales, but there's some dancing in them. And, the painter is fully aware he is part of the picture.

**Fig. 2:** Carroll Dunham, *Study for Horse and Rider (My X) (48)*, 2015, Graphite on paper, 13.3 x 9.2 cm, Gladstone Gallery, New York and Brussels.

**Masha Tupitsyn**

# Editing as the Practice
# of Criticism

There are many adages about writing. Many of them are about editing. Some writers claim to first write and then edit, leaving revision for the end. Others, me included, say that writing is editing. Draft numbers suggest both effort and struggle. Too many drafts, however, indicate blocks and failures. Books that go nowhere and that are built on nothing, like Jack Torrance's famous manuscript in *The Shining*. The correlation between writing and editing denotes talent. If a writer is truly good, they shouldn't have to labor very hard at writing. The tight deadlines and quick turnarounds that journalists and reviewers are bound to are built on this premise. Being fast is synonymous with being good. Editing, a version of writer's block, slows writing down. The longer a writer works on an article or book, the more professionally hazardous they are. The more a book becomes a problem; a story about the disasters of creativity rather than a marker of creativity. In other words, too much editing signals trouble.

In movies, there are always two kinds of writers, the ones who write effortlessly (a book gets written in a week or in one sitting) and the ones who can't write at all. The ones who stare at blank pages and screens because they have "nothing" to say. But also because they refuse to edit their way to saying it. It is as if editing were simply a block to creativity—the kind that is both effortless and spontaneous. While writers Flannery O'Conner and Joan Didion tell us that writing reveals *what* we think, editing teaches us *how* to think about writing. What writers, and movies about writers, don't really concede, but what artists, at least contemporary ones, who openly and comfortably employ different formal strategies in their work always admit to, is that to rewrite, rearrange, and reconstruct is not to fail at writing, it is to gain some kind of consciousness through it. Some version of this idea is articulated by O'Conner's "I write because I don't know what I think until I read what I say," although the famous adage conceals how this happens. For O'Conner, writers are the point rather than the method.

When we say we are blocked in writing, what do we think we are blocked from? When writing is going well, a movie compresses the time of writing into a montage, ironically editing out the process through editing. The time of writing simply "flows." In the true crime genre, as in scholarship, investigation is central, and writer's block is often the result of an assignment that is a de facto truth procedure: You can't write what you don't know. What you don't understand yet. What you have failed to see. It took 20 years for *San Francisco Chronicle* cartoonist Robert Graysmith to write his book on the unsolved serial murders committed by the "Zodiac Killer." Reporter Camille Preaker's existential plight is what eventually enables her to write her best article on the murders of two Missouri girls in HBO's *Sharp Objects*. In the true crime genre, the uncompleted draft is unsolved detective work. Editing is not what one says, or how one says it, but how one comes to be *able* to say it.

"It's not a coincidence that in Antonioni's film *Blowup* (1966) and Brian De Palma's *Blow Out* (1981), it is the artists—a photographer and sound effects technician respectively—who turn into murder investigators," multi-media artist Lawrence Abu Hamdan states in an interview with *Ocula Magazine*. "That's because they are trained to see at the very threshold of images or sound, listening so intently to the world that things emerge…

I'm interested in this procedure as a continuation of an artist's project—an investigative strategy that I see, at its core, as an aesthetic practice." Coincidentally, I have written about both *Blow Up* and *Blow Out* myself, exploring the very same questions in essays like "Behind The Scenes." "Being trained to see at the very threshold of images or sound," as Hamdan puts it, tells us something about what a block might really offer. The way blockage might actually be a gateway for something else; a continuation that pushes us through—and past—what is expected of us in a given medium. It is also one way to think about what we call the politics of representation. In my case, to write was to go beyond writing. In my durational films, *Love Sounds* (2015) and *DECADES* (ongoing), the work is to investigatively listen to the alternate and unseen history that cinematic sound has produced.

At a 2018 talk at The New School in New York City, the writer and artist Moyra Davey was asked two central questions about her work: Why focus so much on process and why combine writing and photography? Like the detective and editor, Davey is being asked to explain her emphasis on (and preference for) construction and linkage rather than narrative. "I had a lot of problems with blockage until I diversified," she admits. "Once I combined writing, photography, and film, I never seemed to have that problem again. It became self-generative. The whole process of writing, taking photographs, and making films, would just suggest other ideas, other combinations." But how does one discover what writing needs? What other forms writing can take? How does a writer move beyond writing?

Like in the detective genre, sometimes the mystery of writing needs cracking. For Davey, and for me, the vocation itself is somewhat prohibitive. A dead end. The fact that I go to artists rather than writers for answers to questions about writing, might tell you something. In today's transmedia world, writing needs to be rethought;

combined with and made using other mediums. In my case, blockage meant saying and seeing more than what a single medium like writing permits one to say and see, which is how and why I wrote my multi-media book, *Love Dog*, online in 2013. For Davey, the idea of writing itself is revised and rewritten—through photography, through film. For me, writing consists of different disciplines. Davey could have simply lamented that she wasn't a good enough writer to write without also doing other things. She could have yielded to the strict conventions of writing. I could have too. Instead, she acknowledged that what she wanted to do in writing, she couldn't do through writing alone. To be able to write at all requires additions that are not strictly textual, not strictly on the page. The rules are revised in order to do something different.

As I have written elsewhere[1], the work of editing is also the practice of criticism. One way to edit is to make disciplines act as other disciplines. What if, as I ask in *Love Sounds* and *DECADES*, we haven't been looking at the right things in the right ways? What if instead of looking, we had been listening? What if instead of making more to see, we listen to what we have already seen? What if instead of watching movies with our eyes we watch them with our ears? In the same way that Davey uses photography and film to write her essays, to "continue" her ideas, the French filmmaker Robert Bresson described film as an act of writing, not a play or filmed theater. He referred to actors as models, to viewers as interpreters; called for thought over spectatorship. Celluloid turns into a fabric that must be "ironed" flat rather than animated. Rhythm, said Bresson, not image,

---

1    In my book *LACONIA: 1200 Tweets on Film* (Winchester: ZerO Books, 2011), borrowing from film scholar Robin Wood, I introduced the idea of criticism as a form of living. In my film work, *Love Sounds* and *DECADES*, I have extended this idea to editing, writing about it in publications like the catalogue for *Love Sounds* (Los Angeles: Penny-Ante Editions, 2015), *This Long Century*, *Lenny*, and *Fanzine*.

is the guiding principle. "Something that would have been forgotten right away becomes unforgettable when it's encountered inside of a rhythm." Rhythm is arrangement. Rhythm is editing. Cinematography, as Bresson called cinema, is the art of relation. The means through which rhythm is created or discovered. The art of relation is knowing where things go; what image goes with what image. In *Notes on the Cinematographer*, Bresson refers to the work of editing, which is the study of relation, as "to know thoroughly what business that sound (or that image) has there." To know, not to see. For me, art always begins with this question: what do we have to do in order to know something thoroughly? To know where something goes? Editing is a practice of thoroughness. It allows us to ask, what am I looking for?, through the search itself.

**Fig. 1:** *Happy Together*, Director: Wong Kar-Wai, color, 96 min., 1997.

**Fig. 2:** *Children of a Lesser God*, Director: Randa Haines, color, 119 min., 1986.

**Fig. 3:** *The Devil Probably*, Director: Robert Bresson, color, 95 min., 1977; still taken from *DECADES*: 1970s, Masha Tupitsyn, film/video, 2017.

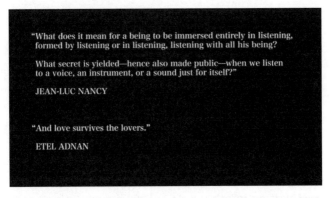

"What does it mean for a being to be immersed entirely in listening, formed by listening or in listening, listening with all his being?

What secret is yielded—hence also made public—when we listen to a voice, an instrument, or a sound just for itself?"

JEAN-LUC NANCY

"And love survives the lovers."

ETEL ADNAN

**Fig. 4:** Title quotes for the opening of *Love Sounds*, Masha Tupitsyn, 2015.

For Bresson, like Hamdan, different elements—music, images, sound, words—need to transform one another. To be something else. To not be itself. To switch places. To look beyond disciplines. That is their business. For Hamdan, Davey, and me, Bresson's idea of combination and addition within cinematography—as he defines it— extends beyond the confines of a single discipline. In my case, to make films using other films is to be something other than a filmmaker. Something other than a writer. What am I looking for?

When it comes to literary writing, too much thinking is often frowned upon. Critical thinking is not seen as the point of "great" literature—pure invention is. The common definition of invention in contemporary literary fiction is, again, different from definitions of invention in contemporary art, where appropriation, mixed media, and the use of found material are all elements of creativity rather than failure. As the art of serious criticism dwindles and memoir replaces it, where do you go to think in writing? In my case, I did not want to be a scholar—of literature or cinema—though I had studied to be one, and there is an aspect of scholarship, and therefore intertextuality, in all of my work. Mostly, I didn't think the invention of a brand new story was ever the point—thinking imaginatively and sustainably was. What philosophy had taught me to accept and embrace was the aesthetic value of relating to other texts and objects, and the often slow pace of that relating. Perhaps part of why I left writing for a time, and why I have been able (to my great surprise) to return to it, is because I turned to and explored other mediums. Like Davey, I needed to diversify in order to continue writing. To see past the threshold of writing in order to see and hear better. To do that, I was willing to give up being a writer. In order to think with and through other forms, I pursued writing in other ways, using cinema (using being the operative word) to make philosophical films about what it means to watch and think about film—studying time, studying voice, studying sound, studying love. Listening.

**Fig. 5:** *Deliverance*, Director: John Boorman, color, 110 min., 1972; still from *DECADES*: 1970s, Masha Tupitsyn, film/video, 2017.

In the prologue to his book on the *Trauerspiel* (*The Origin of German Tragic Drama*), Walter Benjamin makes a case for editing as a practice of criticism, claiming that "[…] philosophy is—and rightly so—a struggle for the presentation [*Darstellung*] of a limited number of words which always remain the same—a struggle for the presentation of ideas." (37, translation altered). Benjamin's "limited number of words which always remain the same," echoed by Bresson's "...there's a kind of cinema that's akin to a giant barracks, and inside it everyone does the same thing. It's a place of clichés," is evoked as a set of found material that asks to be creatively reworked, rethought, rearranged. Equally, to invent anew is less important than imaginatively deciphering what has already been written and made; what is made over and over, remaining the same while posing as new; cluttering the world. In the case of *Love Sounds* and *DECADES*, my aesthetic and critical evaluation of already existing material is another practice of criticism and editing. A new way of being a critic. In my 2011 book, *LACONIA: 1,200 Tweets on Film*, editing is employed as a critical practice in the form of aphoristic writing. To write an aphorism on Twitter, rather than a Tweet, is to choose—and time—your words carefully. Rather than viewing the process of censorship and constraint as wholly restrictive—as though both aren't part of the creative process, or doing is always better that not doing (Susan Sontag in *As Consciousness Is Harnessed to Flesh: Journals and Notebooks, 1964–1980*: "When there is no censorship the writer has no importance. So it's not so simple to be against censorship.")—we must be willing to practice creative vigilance and self-restraint. By viewing the creative process as holistic and precise, not individualistic and habitual as Benjamin notes, creative and intellectual work becomes more necessary rather than less necessary. Rather than the "write no matter what" or "write every day" rule, I adhere to the precept of writing when it feels essential to write. Figuring out why you are doing something seems far more important in the internet age than simply doing it.

In my immaterial writing trilogy, which consists of *LACONIA: 1,200 Tweets on Film* (Twitter), *Love Dog* (Tumblr), and *Love Sounds* (a 24-hour audio-essay and audio-history on love consisting of 80 years of English-speaking movies), constraint is applied as a form of freedom. Formal and conceptual restrictions and limitations are imposed from the start. In all three works, I go against the grain of these highly permissive digital mediums precisely because the temptation and possibility to do whatever I like, whenever I like, is so tempting in the digital age. To keep internet writing innovative and vital, creative and conceptual rubrics can and should be practiced in different ways. Below are some of the methods I employed in *LACONIA*, which turns the minimum (the laconic, the aphorism, the fragment) into a maximum, and *Love Dog*, a multi-media, digital manifesto on love:

1. Each blog post was displayed as a single screen page instead of the usual long stream of posts (texts and images) you scroll through on a blog. I chose this layout to create a book-like economy and laconic (quiet) distribution of ideas/images in a medium that is oversaturated and overrun (even optically) with content.

2. I actively avoided the use of the personal blog as an index and repurposing of already existing visual media. I did not re-blog posts (moving them from one blog to another) without somehow reframing or critically engaging with the content I was citing.

3. Resisting the compulsive posting which is so endemic of the internet, I limited myself to one post per day (sometimes long, sometimes short). I kept a long queue of slated drafts in progress, which I edited and curated carefully on a daily basis, often planning entries in advance. This did not make my work less honest or rewarding, or even less spontaneous. Spontaneity is not simply mean instantaneity (posting something immediately or writing something quickly). The freedom that digital forms offer me is conceptual, discursive, and re-appropriative. Form

and content are interactive as well as collaged. In *LACONIA* (I write about this at length in the book's foreword), I only tweeted original content about a film or idea, and while the book was in progress, I never re-tweeted anyone or included any public correspondence in my RSS feed.

4. Both *LACONIA* and *Love Dog* were conceived and written as books that begin and end; required discipline, crafting, and forethought; move between and across different forms and mediums.

5. Both books stress the difference between time as data flow (a Twitter feed) and time as data storage (a book). All three works, particularly *Love Sounds*, a durational work organized into eight chapters/sections, employed editing as a practice of meticulous arrangement and curation over time.

In an interview about his 1983 film *L'Argent*, Bresson stated, "Editing is also the reward of all our efforts." Nicolas Roeg, director of *Don't Look Now* (1973), who rarely made films from scratch, stated, "Finding reality is much more exciting than trying to invent it." For Roeg, like Benjamin, the images in *Don't Look Now* are "part of a puzzle." A puzzle Roeg makes and solves at the same time. For Bresson, editing is a way of thinking rather than making. Editing marks the act and place of discovery with a cut. In *Love Sounds* and *DECADES*, I use and study movies to conduct a search, to solve a puzzle, to discover what I do not know but seek to find. In most writing, the practice of editing gets divorced from the larger conceptual vision of a creative work. Magazine and book editors often impose edits on texts to fix (punish?) what is supposedly unclear, but also to (belatedly) regulate what does not conform. Outside edits typically enforce conventional logic and legibility.

As a practice, editing is a job and skill that belongs more to cinema than it does to writing. A mainstream film cannot exist without an editor. When it comes to movies, editing is the ultimate praxis because it gives raw material—however inspired and deliberate—form, purpose, and meaning. A way to think about an image, a character, a story. Until the editor steps in to cut, to make a thousand decisions and choices, raw footage can be anything and go in any direction. Can succeed or fail. Be ruined or elevated, potentially making editing the most imaginative, subjective, and decisive aspect of filmmaking.

In my work, there have been other combinations and failed approaches. I eventually turned to the politics of listening because I had trained as a classical musician in my childhood. Yet, I did not want to play an instrument or perform music on stage. Like Roeg, I do not necessarily want to invent a story from scratch, or even make a feature film. As a child, I could not figure out how to work with sound or music without being a performer, so I began to write. Not to be a writer, per se but to give myself a tool with which to study the world. Looking back, the constellation of film, voice, and sound had always been at the forefront of my thinking about language. Specifically, the things people say and the way people sound when they say them. Language has always been a readymade. This is to say, that in my work all forms—whether invented or found—are for this: to think. To edit *Love Sounds* and *DECADES* is also to approach cinema, language, and music as a synaesthetic practice. That is: to think about time, to conserve rather than consume, to contemplate rather than produce, to use old forms to make new forms, to search for what is not in the diegetic story, to listen to what is not being said, to find hidden rhythms, to develop new taxonomies, to recover lost worlds, to invent alternate histories.

**Maria Fusco**

# ECZEMA!

The text you are about to read is extracts from the script of my experimental play *ECZEMA!* which was commissioned by National Theatre Wales to celebrate the 70th anniversary of the UK's National Health Service in 2018. I chose to write about something I know intimately—the skin disease eczema—which I have lived in "co-occupation" with since I was born.

> *Skin wrinkles, adapts, reigns between organs and contains complex paths that link them; more than just a medium of the sense organs, our skin is a mixture of them, a palette.*
> —*The Five Senses*, Michel Serres

In writing *ECZEMA!* I wanted to embody my chronic and embarrassing condition: a condition that necessitates return and persistence and unreasonable frenzy and turns them into a normative process. Scratching, and picking scabs, is a form of critique, a desire to edit my skin, to improve it through reordering the visible surface: I peel off a scab to see more precisely what is under it. This desire for improved clarity of vision is nonsense of course, the scratching and the picking disimprove my skin's totality; they are rather gestural articulations of editorial violence, they are the material ways of "doing" a life-long apprenticeship to eczema, of being an amateur. I am making a direct link here between this, between my, embodied irrationality, and the seemingly "rational" critical process of traditional academic writing. It is certainly true that both ways of writing require attention, stamina and rigor, but to willfully detach from bodily and affective imperatives within academic activities is, in my opinion, at best unrealistic, and at worst dishonest.

> *How does the skin come to be written and narrated? How is the skin managed by subjects, others and nations? Skin, like, writing, can be "cut off" and made to signify anew. It can acquire new meanings, new forms, new shapes.*
> —*Thinking Through the Skin*, edited by Sara Ahmed and Jackie Stacey

In Dante's Eighth Circle in the *Inferno*, falsifiers are sentenced to eternal itching, their hands put to use upon themselves rather than in perfidious acts: the implication being that they must critically reflect inwardly rather than trying to impress outwardly. I am suggesting that scratching and writing are the repeated actions, the gestures, the habits that most succinctly demonstrate the leaky border between our inner and outer selves: they are bi-modal means. The presumed dichotomy, therefore, of inside and outside, makes a case for "pure," unbiased, critique by actively keeping such factors apart. I do not agree with this. The leaking boundaries of the skin, the re-ordering actions of scratching and editing glue expression, knowledge and critique together: I think I know when to stop scratching even if I do not really want to.

> *We were confronting, as it were, a new and infinitely delicate point in the texture of reality, from which something far greater than ourselves, yet indescribably immature, seemed to be appealing to us as if seeking help.*
> —*Primal Sound*, Rilke

The excessive and obsessional scratching dermographically demonstrates a tendency, my tendency, towards critique. This is an essential requirement of writing in an interdisciplinary way because I have no presupposition of form when I sit down to write: I must meet it anew each time, I must scrape it into existence. Whilst I am my primary and most savage critic, I am also aware that I am the one who persists in scratching, who persists in writing, against all caution, and in this sense perhaps the critique is stable because it is repeatable and I have inadvertently created a methodology.

I am skin that walks. Thrown out by heat, I wear this skin for a lifetime. I recognize the word ECZEMA like I recognize my own name. There's nothing deeper than my skin: it is so much craftier than me. We often disagree. My skin attacks the everyday. My skin is a riot! Where my skin twists and splits and thickens, ECZEMA wields its story.

The messages I scratch into my skin can't be translated: they are simply themselves. Bold brassy rips. I communicate without words, I scratch in order to find out. I would wrench my skin off, if I could. Rend the gore from my bones, scratch my heart out, root behind my eyeballs, stick a knitting needle in my ear, ratchet deep about my folds and rasp the tender places. I would never share a scratch. My hands are strong. Nothing is as fantastic as scratching: all other sensations steam pallid. Monogamy. A soul-chomping commitment to scratching, ravishing across body, across time, across reason.

She asked me what I would do if my ECZEMA disappeared tomorrow. I had no answer. I told her I would think about her question. I am still thinking.

I answer the hum of a healing scab, a scab the size of a two-pound coin near my right ankle. It's relatively safe to scratch this scab, I think. The song of flaking skin on my left, inner eyelid is scaling through my eyebrow, up along my forehead and into my hairline, now screaming hot. The inside of my left elbow (sleeved in 100% cotton to stop skin touching skin) has its own persistent pitch, cranking when I use my arm in any way. Inside my right ear, there's an aluminum ache: I've learnt this is also ECZEMA, how the ECZEMA inside my ear rhymes. It's tricky to scratch, hazardous if I poke something in there to help. The ache sings outwards through my cheekbone. Numbing and tantalizing. An itch stretches the length of my tired neck. I winch my neck backwards pulling the skin taut, I scratch with both hands in long vertical strokes. I can't wear collars, not even to hide the damaged skin. The deep scratching I enjoy on the front of my neck doesn't work on the back, here I need stubby stabs, wheeling out to thumb-length loops. Naturally, I inch upwards to the scales behind my ear. Greasy and resilient. What's under these scales never heals. The fingers on my right hand are thrumming. Healthy skin has sloughed to train infected blisters. Best scratched against synthetic carpet, brickwork, a toothbrush, a nutmeg grater, but not with another finger, that way relief does not work (however temporary). I thrash my hand into my back jeans pocket and rub furiously. Reprise of my left eyebrow, I'm listening carefully. It's so easy to scratch an eyebrow and watch all the hairs come away between your fingers: that's a bad song.

At the end of desire comes persuasion. I must eventually stop scratching. Somehow, I've peeled that scab off my leg and am now lightly chewing it.

## MONDAY

I'm standing almost naked in an upright metal cham-ber. I'm wearing what looks, and feels, like a welder's mask. When the mask was being fitted, inside, where the padded supports poorly hug my whippet skull, I spied that they were littered with someone else's dry skin: the previous patient's. I am not alone. The light tubes are switched on from outside, chuckling into life. This whir-ring, healing chamber: I hope. I experience the shining light through my skin, the light is bleached well-being. I am flammable. I can't feel the light on my face because of the welder's mask. I worry the tantrum'd skin won't heal there. I love the light. I can smell my skin burning.

TUESDAY

I'm collecting my prescription from the chemist's. I'm ashamed each week when I do this because I always have the most, and the heaviest, bags. Plastic sacks full of antibiotics, immunosuppressants, steroids, and tanks of slippery disinfecting agents. Milligrams. Kilograms. Milliliters. Liters.

0.05%

1%

2.5%

Mountains. Peaks. Oceans. Troughs.

I struggle home. Soon I won't be able to carry this weight, I'm getting too old. At home, I unpack and stack the load out of sight. ECZEMA is all about making space.

## WEDNESDAY

I'm wearing a red clicky counter tied round my neck on a length of string. It's hanging over the top of my school uniform. Each time I touch my skin, I've been told to click the counter. The actual feeling of string round my neck is making me itchy anyway, so I'm sure just wearing it will increase the number of clicks. I know this counter is meant to make me realize how much I touch myself, make me realize this by trying not to touch myself, by trying to keep my hands to myself, but I touch myself much more than I would normally. I am anxious to be average. With each touch I fail: measured out in clicks.

THURSDAY

I'm being examined in a university teaching hospital. Around me, tight as a knot, six medical students are conferring. All of these students are male; all of them are younger than me. My nipples are shredded with the scratching. I've had to take my bra off for these boys to see. "May I?" the one closest asks, and lays his hand, palm down, flat against my burning sternum where my mad skin is cheating itself. I flinch, but then I feel a cold, dry comfort communicating from his hand. Why have I agreed to this? Well, I've agreed to let these boys scrutinize me, to handle me, to help those, myself included, who have to keep coming here for treatment, year after year after year after year.

A scab is a drawbridge, constructed from biological materials hardening for protection. A scab is so frustrating because it hides what is going on below. This is unwelcome to ECZEMA, the most visual of diseases. The last peel of a scab is the saddest. A crisp brown poppy. With anticipation (and a slightly shaking hand) I loosen the scab, persuading the edges away from their knitted hole, tentative, like trying to calm a growling dog. The healthy skin below is so heartbreakingly innocent that I can't resist giving it a brisk scratch even though it isn't really that itchy.

I dropped my newborn baby once, so occupied was I in scratching.

FRIDAY

I'm having blood taken. I know this will take a long time because the skin on my inner elbows is ridged: thick as jumbo corduroy. The nice young nurse attempts her usual routine to no avail. Her skin is perfect. How deeply embarrassing that I, whose skin is shuddering in crimson blooms, splitting in port ravines, suppurating primrose, should be witnessed by this complete parchment; this smooth proposition.

My veins are not assertive enough to perform through my scarred skin. She pulls the tourniquet tighter: the tips of my fingers tingle purple. I'm used to this. With each attempt she grows braver, more aggressive, poking the needle forcefully towards something that she can't actually see. A posy of pricks brims neatly with blood. She locates a vein and rushes the needle in. After she has drawn the blood, the plaster she tries to apply won't stick, of course, because of the emollient I applied this morning.

A scar is a scab that's stopped: it cannot be undone. Slubbed monuments. I have hundreds, thousands, thousands of monuments cross-hatching my entire body. Private monuments to my private scratching. I am legion with such monuments. Not all scars are raised though: many are flush, washed-out, where the scar has drained melanin. A scar stops time, marking exactly when a skin event has finally come to an end. Time expressed through stubborn cells. A scar cannot go back. Decades of ECZEMA have both thickened and thinned my skin. Thickened: an elephant's, a donkey's skin. Thinned: steroids encourage quicker healing but parse the skin's surface to tiny bloody mouths.

Scars chart of my lifetime of scratching. My skin remembers that which I cannot.

## SATURDAY

My house is on fire! I do not sweat. No sweat. No sweating. I don't need a deodorant. My house is on fire! I am tinder dry. Voracious bonfire. Licking. Sparking. My hectic glow. My house is on fire! All doors locked. All windows sealed. My house is on fire! The hottest day you can imagine. Stifling. Can't catch breath. My house is on fire! Turbulent heat. My house is on fire! Needs to be stoked. Rollicking combustion. My house is on fire! Nothing can get out. The heat flows inward. My house is on fire! Flames lick under my skin. I cannot extinguish them. I am being burnt alive. I am Joan of Arc. My house is on fire!

## SUNDAY

The skin on my shoulders has been burnt by the light treatment and is oozing in protest against the assault. I am lying in bed now trying to sleep. My wet shoulders stick to the thin tee shirt I'm wearing: I peel it off and lie on my front where the skin is volcanic, but not yet broken. My skin smells like a sick toffee apple. Yes, I am trying to sleep. I have been told ECZEMA is something that is working its way out ... working its way out ... I believe ECZEMA is working its way in ... working its way in.

Was there a time before ECZEMA? I'd like to believe. I don't believe. I know there was no time before ECZEMA. I drift off. I don't dream anymore, not for years. I wake. I'm happy because I've been able to sleep for nearly an hour. I am scrunched into a sticky human ball, adhered to the sheet, crusted in crunchy ochre.

**Thomas Glaser**

# Roland Barthes' Critical Writing from the Materials of Cy Twombly—and the Criticism of Form in the Early Texts of Lukács and Benjamin

At the latest since early German Romanticism, the concept of "form" has been an irritation for aesthetics, insofar as it repudiates its aesthetic conception of being the (external) appearance of a content that manifests itself within it. After a century in which a concept of form, clamped in the dualism of meaning and (its) shape, was still virulent and decisive for art-critical discourse, two texts, located within the context of neo-Kantian thought in Germany, and published towards the end of the First World War, revived this complex dealing with form as it is inherent in German Romanticism. Georg Lukács' "Die Subjekt-Objekt-Beziehung in der Aesthetik" (The Subject-Object Relationship in Aesthetics), published in the seventh issue of *Logos* magazine (1917/18, under the name "Georg von Lukács"), and Walter Benjamin's dissertation "Der Begriff der Kunstkritik in der deutschen Romantik" (The Concept of Art Criticism in German Romanticism),[1] defended in 1919, are completely differ-

---

1   Benjamin's doctoral thesis was published in 1920. See Walter Benjamin, "The Concept of Art Criticism in German Romanticism," in Walter Benjamin, *Selected Writings, Volume 1, 1913–1936*, ed. Marcus Bullock and Michael W. Jennings (Cambridge MA: Belknap Press of Harvard University Press, 1996), pp. 116–200, here p. 123.

ent projects in terms of preconditions, methodology, and objective, but they are both in agreement with regard to the avoidance of an aesthetic concept of "form" which reduces it to the manifestation of a production process, an (ingenious) subject, or an idea—with far-reaching consequences for art criticism. An analogous irritation reappeared around the mid-twentieth century, when criticism no longer strove to reconstruct something underlying forms for the sake of comprehensibility, but rather aimed to reconstruct the formation of form in itself. This is evident in Roland Barthes' critical writings on visual art since the late 1960s. It is his texts on Cy Twombly's pictures, however, that link the emerging criticism of form to the conditions of its material representation and thus, already around 1979, represent something akin to a *material turn* of art criticism. This shall be investigated further in the following.

In contrast to the connection established since the nineteenth century of Romanticism with historicism and irrationality,[2] Benjamin's investigation accentuates Friedrich Schlegel's "objective grounding of the concept of art criticism," which is solely concerned with "the objective structure of art as idea, and with its formations, its works."[3] By rejecting the platitude of empty subjectivity in the writings of Schlegel, which can be traced back to Hegel, Benjamin positions himself not only against the contemporary criticism of Romantism, but also against the prevailing art criticism: Whereas Schlegel's reflection-theoretical concept of criticism overcame both "aesthetic dogmatism"—judgement according to rules—and "the skeptical tolerance that is

---

2  For more on the "German dominants," historicism on the one side, which was still being asserted through the end of the twentieth century, and irrationalism on the other, as well as the latter's identification with "Romanticism," see Karl Heinz Bohrer, *Die Kritik der Romantik* (Frankfurt am Main: Suhrkamp, 1989), p. 25. Here, Bohrer draws attention to the curious juxtaposition of these mutually exclusive labels.

3  Benjamin, "The Concept of Art Criticism," p. 118.

traceable, in the end, to the boundless cult of creative power understood as the mere expressive force of the creator," the criticism of the nineteenth and twentieth centuries had once again "fallen away" from this standpoint.[4] "Criticism, which for the contemporary understanding is the most subjective of things, for the Romantics was the regulator of all subjectivity, contingency, and arbitrariness in the genesis of the work."[5]

Even Lukács' early critical texts, published before the First World War, could have exempted Benjamin from his criticism of the "degeneration" of the criticism of his day. According to these texts, the critic may indeed experience the forms of works of art, but this experience is based on objective knowledge of general forms, which are radically separated from their material content. In the essay collection *Die Seele und die Formen* (Soul and Form), which then twenty-six-year-old Lukács published in 1911 with Egon Fleischel in Berlin, the introductory essay "Über Form und Wesen des Essays" (On the Nature and Form of the Essay),[6] conceived as a letter to his late friend Leo Popper, explicitly addresses the problem of aesthetic criticism and form. Form and content should provide differential criteria for various forms of discourse: "Science affects us by its contents, art by its forms; science offers us facts and the relationship between facts, but art offers us souls and destinies."[7] Destiny [*Schicksal*], as a principle ordering of the things of the world, "condenses" that which is unique and coincidental in art and develops its forms. From that the "substance" of these forms comes into being by this very act of condensation or formation; it is not prior to it.

4  Ibid., p. 154.
5  Ibid., p. 160.
6  György Lukács, "On the Nature and Form of the Essay," in György Lukács, *Soul and Form*, ed. John T. Sanders and Katie Terezakis, with an introduction by Judith Butler (New York: Columbia University Press, 2010), pp. 16–34. Lukács concludes the letter with "Florence, October 1910." Leo Popper died in 1911.
7  Ibid., p. 18.

The forms themselves are already "something finished," come "from outside," "set limits around" that which would otherwise "dissolve like air in the All." Forms are not instruments "of a will or desire or personal expressivity that precedes them."[8] In contrast, critical writings are deprived of destiny with its formative power; they lack "any natural inclination or possibility of condensing themselves into form."[9] They always speak only "of something that has already been given form,"[10] namely the forms of poetry.[11] This can, however, be experienced by the critic: "Form is his great experience, form—as immediate reality—is the image-element, the really living content of his writings."[12] And this experience of form does not result in criticism as subjective evaluation, but as a practice of existential significance: "Form is reality in the writings of critics; it is the voice with which they address their questions to life."[13]

Conceptually and methodically indebted to the southwest German neo-Kantianism of his teachers Heinrich Rickert and Emil Lask, the work Lukács published seven years later[14] aims to demonstrate that, in contrast to the theoretical and ethical "sphere of value," a subject-object relationship can be assumed solely for the aesthetic in which both poles are equally valid. Lukács assumes a subject vis-à-vis an object, the work of art, within

**8** Judith Butler, "Introduction," in Lukács, *Soul and Form*, pp. 1–15, here p. 4.
**9** Lukács, "On the Nature and Form of the Essay," p. 23.
**10** Ibid., p. 26.
**11** Konstantinos Kavoulakos, "Kritik der modernen Kultur und tragische Weltanschauung. Zu Georg Lukács 'Die Seele und die Formen'," *Zeitschrift für Kulturkritik* 8 (2014): pp. 121–135, here p. 128: "The essay sees the fateful […] in the finished forms of art […]." [translated by G. A. Goodrow].
**12** Lukács, "On the Nature and Form of the Essay," p. 23.
**13** Ibid., p. 24.
**14** Apart from this text that represents the first chapter of the second part of Lukács' postdoctoral project on aesthetics, the latter remained unpublished during the author's lifetime. See Konstantinos Kavoulakos, *Ästhetizistische Kulturkritik und ethische Utopie. Georg Lukács' neukantianisches Frühwerk* (Berlin: de Gruyter, 2014), pp. 36–42.

which it strives to fulfill its "subjectivity." For the subject's focus on its immanence, its total "reduction," requires it to become a "vehicle of totality, [...] an all-encompassing seclusiveness," a "microcosm,"[15] which is achieved in relation to an object that is absolutely complete and at the same time represents a whole that is not limited by anything external, but is rather inherently delimited. Here, form is not to be understood in the narrower aesthetic sense as a shape, but rather as an intentional reduction of the subject. This is, however, by no means present in its totality in the form of the work. The intentional reduction to the work is an "infinite and in principle unfinishable process which—from the point of view of the creative subject—must end with a resignation, with a simple 'abandonment' of the work."[16] Thus, in the finished work, the only result can be an "objectivity that is completely detached from the subject"; the infinite task of completing subjectivity can only be accomplished as a "leap, as the setting of an object absolutely independent of this."[17] The paradoxical universal validity of the aesthetic experience, or—in keeping with Immanuel Kant—the communicability of feeling, is guaranteed by the aesthetic form, free from any external determination, as well as from the enclosed content, which is "that of the experience itself." In so far as this form is general and communicable, it refers "to the general foundations of experience-ability; it 'encloses' its content of experience in such a way that it becomes experienceable—as the content of experience."[18]Aesthetic form thus by no means enables the repetition of an experience, its circulation between producer and recipient, but rather denotes an unfinishable intentional orientation that is generally valid in

15 Georg Lukács, "Die Subjekt-Objekt-Beziehung in der Ästhetik," Logos 7 (1917/18): pp. 1–39, here p. 10 [translated by G. A. Goodrow].
16 Ibid., p. 23.
17 Ibid., p. 25.
18 Ibid., p. 31.

the general conditions of experienceability. For criticism, this means, on the one hand, the impossibility of attributing the subjectivity of the producer to the form of a work of art; Lukács makes this very clear by categorically separating the attitudes of the producer and the recipient, analyzing form from the perspective of the producer, as *forma formans*, differently than from the perspective of the recipient, as *forma formata*. On the other hand, criticism is unable to "grasp" how a complex of forms is capable of uniting specific contents of experience into a "closed, self-sufficient whole."[19] Precisely because the criticism of aesthetic forms has to reckon with an absolutely irreducible subject-object relationship, it cannot be nourished by critical acts that would in any way relate one pole to the other. Criticism can understand aesthetic form with regard neither to its absolute subjectivity nor to its constitution as a whole.

With the Romantic conception of the work of art, Benjamin's dissertation aims to demonstrate the possibility of a positive criticism that refers to the "laws of the spirit," which Schlegel located in the work of art itself, instead of making this "a mere by-product of subjectivity, as so many modern authors, following the train of their own thinking, have misunderstood" Schlegel's approach.[20] Although it was keen to join the Romantic repudiation of rule-led criticism, contemporary criticism failed to recognize its positive preconditions, which first and foremost secure the basic concept of the "work" free of external determinations: "For not only did Schlegel's concept of criticism achieve freedom from heteronomous aesthetic doctrines, but it made this freedom possible in the first place by setting up for artworks a criterion other than the rule—namely the criterion of an immanent structure specific to the work itself." This

19  Ibid., pp. 31–32
20  Benjamin, "The Concept of Art Criticism," pp. 154–155.

criterion has nothing to do with central concepts of the aesthetics of the eighteenth century, with harmony or organization, but is related to Schlegel's theory of art "as a medium of reflection and of the work as a center of reflection."[21] This is why Benjamin can introduce his chapter on "The Work of Art" with the programmatic statement: "The romantic theory of the work of art is the theory of its form." For "form is the objective expression of the reflection proper to the work, the reflection that constitutes its essence."[22] With the concept of reflection, Johann Gottlieb Fichte's Doctrine of Scientific Knowledge is called upon, from which, however, according to Benjamin's interpretation, the early Romantics distanced themselves decisively. Form is the intellectual act of thinking, which, insofar as it is directed at itself, is form of form, i.e. reflexive. Whereas, for Fichte, reflection is ontologically determined as a correlate to the setting and refers to the I, for the early Romantics it refers to thinking itself, so that—in contrast to Fichte—it is, in principle, infinite. This is not an empty infinity of progress, but rather a "full infinitude of interconnection."[23] In this, as in a medium of reflection, the objects of thought, natural as well as artistic, are formed, in that the reflection limits itself. As a threshold value of reflection, they are objects only in relation to the endlessness of reflection, so that each object is always only a fragment and cannot be recognized in any other way than in its final completion in relation to the thinking absolute. Accordingly, knowledge of objects should be consummated within the medium of thought, within the "context of thinking relationships"; it should not be the recognition of an object by a subject, but rather, in principle, self-recognition: "All knowledge is self-knowledge of a thinking being that does not necessarily

21   Ibid., p. 155.
22   Ibid., p. 156.
23   Ibid., p. 126.

need to be an I."[24] According to Benjamin, this should be ensured by the Romantic experiment, which is not set up by an experimenter, carried out on an object and observed, but in which an observer, as a center of reflection, evokes the "nascent consciousness of the object"[25] in himself. For the recognition of objects, the subject-object correlation is thus suspended. Criticism is nothing other than observing objects of art within the infinite medium of reflection—art. Like the observation of an object, criticism should be an experiment on the artwork, "one through which the latter's own reflection is awakened, through which it is brought to consciousness and to knowledge of itself."[26] It is thus only in an irreducible way that the "work" can become the object of criticism. For, in its form, it can be reduced neither to a subject of its creation nor to objects of its destiny: "Every form as such counts as a peculiar modification of the self-limitation of reflection; it needs no other justification, because it is not a means to the representation of a content."[27] Just as recognition must relate its objects to endless reflection, as the threshold value of which they take form, and always has to complete this only partially, the same holds true for criticism. This is positive in that it allows its objects to become within themselves, completes them—but also dissolves them by referring them to their infinite connections and ultimately to the endless medium of reflection of art. Criticism is therefore "formative, not in the pedagogical sense of the term [...] but in the specific sense of the formation of putting-into-form."[28] The criterion for the judgement can thus only be the success or failure

---

**24** Ibid., p. 145.
**25** Ibid., p. 148.
**26** Ibid., p. 151.
**27** Ibid., p. 158.
**28** Philippe Lacoue-Labarthe and Jean-Luc Nancy, *The Literary Absolute: The Theory of Literature in German Romanticism*, trans. Philip Barnard and Cheryl Lester (Albany: State University of New York Press, 1988), p. 114; the authors refer here to Benjamin.

of resolution or formation, and the instance of judgement can only be the art itself, not an evaluative critic. And it is precisely this, according to Benjamin, that distinguishes the conception of early Romantic criticism from that of his own time.[29]

The concepts of a form that should not be reducible to the representation of content, the manifestation of a production process, and of a criticism that understands itself not as a protocol of such reduction, but as both production and resolution of the form—which, precisely not in the pedagogical sense, is formation—also run through critical texts after the mid-twentieth century. New perspectives—also on Benjamin's concept of criticism—are opened up precisely where art criticism does not refer primarily to literature, as in early Romanticism, but also to the visual arts—as in the critical writing of Roland Barthes. Barthes' literary-critical beginnings shortly after the Second World War[30] operate with the concept of a form which, since the end of the eighteenth century, has become "concrete" and thus visible as that moment of literary writing that pushes itself between things and their linguistic expression in order to "elicit those existential feelings lying at the heart of any object [...]."[31] The writers reacted to this in their "mode of writing." But in their modes of writing as a specific application of form, the writers are stuck in a dilemma: As "the choice of a human attitude," as "the affirmation of a certain Good," writing means "the relationship between creation and society"[32]; it has the claim of uni-

29 Also "[...] criticism in its central intention is not judgement but, on the one hand, the completion, consumption, and systematization of the work and, on the other hand, its resolution in the Absolute." Benjamin, "The Concept of Art Criticism," p. 159.
30 Barthes' *Le degrée zéro de l'écriture (Writing Degree Zero)* was published by Éditions du Seuil in 1953 (with parts appearing in print as early as 1947 and 1950).
31 Roland Barthes, *Writing Degree Zero*, trans. Annette Lavers and Colin Smith (New York: Farrar Straus & Giroux, 1990), p. 4. In the original, Barthes refers to "ce phénomène dramatique de concretion."
32 Ibid., p. 14.

versal validity to be "literature"; at the same time, however, it shows itself in its partiality, conditioned by the
social determination of the writer, tragically excluding
him or her "from this social finality"[33] and making him
or her a writer "without Literature." This is precisely
the "Orphean problematics of modern Form,"[34] with
which Barthes implicitly refers here to Jean Wahl.[35] In
this early text, Barthes shifts form—which should not
be substance but rather function, and which, as merely
fragmentary, remains related to a "literature" that is
nevertheless impossible—into the realm of socially-
determined ideologies. His critical writing can thus
tell the story of the literary modes of writing that, at
the same time, unite "the alienation of History and the
dream of History"[36] and that do not escape the problem
of form. The fact, however, that the problem of form
infests Barthes' critical writing itself, becomes a primary theme in the later ideology-critical works, such as
*Mythologies*, especially those that focus on semiology.
But only its textual delimitation, from roughly 1968
onwards, makes criticism—in "abandoning the structural model and resorting to the practice of the infinitely different Text"[37]—a "reading," and the activity
of reading a further writing. This culminates in Barthes'
"readings" of Cy Twombly's pictures, in the manner of
a de-differentiation of form and matter, and thus refers
back to an analogous aspect in Benjamin's reading of
the early Romantics, as will be shown.

---

**33**  Ibid., p. 23.
**34**  Ibid., p. 61.
**35**  Compare Jean Wahl, *Existence humaine et transcendence* (Neuchâtel:
La Pacennière, 1944), for example, p. 95: "[Le poète] se détruit lui-
même, en même temps qu'il s'affirme lui-même par l'expression. Il
est Orphée ressuscitant Eurydice, mais sous le masque de la Ménade
qui le tue […]."
**36**  Barthes, *Writing Degree Zero*, p. 87.
**37**  Roland Barthes, "Introduction: The Semiological Adventure" [1974],
in Roland Barthes, *The Semiotic Challenge*, trans. Richard Howard
(Berkeley and Los Angeles: University of California Press, 1994),
pp. 3–9, here p. 7.

Barthes' critical writing on visual art[38] is based on a structuralist problem: the structural incompatibility of language and painting. In his text "Is Painting a Language?" (1969),[39] he reports on Jean Louis Schefer's *Scénographie d'un tableau* and refers to his position that runs counter to the "professional criticism of painting." In contrast to this, Schefer emphasizes the textuality of the image and thus the manifold, but by no means contingent, readings that first and foremost constitute the image as activities of further writing: "The picture, whoever writes it, exists only in the *account* given of it (*le récit que j'en donne*); or again: in the total and the organization of the various readings that can be made of it: a picture is never anything but its own plural description."[40]

These activities of reading and writing are not contingent, because they find their organization in the image itself, even when this does not represent a fixed structure, but rather a dynamic system. There can thus be no neutral description from outside, no denotation; at the same time, however, the image is not only a place for subjective occupations: It is "neither a real object nor an imaginary object." Rather, it constantly postpones its identification, postpones its signification, "for it is only a series of nominations, as in a dictionary,"[41] whereby the flight of its significations is nothing other than the dynamic system of the image that organizes its readings. Schefer's analysis of Paris Bordone's *Chess Game* is thus not about revealing a structure of this image, but only the activity by which it is structured, its *structuring*. The

---

38  This began in the late 1960s after the lecture tour on the "Empire of Signs," with texts on Masson, Réquichot, Erté, Arcimboldo, Cy Twombly, Pop Art, Steinberg etc.

39  Roland Barthes, "Is Painting a Language?" [1969], in Roland Barthes, *The Responsibility of Forms: Critical Essays on Music, Art, and Representation*, trans. Richard Howard (Berkeley and Los Angeles: University of California Press, 1991), pp. 149–152.

40  Ibid., p. 150.

41  Ibid., p. 150.

reading of the textual structures that define the image can therefore be nothing other than a (further) writing: "there is no longer a critic, nor even a writer talking painting, there is the *grammatographer*, someone writes the picture's writing."[42]

Ten years later, in two catalogue contributions,[43] Barthes, as a grammatographer, continues the writing in Cy Twombly's works—the writing which is intended to be its key *sujet*: "TW's work […] is a kind of writing" ("L'oeuvre de TW […], c'est de l'écriture").[44] The clumsiness of what is written there, its confusion and carelessness, refers to the gesture, the dismissive, the ancillary aspect of a writing that serves communication; and for this very reason, the "essence of the writing" should be legible in the gesture: "The essence of an object has some relation with its destruction: not necessarily what remains after it has been used up, but what is *thrown away* as being of no use. This is the case with TW's 'writings' […]."[45] It is the writing, the ductus, which Twombly shows in the gesture, Barthes emphasizes on that activity of structuring which, according to Barthes' readings of Schefer, is to be (further) written by the grammatographer: "We are not asked to see, to conceive, to savor the *product*, but to review, to identify, and, so to speak, to 'enjoy' the *movement* which has ended up *here*."[46] With the continuation of writing, "seeing" and "enjoying" are thus the first things to set in. The activity of the gesture, of the thoughtless, if not aimless stroke that pays no attention to any

42  Ibid., p. 151.
43  *Cy Twombly: catalogue raisonné des œuvres sur papier, 1973–1976*, ed. Yvon Lambert (Milan: Multhipla Edizioni, 1979); Cy Twombly: *Paintings and Drawing 1954–1977*, exhibition catalogue (New York: Whitney Museum of American Art, 1979).
44  See Roland Barthes, "Cy Twombly: Works on Paper" [1979], in Roland Barthes, *The Responsibility of Forms*, pp. 157–194, here p. 158. In this essay, Barthes consistently writes "TW" for Cy Twombly.
45  Ibid., p. 158.
46  Ibid., p. 164.

goal, should be visible in its result, the production in the product—as its "reality."

But the "critical function" of the "'clumsiness'" of the writing, which Barthes' writing addresses "here, where we don't speak about [Twombly] in the language of art criticism,"[47] is not achieved solely by the theoretically distanced and classically receptive act of "seeing," "identifying," and "enjoying." In the two texts on Cy Twombly, a shift can be read which simultaneously specifies and jiggers the activity of the grammatographer. According to the Schefer essay, if the grammatographer is to continue writing the structuring activity of an image after she or he has brought it to light, she or he is the sole protagonist; in the two Twombly texts, the artist enters as the *sujet* of the event, which, *as* the *sujet* of his pictures, spills over onto the body of the reader-writer. Here, Barthes already locates the difference between *product* and *production*, which should guide the work of the grammatographer as a methodical concept; in Twombly's work itself, as its foundation: the entire work of Twombly is based on "the distinction between product and producing."[48] And this distinction becomes productive there by baiting the reader-writer, luring him or her on. The visibility of the production in the product is not a bringing-to-light by the one who— theoretically—sees, or it is not only this: rather, Twombly's work itself acts, exerts a compulsion on its reader-writer to see the production in the product:

> This oeuvre conducts TW's *reader* (I am saying: reader, though there is nothing to decipher) to a certain philosophy of time: he must retrospectively see a movement, what was the hand's *becoming*; but then—a salutary revolution— the product (any product?) appears as a kind of bait [...].[49]

47 Roland Barthes, "The Wisdom of Art," in *Cy Twombly. Paintings and Drawing 1954–1977*, pp. 9–22, here p. 18.
48 Barthes, "Cy Twombly: Works on Paper," p. 172.
49 Ibid., p. 172.

The reversal comes from Twombly's work itself: Its product presents itself to the viewer as bait in order to see its reality, its production. The distinction between product and production is therefore the basis of Twombly's work, because, there, its production is "delicately imprisoned, enchanted within that aesthetic product which we call a canvas, a drawing [...]."[50] The product is laid out in Twombly's work for the reader-writer in order to solve (or liberate) the production enchanted within it, to see it.

The work itself should be the protagonist, the hero of the revolution in this event—but so are the viewers and the writers: They are not only baited as distanced seers, but solely because they themselves are subjects of production—in *imitation*:

> I very slowly look through a book of TW's reproductions, and I frequently stop in order to attempt, quite quickly, on slips of paper, to make certain scribbles; I am not directly imitating TW (what would be the use of that?), I am imitating his *gesture*, which I, if not unconsciously, at least dreamily, infer from my reading; I am not copying the product, but the producing, I am putting myself, so to speak, *in the hand's footsteps*.[51]

And in this imitation of the *tracing*, the work "retrospectively" forces one to see the production, the movement. But even the imitative action is one that emanates from Twombly's work. To be more precise, it emanates from the respective *sujet* of the pictures in its double meaning of "object" and "the human being who produces himself through it." If the subject of Twombly's pictures "is only a written allusion, the whole weight of the drama falls back again on the person who is producing it: the sub-

---

50   Ibid., pp. 171–172.
51   Ibid., p. 171, emphasis in the original.

ject is Twombly himself."[52] Yet, Barthes continues, the *sujet* of the pictures should also be their viewers, inso- far as the supposed simplicity of Twombly's art *entices* them to repeat the production, to imitate it:

> The "simplicity" of Twombly (what I have analyzed under the name of "Rareness" or "Clumsiness") calls, attracts the spectator: he wants to be reunited to the picture, not to consume it aesthetically, but to produce it in his turn (to "re-produce" it), to try his hand at a technique [...].[53]

Three *sujets*—object, artist, observer—outline in their in- difference a scene of temptation and seduction. For, in imitation, a significant default, a failure is experienced, which is essential for seduction—as well as for desire. Twombly's stroke is inimitable, as imitators must inevi- tably experience. "Now what is ultimately inimitable is the body; no discourse, whether verbal or plastic [...] can reduce one body to another body. TW's work reveals this fatality: my body will never be yours."[54] The work thus proves to be a scene of seduction: In so far as it is inimi- table, in so far as, in imitation, that which is desired, the body of Twombly, remains elusive, the latter, or rather his sensual surrogates—his art, his writing—seduce the body of the beholder, confuse him or her. Only in this way can desire continue in imitation and thus continue itself.

Tempted to constantly imitate, and constantly failing to do so, the reader-writers explore their powerlessness— "and at the same time, as it were in relief, the power of the artist."[55] This is what distinguishes Barthes, the fact that he "prevents himself from wanting too much; he succeeds in a way which is not unrelated to the erotic

52 Barthes, "The Wisdom of Art," pp. 19–20.
53 Ibid., p. 20.
54 Barthes, "Cy Twombly: Works on Paper," p. 170.
55 Barthes, "The Wisdom of Art," p. 21.

art of the Tao: intense pleasure comes from restraint."[56] Twombly's writing, his stroke, is, according to Barthes, clumsy but not stupid—or precisely because of this not stupid. It should not represent anything analogously; it is free and yet by no means arbitrary:

> And from this I understand that Twombly's art is an incessant victory over the stupidity of strokes: to draw an intelligent stroke: here, in the last analysis, is what makes the painter different. [...] no stroke seems endowed with an intentional direction, and yet the whole is mysteriously oriented.[57]

The artist incorporates his body into the writing, thwarts the standards of culture, but subtly, not by overwriting them, imposing his imprint on them, or representing them first and foremost in his own ductus.[58] It is precisely here that he restrains himself, "composes" what his culture has brought forth and in which his body persists; in which he, as it is called in Tao, expresses a "subtle vision of the world" (*vision subtile du monde*).[59] Herein lies the restraint of the artist, which brings intense pleasure.

In Barthes' re-reading of this subtle eroticism of restraint in the Marquis de Sade, namely in his "principle of delicacy" (*principe de délicatesse*)[60], which de Sade accepted as the reason for the preferences and fantasies of his protagonists, a central concept of classical aesthetics—and thus classical aesthetics itself—experiences that

---

**56**  Ibid., p. 21.
**57**  Ibid., p. 22.
**58**  Insofar as Barthes reads Twombly's "stroke" explicitly as free and subtle, devoid of any intentionality or imposition, a traditional system of sexual connotation is exposed and undermined which deals with the painter's stroke as a means of (sexual) imposing or imprinting, with the masculine form as a forceful penetration of the feminine substance.
**59**  Barthes, "Cy Twombly: Works on Paper," p. 173.
**60**  Ibid., p. 174.

"torsion" which Barthes' autobiography lays claim to for the old category of the aesthetic, that contortion or distortion that "alienate[s] it from its regressive, idealistic background and bring[s] it closer to the body, to the *drift*."[61] While in sensualist aesthetics, such as that of Dominique Bouhours, *délicatesse* described the sense for the "barely perceptible qualities of a work,"[62] the ability to suddenly recognize a huge abundance of *rapports*, Sade's *principe de délicatesse*—in Barthes' re-reading—takes effect within the body, or rather: between the bodies, in their manifold rapports. It organizes the "*postures combinés*," their "*figures*," and "*épisodes*"[63] in order to intensify pleasure in such mandated deferral. Accordingly, for Barthes it is not a capacity for cognition, but a physical drive, a *pulsion*. And from this, from the restraint of the artist, results that which is clumsy, rare, and sparse in Twombly's pictures, which ignites the pull effect, *une dérive*, a pull of the material background, from the void, from the space in between: "of course there is a silence, or, to be more accurate, a very faint buzzing of the surface, but this ground itself is a positive power; inverting the usual relation of classical production, we might say that the line, the hatching, the shape, in short the graphic event, is what permits the surface or the sheet of paper to exist, to signify, to take pleasure [...]."[64]

What appeared as an empty sheet of paper, as a white surface, as a background to be merely a carrier medium that allowed the markings, the notches on it to narrate, to represent, to generate depth of content, functions—in the clumsiness, rarity of the markings—as a

---

**61** Roland Barthes, *Roland Barthes by Roland Barthes* [1975], trans. Richard Howard (New York: Hill and Wang, 1977), p. 84.

**62** Burkhard Meyer-Sickendiek, *Zärtlichkeit. Höfische Galanterie als Ursprung der bürgerlichen Empfindsamkeit* (Munich: Wilhelm Fink, 2016), p. 40 [translated by G. A. Goodrow].

**63** Roland Barthes, *Sade. Fourier. Loyola* [1971], trans. Maren Sell and Jürgen Hoch (Frankfurt am Main: Suhrkamp, 1986), pp. 35–36.

**64** Barthes, "Cy Twombly: Works on Paper," p. 175.

*puissance positive*, as a positive, superimposing power on the reader-writer. In this way, however, the treated space, *l'espace traité*, eludes an order that can be prescribed, narrated, or abrogated by the depth of the markings' content; instead, it represents a multifaceted whole composed of strokes, gestures, streaks, pencil marks, canvas, paper, fiber grids, folds, wrinkles, etc. in a variety of ways. "The space treated is no longer reckonable [*dénombrable*], though it does not cease to be plural [*pluriel*]."[65]

This is precisely what Barthes writes further—like Twombly, referencing antiquity—by quoting Pliny's aphorism about reading: *"Non multa, sed multum"* stands for *"aiunt enim multum legendum esse, non multa"*: They say one should indeed read much, but not many things. Twombly's *multum* is the multifaceted *espace traité*, within which the material ground represents a positive power that subverts the countable order of markings, *multa*.

If Barthes' critical writing about Cy Twombly is oriented towards the experience of the material ground, the clumsiness, sparsity as a positive power, to be able to be a criticism of that arrangement of the markings that rises up in the negation of this power, then it makes sense to read this from the perspective of an analogous aspect in Benjamin's reading of the early Romantics. Benjamin reads Schlegel's mysticism as an attempt to grasp the system absolutely, in an intuition [*Intuition*] which, however, is not meant to be intuition in a Kantian sense [*Anschauung*], let alone intellectual. The early Romantics are said to have found the possibility for this in language: "Schlegel's thinking is absolutely conceptual—that is, it is linguistic thinking."[66] This addresses the literalness of language. Benjamin proves this with the Athenaeum Fragment 414, where there is talk of the connection between "mysticism" and "grammati-

---

**65**  Ibid., p. 175.
**66**  Benjamin, "The Concept of Art Criticism," p. 140.

cal sense"[67], by which, as footnote 105 clarifies, the *ety-mological* sense is to be understood: that is to say the sense for the historical shifts of the letters and the meanings that resulted from this.[68] Meaning is thus located *in* the letters themselves, instead of understanding it as their other, as an intellectual thing *above* them, which arranged them and organized their history. From this perspective, Barthes' reference to the positive power of the material ground can be read as an appeal to understand the meaning of material marks not as their other, as what governs them, but rather as being located in themselves, as an effect that can constantly shift within other arrangements of their material components—in their (material) *representation*. In turn the "sobriety," the "prosaic" aspect, which, according to Benjamin's reading of the early Romantic philosophy of art, should characterize poetry, because in it the principle of reflection "appears uppermost,"[69] can be read in correspondence with the clumsiness, the sparsity, which, according to Barthes, drives the positive power of the material ground forward. The prosaic aspect, the sobriety, of the medium of reflection that limits itself (in the form) then presents itself as an enticement to interrupt the inevitable order of forms and to experience in their changing constellations the positive power of the medium of reflection as a material background. Criticism must then take into account the fact that its *sujets* have always depended on their material representation, on the materials of their appearance.

Given that, for Barthes, every discourse is aesthetic which is "not uttered in the name of the Law and/or of Violence,"[70] but is rather a remnant or supplement of all

---

67  Ibid., p. 140.
68  The footnote further refers to a statement made by Schlegel in a letter to Novalis: "The letter [Buchstab'] is the true magic wand [Zauberstab]." Ibid., p. 190, note 108.
69  Ibid., p. 175.
70  Barthes, *Roland Barthes by Roland Barthes*, p. 84.

scientific, political, or religious statements, his criticism is aesthetic insofar as it is political—as a suspension of the significate, as well as a subversion of order. Accordingly, the aesthetic criticism that Benjamin calls for could be read as political: as an interruption of an order of forms with regard to their suspension in the infinity of the literal or material medium of reflection. Just as, according to Lukács, it should be impossible to understand the emergence of form, for Barthes this applies to production: The product in no way makes it intelligible, but rather baits the recipients to imitate it as something opaque (and to fail in this). And just as, according to Benjamin, it should be impossible to categorically distinguish the completing, resolving criticism from its sujets, in as much as it, like this, is poetry, for Barthes as well, semiological work cannot be categorically separated from its objects.[71] The délicatesse, which Barthes reads from Cy Twombly's materials, would determine his further critical writing. This would be delicate, ténu, restrained in the analysis of the processes of meaning, not imposing his own writing on the objects, but "composing" both—and develop political power precisely in this. Following on from his Mythologies, in the Chroniques (Chronicles), brief cultural readings that Barthes wrote in the last year of his life, he appeals to this very power of gentleness, the "douceur": "But there is, after all, a struggle for gentleness: Does it not become a force from the moment one decides in favor of gentleness? I write tenuously for morals."[72]

*Translated by Gérard A. Goodrow*

---

71  Compare Roland Barthes, "Leçon/Lektion" [1977], inaugural lecture at the Collège de France, trans. Helmut Scheffel (Frankfurt am Main: Suhrkamp, 1992), pp. 59–61.
72  "Mais après tout, il y a un combat pour la douceur: à partir du moment où la douceur est décidée, ne devient-elle pas une force? J'écris ténu par morale." Roland Barthes, "Pause," in Roland Barthes, *Œuvres Complètes III* (Paris: Le Seuil, 1995), pp. 990–992, here p. 991 [translated by G. A. Goodrow].

# The Scene as Form

**Bettine Menke**

# Gesture and Citability

## Theater as Critical Praxis

In their references to the word "gesture" and its repeat-
ability, and to the relation between stance (*Haltung*) and
halting (*Halt*), some of the formulations in the conference abstract for "Critical Stances – Critique as Practice"
seem to refer to Walter Benjamin's essay(s) "What is the
Epic Theater?," the first version of which was stopped
in the printing process in 1931, and the second version
of which appeared anonymously in 1939.[1] Fundamental features of Benjamin's philosophy and readings are
indicated by the concepts of *gesture, interruption,* "dialectics at a standstill," and *citability*. Moreover, these

1   In 1931, Walter Benjamin wrote "Was ist das epische Theater? Eine
    Studie zu Brecht" at Siegfried Kracauer's invitation to review the cur-
    rent production of Brecht's play *Mann ist Mann [A Man's a Man]*.
    The text was to be published in the newspaper *Frankfurter Zeitung*,
    and was already typeset, but the editor Bernhard Diepold stopped the
    printing process at the last minute. (Proofs and document published
    in Erdmut Wizisla, ed., *Brecht und Benjamin. Denken in Extremen*,
    exhibition catalogue [Berlin: Suhrkamp, 2017], pp. 71–80). A revised
    version, "Was ist das epische Theater?," was eventually published
    anonymously in the bimonthly magazine *Maß und Wert* 2/6 (1939).
    Both texts are included in Walter Benjamin, *Gesammelte Schriften*
    II, ed. Rolf Tiedemann, Hermann Schweppenhäuser (Frankfurt am
    Main: Suhrkamp, 1977) [hereinafter referred to as *GS* II], pp. 519–531
    and pp. 531–539. For further information on the history of publica-
    tion, see the editors' annotations, p. 1374 and pp. 1379–1381. Refer-
    ences in English for both texts are based on "What is Epic Theater?
    A Study on Brecht," in Walter Benjamin, *Understanding Brecht*, ed.
    Stanley Mitchell, trans. Anna Bostock (London and New York: Verso,
    1998), pp. 1–14; hereinafter referred to as (1.); and "What is Epic The-
    ater?," in Howard Eiland and Michael W. Jennings, eds., *Walter Ben-
    jamin: Selected Writings, vol. 4: 1938–1940* (Cambridge MA: Belknap
    Press of Harvard University Press, 2006), pp. 302–309; hereinafter re-
    ferred to as (2.). All translations of Benjamin's texts are modified
    where necessary or translated by the author or by the translator.

concepts have a particular relevance for the theater—
and not only for the "epic" or "gestural" theater, as Benjamin defines it.[2] I prefer to speak of the "gestural" in
order to avoid the misunderstanding of the epic theater as a genre.[3] In short, the relevance for the theater
inheres in the fact that in gesture, which as an interruption becomes knowable, that is to say "citable," the
split: *Entzweitheit*, that divides theatrical presentation
in itself between what is shown, and this showing itself,
is displayed. On the one hand, its split and doubling
constitutes theatrical presentation as such. On the other
hand, in gesture, Benjamin discerns the specific trait
of *this* theater, *the* trait of gestural theater, by which it
relates in a theatrical manner to the theater and to acting, and with which theatrical presentation sets itself
apart—from itself.

In gesture, according to Benjamin, in the "Auseinandersetzung," the setting-apart[4] of showing and what is
shown that makes itself felt therein, a "different, distancing mode of representation" can be identified,[5] which is
attained by theater's "latest experiments" ("neueste [...]
Versuche").[6] This mode of distancing theatrical presenta-

2    See Benjamin (1.), p. 3 [*GS* II, p. 521]; "Studien zur Theorie des epischen
     Theaters" (1931) [*GS* II, pp. 1380–1382, here p. 1380; (2.), p. 305 [*GS* II,
     p. 536].
3    Above all evaluating the genre by the question of how it fits the
     (later) Brechtian "epic theater" should be avoided; what is wrong
     with this approach can be seen in Tomislav Zelic, "Walter Benja-
     min über objektive Ironie im epischen Theater Bertolt Brechts," in
     Bärbel Frischmann, ed., *Ironie in Philosophie, Literatur und Recht*
     (Würzburg: Königshausen and Neumann, 2014), pp. 113–134. On
     the contrary: "Das 'epische' als 'gestisches Theater' hat letztlich nur
     in Benjamins Text existiert." Nikolaus Müller-Schöll, *Das Theater
     des "konstruktiven Defaitismus". Lektüren zur Theorie eines Theaters
     der A-Identität bei Walter Benjamin, Bertolt Brecht und Heiner Müller*
     (Frankfurt am Main and Basel: Stroemfeld/ Nexus, 2002), p. 161; also
     p. 48, pp. 157–158, pp. 175–177, pp. 182–184, pp. 297–298, p. 326.
4    "To set apart" literally translates here the important word "ausein-
     andersetzen"/"Auseinandersetzung" in Walter Benjamin's text. (1.),
     p. 11 [*GS* II, p. 529].
5    (2.), p. 307 [*GS* II, p. 539].
6    Benjamin, *Ursprung des deutschen Trauerspiels*, in *Gesammelte
     Schriften* I (Frankfurt am Main: Suhrkamp, 1974), [hereinafter re-

tion from itself is distinguished from the Romantic mode of self-distancing presentation. It would be "erroneous" ("irrig") to confuse "Tieck's [...] 'dramaturgy of reflex-ion'" with the way the gestural theater performs the "awareness that it is theater,"[7] as Benjamin states with unusual decidedness. Tieck's *Puss in Boots*, to which Benjamin explicitly refers in the second text (1939), and which he might already have had in mind in the first version, "reflected" the theatrical play, its play-acting, and its framing conditions *into* the play and as the "dramaturgy" of the play *within* its frame, on the stage, so that the reflection of the theatrical play *into* and *in* the play becomes dramatic action. Tieck's com-edies are well known as offering examples of "romantic irony," of the romantic "ironizing" of form.[8] According to Benjamin's doctoral dissertation, *On the Concept of Art Criticism* [Kunstkritik] *in German Romanticism*, the "[c]ritique of a work ["die Kritik des Werkes"] is [...] its reflection,"[9] which "drives [its form] out of itself" ("aus sich heraustreibt").[10] For the form of the work "is" as or by means of self-limitation, and therefore "is" not, but

ferred to as *GS* I], pp. 203–430, here p. 390; wrongly translated as *The Origin of German Tragic Drama*, trans. John Osborne (London: Verso, 1998) [hereinafter referred to as *OGT*], p. 216. The new 2019 Harvard University Press edition, which unfortunately was not yet available when I was writing this text, avoids the notorious mistranslation by translating *Origin of the German Trauerspiel*.

7 (1.), pp. 11, 4 [*GS* II, pp. 529, 522]; (2.), p. 307 [*GS* II, pp. 538–539].
8 (2.), p. 307 [*GS* II, p. 538]. See Benjamin, *Der Begriff der Kunstkri-tik in der deutschen Romantik*, *GS* I, pp. 7–122, here p. 84; also Paul de Man, "The Concept of Irony," in Paul de Man, *Aesthetic Ideol-ogy* (Minneapolis: University of Minnesota Press, 1996), pp. 163–184, here p. 178.
9 Benjamin, *Der Begriff der Kunstkritik in der deutschen Romantik,"GS* I, p. 78. In English: "The Concept of Criticism in German Romanticism," in Marcus Bullock and Michael W. Jennings, eds., *Walter Benjamin: Selected Writings, vol. 1: 1913–1926* (Cambridge MA: Belknap Press of Harvard University Press, 2002), pp. 116–200, here p. 159. The "cri-terion" ["Maßstab"] of "immanent critique/cism" is the "immanent tendency of the work," its "reflection" of its form. (p. 159 [*GS* I, p. 77]).
10 Benjamin, "The Concept of Criticism in German Romanticism," p. 156, [*GS* I, p. 73]; "the unity of the single work" is "continually being shifted [from itself] in irony and criticism." (p. 164, [*GS* I, p. 86]).

rather remains bound to what is external to it (Benjamin speaks of the "accidentality", *Zufälligkeit*) and to its exclusion; in order not to remain "limited," it must relate itself to its own constitution and refer to the formlessness from which it has emerged (and which it excludes while delimiting itself). "Critique fulfills its task by [...] resolving [...] the original reflection" (whose "objective expression" is form as "the work's own reflection") "into a higher one and goes on in this way," since this displacement out of itself always attains form again.[11]

"Critique" was proposed as a counterpart to "crisis" in the title of the journal *Krise und Kritik*, conceived by Brecht and Benjamin in 1930–1931, with obvious reference to the exigent events of the times.[12] But epic theater withdraws, according to Benjamin, from "professional" criticism and contests this and its failed standards,[13] and indeed does so with the distance the play takes (from itself), by letting "intervals" into itself, which allow the spectators to take a "critical stance" ("kritische Stellungnahme"):

So entstehen Intervalle, die die Illusion des Publikums eher beeinträchtigen. Sie lähmen seine Bereitschaft zur Einfühlung. Diese Intervalle sind seiner kritischen Stellungnahme

---

11  Ibid. p. 156 [*GS* I, p. 73]. "Formal irony [...] presents a paradoxical venture: to build on the structure even through demolition [am Gebilde noch durch Abbruch zu bauen]." (p. 165 [*GS* I, p. 87]). This venture or attempt is referred to by the conference's proposal relating it to "anti-form (F. Schlegel)" or "informe (Bataille)".

12  On "Krise und Kritik," see "Konzeptgespräch" (Benjamin Archiv Ts 2463, in Wizisla, ed., *Brecht und Benjamin*, pp. 102–104): "[Benjamin] Kritik ist heute die richtige Haltung der Intelligenz," "[Brecht] Das finde ich gefährlich. Dann kann man sagen, die Intellektuellen sollen nichts tun. [...] [Benjamin] Kein Intellektueller darf heute aufs Katheder gehen und Anspruch erheben, [...] wir [...] führen nicht." (pp. 103–104). It is necessary to draw "radical conclusions from the unfoundedness and untenability of authority" ["die radikale Konsequenz aus der Grund- und Haltlosigkeit jeder Autorität"]. Müller-Schöll, *Das Theater des "konstruktiven Defaitismus"*, p. 310.

13  The critics and their critique have to notice: "ihren Agentencharakter aufgedeckt und zugleich außer Kurs geraten" ([1.], p. 10, see also pp. 9–10. [*GS* II, p. 528, see also pp. 527–528]).

(zum dargestellten Verhalten der Personen und zu der Art, in der es dargestellt wird) vorbehalten.

Thus intervals emerge which rather undermine the illusion of the audience and paralyze its readiness for empathy. These intervals are reserved for the audience's critical stance to the behavior of the persons and the way they are presented.[14]

Through his acting, the actor must demonstrate ("in seinem Spiel auszuweisen")[15] the "intervals" and interruptions let into the theatrical presentation in the action on the stage, opened up into the representational order to give the audience space for their "critical stance": in the self-distancing of acting from what is represented and from its presentation. There is no place for a position, no certain ground for critique.[16]

Epic theater, because it is interruptive and therefore *gestural: gestisch*,[17] according to Benjamin, is to be characterized by its "Vorstellung des 'Theaterspielens'": its notion of "putting on a show of 'theater-playing'" in the praxis of acting that is playing (*schauspielen*).[18] Ben-

14  (2.), p. 306 [*GS* II, p. 538]. See also Benjamin, "Das Land, in dem das Proletariat nicht genannt werden darf," *GS* II, pp. 514–518, here pp. 515–516; (1.), pp. 6–8 [*GS* II, pp. 524–526].

15  (2.), p. 306 [*GS* II, p. 538].

16  Critique cannot "rely on authorities" ["[sich] im Ganzen nicht auf Autoritäten stützen"] according to the "Memorandum" to "Krise und Kritik," in Walter Benjamin, *Gesammelte Schriften* VI, ed. Rolf Tiedemann, Hermann Schweppenhäuser et al. (Frankfurt am Main: Suhrkamp, 1972) [hereinafter referred to as *GS* VI], p. 619. "Narren, die den Verfall der Kritik beklagen. Denn [...] Kritik ist eine Sache des rechten Abstands." Benjamin, "Diese Flächen sind zu vermieten," in Walter Benjamin, *Einbahnstraße, Werke und Nachlaß. Kritische Gesamtausgabe*, vol. 8, ed. Detlev Schöttker et al. (Frankfurt am Main: Suhrkamp, 2009], pp. 59–60. Instead of "forcing open our state of things from outside" ["von außen her unsre Zustände einzurennen"], Brecht is said to have let them dialectically criticize themselves ["vermittelt, dialektisch sie sich kritisieren [lassen]" ([1.], p. 8 [*GS* II, p. 526]).

17  (1.), p. 3 [*GS* II, p. 521]; see "Studien zur Theorie des epischen Theaters," *GS* II, pp. 1381–1382; (2.), p. 305 [*GS* II, p. 536].

18  (2.), p. 306 [*GS* II, p. 538].

jamin accounts for this with the old phrase: "an actor
should reserve for himself the possibility of falling out
of character artistically." ("Der Schauspieler soll sich
die Möglichkeit vorbehalten, mit Kunst aus der Rolle zu
fallen.")[19] Thus, Benjamin brings the concept of *parekbasis* and thereby the paradigmatic figure of "romantic
irony" into play, while he immediately rejects romantic
irony as a flawed analogy for the epic theater. *Parekbasis* is a gesture of speech, with which a figure on the
stage turns away from the scene of dramatic speech.
Traditionally chalked up to being a failure of ancient
comedy, Friedrich Schlegel re-evaluated this gesture,[20]
which interrupts the dramatic illusion of what is taking
place on the stage.[21] In the aside, playing along the *the-
atron*-axis and addressing the audience, *parekbasis* comments on what is happening on the stage. In the speakers' turn away from the represented action, out of the
contours of the dramatic person and out of the scene of
dramatic speech, the speakers address these others (the
audience) who do not belong to the represented action
and who, according to Diderot, should be excluded (or
forgotten) by what is represented, as well as those who
are presenting—to allow the audience's illusion and
empathy. Diderot's fictive fourth wall represented the
closure or containment of the play in itself. Benjamin
refers to this self-containment by speaking of the "pit"
("Graben") into which the "abyss" ("Abgrund") had
been transformed, "which separates the actors from the
audience as the dead from the living," and which "bears
the most indelible traces of its sacral origin"[22] and there-

---

19  (2.), pp. 306–307 [*GS* II, p. 538].
20  Friedrich Schlegel, "Vom ästhetischen Werthe der Griechischen
    Komödie," *Berlinische Monatsschrift* 24 (1794): pp. 485–505; on the
    attic comedy see August Wilhelm Schlegel, *Vorlesungen über drama-
    tische Kunst und Literatur: Dramaturgische Vorlesungen, Kritische
    Ausgabe*, vol. I, ed. Giovanni Vittorio Amoretti (Bonn and Leipzig:
    Kurt Schröder, 1923), p. 6.
21  See de Man, "The Concept of Irony," pp. 178–179, pp. 177–180.
22  (2.), p. 307 [*GS* II, p. 539].

fore has lost its function. It is decisive that—according to Benjamin—"what matters in theater today [das, "[w]orum es heute im Theater geht"] can be defined more precisely in terms of the stage than in terms of a new form of drama" (thus begins the text from 1931 and thus concludes the text from 1939);[23] thus by its relating otherwise to the stage that has been transformed into a "podium," whereas the regular old theater business continues to operate an "obsolete" "stage apparatus."[24] But no "apparatus of production" ("Produktionsapparat") should be supplied, Benjamin postulates elsewhere, without changing it, occupying it, or giving it a new function.[25]

*Parekbasis* is, as gesture of speech, an act or event (not of something): a turning away and a suspension. Tieck's *Puss in Boots* carries out the reflection of the play through its most "evident" ("offenkundige") "technique" of the "play within the play," as Benjamin referred to in *The Origin of the German Trauerspiel*, which mirrors or folds the game of the play into the occurrences on stage, so that a stage "is set up on the stage, or the spectators' space is extended onto the stage-area."[26] In *Puss in Boots*, the actors assert themselves, as they "fall out of character,"[27] alongside the dramatic figures, emphasizing the duality

23  (1.), p. 1 [*GS* II, p. 519]; (2.), p. 307 [*GS* II, p. 539].
24  (2.), p. 307 [*GS* II, p. 539]. "Auf diesem Podium gilt es sich einzurichten. Das ist die Lage. Wie aber vielen Zuständen gegenüber, so hat sich auch bei diesem der Betrieb ihn zu verdecken vorgesetzt, statt ihm Rechnung zu tragen." ([1.], p. 1 [*GS* II, p. 519]; see [2.], p. 307 [*GS* II, p. 539]).
25  Benjamin, "Der Autor als Produzent. Ansprache im Institut zum Studium des Fascismus in Paris am 27. April 1934," *GS* II, pp. 683–701, here pp. 691–692. In English, "The Author as Producer. Address at the Institute for the Study of Fascism, Paris, April 27, 1934," in Michael W. Jennings, Howard Eiland and Gary Smith, eds., *Walter Benjamin: Selected Writings, vol. 2, part 2: 1931–1934* (Cambridge MA: Belknap Press of Harvard University Press, 2005), pp. 768–782, here pp. 774–775.
26  *OGT*, p. 82 [*GS* I, p. 261]. Tieck's play doesn't decide where the parterre in (the) play is situated.
27  In "the plays of his friend Tieck [...] the parabasis is constantly being used." de Man, "The Concept of Irony," p. 178.

of the actors and the dramatic figures. Thus, aside from kings and cats, actors, the director, machinist, poet, and enthusiastic as well as annoyed audience also belong to the action represented on the stage. In this way the *parekbasis* is set into and thus contained in a new frame and the interrupting turn away, which refers the form out of itself, is included into the dramatic action with "Tieck's old dramaturgy of reflection," which would produce a rather dull satire of philistines in the theater. But the presentation is not *one;* it is not homogeneous and is always only provisional,[28] which means that it is undecidable *where* its frame actually is, therefore between form and its (self-) suspension. The reflection of the play—this is what makes it paradoxical—performs the constitution of what may become presented by means of its delimiting, folded into the reflected play and its framework, in that it presents the *processes* of constitution, which must continually be carried out as figural separations between that which belongs, form, what is "actually represented" (on the one hand), and the digressions, additions, or marginal phenomena, what is merely contingent, or not meaningful (on the other hand): without reaching a conclusion and therewith a detachment of form or figure from the formless or the (figure's) ground. In the potentiated (*potenzierte*) suspension or transgression of delimited form and its framework, the border that decides about form becomes always again and still uncertain,[29] becomes always again

28  On provisionality and its incompatibility with drama, see Peter Szondi, "Friedrich Schlegel und die romantische Ironie. Mit einer Beilage über Tiecks Komödien," in Peter Szondi, *Schriften II*, ed. Jean Bollack et al. (Frankfurt am Main: Suhrkamp, 1978), pp. 25–31, here p. 26. In English, "Friedrich Schlegel and Romantic Irony, with Some Remarks on Tieck's Comedies," in Peter Szondi, *On Textual Understanding and Other Essays*, trans. Harvey Mendelsohn (Manchester: Manchester University Press, 1986), pp. 57–73, here pp. 68–69.
29  In the potentialization of the folding of what presents into what is represented, it is uncertain where the contour between the "inside" and the "outside" is: does the puss in boots fall out of his role when he climbs up a tree in fear? Or does the actor fall out of his

and still unrecognizable, its contours diffuse in an unde-cidable manner.

When (limited) form interrupts itself *ironically* and *reflects itself,* it still does not escape the constitutive delim-itations of the theater; rather, the play (*Spiel*) is potenti-ated (*potenziert*) in the paradoxical "reflection of appear-ance and play"[30] *in* the play. Friedrich Schlegel defines Romantic irony *tout court* as "a permanent *parekbasis.*"[31] The ironizing turn of the representation away from and out of itself, which splits what has become in itself and distances it from itself, will have to be continued as/in the indefinite suspension, as the "irony of irony"[32] and in this way does not allow something else as (really) meant to be understood, but rather suspends the decision about the position of speech, its object, and its addressee, in favor of its potential deferrals. De Man reformulates the "permanence" of the *parekbasis* of Romantic irony as a self-disruptive turning-away, which displaces (itself) ever again and can occur or may have occurred anytime, *everywhere,* and *at every moment.*[33]

Yet it would be wrong, according to Benjamin, in this moment, in which the actors of the gestural the-ater take distance from the represented action and from their acting (*schauspielen*), "to be reminded at such a moment of romantic irony, as handled by Tieck in his

role into the role of the puss in boots? Or something else? In this fall-ing out of the role, what is shown in Tieck's comedies, according to Szondi, is not the actors, but rather the "role," which takes distance from their "dramatic existence." Szondi, "Friedrich Schlegel and Ro-mantic Irony," pp. 68–75. ["Friedrich Schlegel und die romantische Ironie," pp. 28–31].

30   *OGT,* p. 82. [*GS* I, p. 261].

31   "Die Ironie ist eine permanente Parekbase." Friedrich Schlegel, "Zur Philosophie (1797)" [Fr. 668], in *Kritische Friedrich-Schlegel-Ausgabe* [hereinafter referred to as *KA*], XVIII, ed. Ernst Behler et. al. (Pader-born: Schöningh, 1963), p. 85.

32   Friedrich Schlegel, "Über die Unverständlichkeit," in *KA* II, pp. 363–372, here p. 368. See also Eckhard Schumacher, *Die Ironie der Un-verständlichkeit: Johann Georg Hamann, Friedrich Schlegel, Jacques Derrida, Paul de Man* (Frankfurt am Main: Suhrkamp, 2000), in par-ticular pp. 9–11, and pp. 218–228.

33   de Man, "The Concept of Irony," pp. 178–179.

*Puss in Boots.*"[34] This may be an objection against its restrictive performance in terms of Tieck's "old dramaturgy of reflection." Yet in his book on Romantic criticism, Benjamin had already pointed out the insufficiency of this concept of critique: as "medial, continuous transposition"[35] of the reflection of form. Critique that "drives [form] out of itself,"[36] according to its Romantic concept, should be (both): "on the one hand, the completion, consummation, and systematization of the work and, on the other hand, its resolution in the absolute" ("einerseits Vollendung, Ergänzung, Systematisierung des Werkes, andererseits seine Auflösung im Absoluten")[37]. If thereby the "unity of the individual work"[38] shall "continually be displaced in irony and criticism," then in this way a continuum of artworks and (the "idea" of) art is conceived,[39] without the conflict of the work and art actually becoming visible. This Romantic concept is deficient in thinking discontinuity, of the relation, which *is* rupture, and which Benjamin invokes as "caesura," in thinking "das *Ausdruckslose*," the "inexpressive" as "critical violence," for which the "Work" called and which shatters "its false totality."[40] In an explicit revision of the Romantic concept of criti-

34  (2.), p. 307 [*GS* II, p. 538].
35  Benjamin, "The Concept of Criticism in German Romanticism," p. 154 [*GS* I, p. 70].
36  Ibid., p. 156 [*GS* I, p. 73].
37  Ibid., p. 159 [*GS* I, p. 78]. "Both of these processes coincide in the end" (p. 159 [*GS* I, p. 78]). "Formal irony [...] presents a paradoxical venture: to build on the structure even through demolition, to demonstrate in the work itself its relationship to the idea." ["Die formale Ironie [...] stellt den paradoxen Versuch dar, am Gebilde noch durch Abbruch zu bauen: im Werke selbst seine Beziehung auf die Idee zu demonstrieren."] (p. 165 [*GS* I, p. 87]).
38  Ibid., p. 164 [*GS* I, p. 86].
39  Ibid., p. 164; see also pp. 165–167, [*GS* I, p. 86; see also pp. 87–89, pp. 90–91].
40  The conclusion of "The Concept of Criticism in German Romanticism" alludes to this with Goethe (pp. 111–115). The Work, a concept for which Goethe stands, needs, as Benjamin has it in *Goethes Wahlverwandtschaften* the caesura as the expressionless [ausdruckslose] interruption, the "critical violence" that applies to the mistaken mythical supposition of wholeness: "This only completes the

cism as awakening (of consciousness) in *The Origin of the German Trauerspiel*, Benjamin claims critique to be the "mortification of works"—as which it operates in complicity with the duration in which the works decay, and endure as ruins.[41] Criticism/critique is thus a mode of the "living-on (and away) of works," ("Fortleben der Werke"), where these no longer belong to art.[42]

According to Benjamin, Tieck merely demonstrates with his comedies' "romantic irony" his being "in the philosophical savvy" ("seine philosophische Informiertheit"): "the world may ultimately prove to be a theater."[43] With this, the presupposed givenness of both "world" and "theater" would merely be confirmed,[44] and the turn out of the frame of the play would be recuperated in a broader dramatic and philosophical framework. Like Tieck "in writing his plays," led only by the "philosophical savvy," such is Benjamin's reservation, "the romantic stage" "despite of all its reflective arts" "never was able to do justice to the relation between theory and practice."[45] Yet what matters for gestural theater is what is taking place in acting, playing and putting on an act (*schauspielen* and *vorspielen*): "die Art des Spiels", "the mode of play" or better: playing, its procedure, and its behavior (*Verhalten*), its practice. And

work, which shatters it into a broken piece [Stückwerk], into a fragment of the true world." *GS* I, pp. 123–201, here pp. 181–183.

41  See *GS* I, p. 357 [*OGT*, p. 182]; Benjamin, ›Fragmente zur Kritik‹, *GS* VI, pp. 170–171. [fr. 135 and fr. 136].

42  Analogously to translation in the notes in the context of "Krise und Kritik" (*GS* VI, p. 174, pp. 70–71), "criticism/critique is interior to the work [...] art is merely a transitional stage of great works. They were something else (in the state of their becoming) and they will become something else (in the state of criticism/critique)." (*GS* VI, p. 172 [fr 138, around 1931]). The scope of Benjamin's concept of "critique"/"criticism" is thus indicated, see also Uwe Steiner, "Kritik," in Michael Opitz and Erdmut Wizisla, eds., *Benjamins Begriffe* (Frankfurt am Main: Suhrkamp, 2000), pp. 479–523.

43  (2.), p. 307; "Die Welt mag am Ende wohl auch ein Theater sein." [*GS* II, p. 538]; see (1.), pp. 11–12 [*GS* II, p. 529].

44  The counterpart to this (which is merely inverted) is the stage as "'the planks, which mean the world'" (1.), p. 2, *GS* II, p. 520.

45  (1.), pp. 11–12 [*GS* II, p. 529].

thereby justice is done "to the relationship between theory and praxis": it takes place *in* the gestural theater as "the ongoing conflict or setting-apart ["Auseinandersetzung"] between the action on the stage ["Bühnenvorgang"] which is shown and the behavior of showing on the stage ["Bühnenverhalten"]."[46]

The text from 1939 (in the next section) proceeds: "The extent to which artistic and political interests coincide in the epic theater can be easily seen in its mode of play and playing" ("die Art des Spiels").[47] That is not so much because of political objects (or roles, as the second text suggests), but rather precisely due to the setting-apart ("Auseinandersetzung") taking place *in* acting/ playing (*Vorspielen*), which allows "the one who is showing— the actor as such—[to be] shown."[48] This also means that "the awareness that it is theater" (which the naturalistic theater must repress in order to "devote itself" *without* being "distracted" to the supposed representation of the supposed real), "is incessantly asserted"[49]—and that *is* politically relevant.

It may be surprising, but the argument can be drawn from Benjamin's essay problematizing "historical drama," which confronts a play of Calderón with a drama of Hebbel, and was written at the same time as *The Origin of the German Trauerspiel*, and as kind of preliminary study to its notion of the play.[50] This (kind of a) detour is justified because, on the one hand, Benjamin's book on the *Trauerspiel* saw the awkward German

---

**46**  (1.), p. 11, "der steten Auseinandersetzung zwischen dem Bühnenvorgang, der gezeigt wird, und dem Bühnenverhalten, das zeigt." [*GS* II, p. 529].
**47**  (2.), p. 307 [*GS* II, p. 538].
**48**  (1.), p. 11 [*GS* II, p. 529].
**49**  (1.), p. 4 [*GS* II, p. 522].
**50**  Benjamin, "*El mayor mónstruo, los celos* von Calderon und *Herodes und Mariamne* von Hebbel: Bemerkungen zum Problem des historischen Dramas," *GS* II, pp. 246–276. In English, "Calderon's *El Mayor Monstruo, Los Celos* and Hebbel's *Herodes und Mariamne*. Comments on the Problem of Historical Drama," *Selected Writings Vol. 1*, pp. 363–386..

Baroque Trauerspiel (not contained as form in itself) as pointing to the coming "latest experiments or attempts" of theater.[51] On the other hand, according to the texts asking about the epic theater, this theater emerges from a non-linear tradition, travelling on smuggler's paths and mule's tracks, of a whole disorderly clan (*Sippe*) of anti-dramatic theater forms, to which the baroque Trauerspiel belonged, that must be read as the constellation of its "pre- and post-history."[52] Benjamin approached "historical drama" as a "problem," since it supposes a "Sinn der Determiniertheit," a "meaning of the determinateness" of the dramatic action, for which the recourse to causality would be insufficient; since history can "only" "claim dramatic truth" as "fate," it must present "history as fate."[53] But it can only do that as and in the "play" that drama is. "The dramatology of the play ["Dramatik des Spiels"], where it stands vis-a-vis historical materials, sees itself obligated to unfold fate as play. It is precisely this cleavage ["Zwiespalt"], that constitutes the 'Romantic tragedy'."[54] The play-character, which the "fate" of the "drama of fate" inevitably has, requires the "romantic," that is the "paradoxical reflection of play and appearance,"[55] which Calderón's plays in particular achieve, as Benjamin claims also with respect to the "historical drama." If the "world of fate"

---

**51** *GS* I, p. 390, [*OGT*, p. 216].

**52** "Vor- und Nachgeschichte" [*GS* I, p. 226]; compare the misleading translation in *OGT*, p. 46. For the relations between Benjamin's concept of the epic theater and the Trauerspiel(book), see Müller-Schöll, *Das Theater des "konstruktiven Defaitismus"*, pp. 110–111, p. 139, pp. 50–51.

**53** Benjamin, "Comments on the Problem of Historical Drama," p. 373 [*GS* II, p. 276, p. 250]; here and in what follows see also Bettine Menke, "Reflexion des Trauer-Spiels. Pedro Calderón de la Barcas El mayor mónstruo, los celos nach Walter Benjamin," in Bettine Menke, Eva Horn and Christoph Menke, eds., *Literatur als Philosophie. Philosophie als Literatur* (Munich: Fink, 2005), pp. 253–280.

**54** Benjamin, "Comments on the Problem of Historical Drama," p. 373 [*GS* II, p. 260].

**55** *GS* I, pp. 261–262, [*OGT*, p. 83].

or rather of "dramas of fate" is "self-contained,"[56] this is none other than the stage (itself), the "strictly delimited space" of the theater-play, in which Calderón "allows fate to unfold playfully."[57] Fate is presented "as play," as the theatrical play (*Schauspiel*) and its framing are "playfully" reflected as a play: mirrored inward, "minimizing" ("verkleinernd") and "framing" ("umrahmend") it: inside of its constitutive delimitations.[58] In this way, Calderón's Herod drama displays the "obvious" "deliberateness" ("offenkundige" "Absichtlichkeit") of the dramatic plot-assemblage through its cumbersome fabrication,[59] which (precisely for this reason) allows for the wildest coincidences of ominous props. By contrast, "fate is postulated as real only in the bad, unromantic tragedies of fate" ("das Schicksal [werde] schlechthin real" "nur in den schlechten, den unromantischen Schicksalstragödien gesetzt").[60] When taken seriously, such "historical dramas" that present history "as fate" must fail.[61] Without the reflection on the play that it is, that is to say, without the disruptive entry of the *theater* into what is represented, the *play* of fate (which

56 Benjamin, "Comments on the Problem of Historical Drama," p. 378 [*GS* II, p. 267], revised in *Ursprung des deutschen Trauerspiels*, GS I, p. 261 [*OGT*, p. 83].
57 Benjamin, "Comments on the Problem of Historical Drama," p. 381 [*GS* II, p. 272].
58 *GS* II, pp. 268–269; *Ursprung des deutschen Trauerspiels*, GS I, p. 262; the "Verkleinerung des Reflektierten" in the play [im Spiel], GS I, p. 306, p. 261.
59 Benjamin, "Comments on the Problem of Historical Drama," p. 376 [*GS* II, p. 264]. Benjamin reports on the plot of Calderón's *El mayor mónstruo, los celos* (1636–1672) in great detail in "Zum Problem des historischen Dramas," *GS II*, pp. 263–264. The deliberateness ["Absichtlichkeit"] of the plot construction gives "Einblick in ihre [Calderóns Dichtung] Auffassung vom dramatischen Schicksal [...] " (*GS II*, p. 264). "Jene Absichtlichkeit [...] zerstreut im idealen romantischen Trauerspiel des Calderon die Trauer. Denn in der *Machination* hat die neue Bühne den Gott." *Ursprung des deutschen Trauerspiels*, GS I, p. 261. The intrigue or *Machination* is a "zufällige[s]" as well as "berechnende[s] und planmäßige[s]" play.
60 Benjamin, "Comments on the Problem of Historical Drama," p. 381 [*GS* II, p. 272].
61 Ibid., p. 384 [*GS* II, p. 276].

cannot be other than deliberate assemblage), unfolded in the theatrical space, will be *forgotten* or *repressed*, and is taken as "simply real." And "unromantic historical dramas" fall to a "realistic" misunderstanding of "fate"—which is made to underpin the determinacy of the sequence as its "dramatic truth."[62]

Against the "naturalistic" confusion of the events on the stage with the extra-theatrical world, that the "naturalistic stage" allows as smirking recognition only through its repression of its "awareness that it is theater,"[63] epic theater is a theater that precisely does *not* act without being distracted, but rather, has a "productive awareness" "incessantly" that "it is theater." That allows epic theater to handle theater as a "Versuchsanordnung," an "experimental disposition" which does not presuppose the (given) "state (of things)" ("Zustände") as to be imitated, but rather always also negotiates their respective framings, in which the "state (of things)" that may stand "at the end of the experiment" are possible,[64] *and* displaces them out of these always only provisional frames. For epic theater, "historical incidents" ("Vorgänge"), according to Benjamin citing Brecht, have the function, precisely, of resisting the "Dramatik des Spiels" or "dramatology of play." Since the course they will follow is known, these incidents do not preoccupy spectators with comprehendingly following (*nachvollziehen*) the course of action. Therefore, according to Benjamin (but not Brecht), theater is allowed "to loosen the [...] joints of the plot [*Fabel*] to the limits of the possible ["bis an die Grenze des Möglichen"]."[65] In this way, it is *not* the

---

62 Benjamin's text from 1931 finds the traces of the interrelation between irony and criticism in Strindberg's Histories, which have "paved the way for the gestural theater" ([1.], p. 8 [*GS* II, p. 526]).
63 (1.), p. 4 [*GS* II, p. 522]; see (2.), p. 307 [*GS* II, p. 539].
64 (1.), p. 4 [*GS* II, p. 522].
65 (2.), p. 303 [*GS* II, p. 533]: the metaphor "wie ein Ballettmeister der Elevin" would have been to be read as very specifically gendered. The Brechtian theory of theater is bound to plot or "Fabel," see Hans-Thies Lehmann, "Der andere Brecht," in Hans-Thies Lehmann,

recognition of the events following the usual patterns that is made possible for the spectators; rather, what is "incommensurable" to the plot and to the "Fluchtlinien der Erwartung" is allowed to appear as its known and presupposed connections are "loosened," interrupting and expanding them.[66] Here, theater makes the contingency of the theater "productive"—in taking the basic stance ("Grundhaltung"): "It can happen this way, but it can also happen quite otherwise." ("Es kann so kommen, aber es kann auch ganz anders kommen").[67] "Where someone experiments, there reigns no necessity; rather, possibilities are obtained," states Christoph Menke.[68] In a deferred (or belated) way, "real states" ("wirkliche Zustände") may be re-cognized in the experimental dispositions. Then not only the events on the stage, but also the real state of things, "wirkliche Zustände" are cognizable as *not* necessary and also as possible otherwise: They could not be, or could be different, and are always (invisibly) accompanied by the shadows of other possibilities.[69]

While this theater is defined, according to Benjamin, above all by its "Vorstellung des 'Theaterspielens'"

*Das Politische Schreiben. Essays zu Theatertexten; Sophokles, Shakespeare, Kleist, Büchner, Jahnn, Bataille, Brecht, Benjamin, Müller, Schleef* (Berlin: Theater der Zeit, 2002), p. 207–281 and "Fabel-Haft," pp. 219–237, specifically p. 230; compare also Hans-Thies Lehmann, *Brecht* Lesen (Berlin: Theater der Zeit, 2016), pp. 147–164, specifically pp. 157–159.

**66** (1.), p. 8 [*GS* II, p. 525]; on the "epic extension" of "historical incidents" ["epische Streckung der "'geschichtliche[n] Vorgänge'"] "by a particular mode of acting/playing, by placards, and by onstage captions" ["durch die Spielweise, die Plakate und die Beschriftungen"] see (2.), p. 303 [*GS* II, p. 533].

**67** (1.), p. 8 [*GS* II, p. 525]. See Lehmann, *Das Politische Schreiben*, p. 368.

**68** That is, the possibility to act otherwise. See Christoph Menke, *Die Gegenwart der Tragödie. Versuch* über *Urteil und Spiel* (Frankfurt am Main: Suhrkamp, 2005), p. 145; English translation *Tragic Play: Irony and Theater from Sophocles to Beckett* (New York: Columbia University Press, 2009), p. 117.

**69** The abandonment of the illusion of the reality of "how it really was" is above all decisive for Benjamin's concept of historiography (especially for "Thesen über den Begriff der Geschichte"; see below).

("notion" or "presentation of theater playing"),[70] this is not to be read as a reference to a Brechtian theoretical concept ("Vorstellung")[71] but rather with respect to the "presentation" of playing *in acting*, which draws attention to play-acting. Differently from what the formula "theory and practice" might suggest, practice does not apply to the real reality outside of the theater as opposed to the illusionary theatrical play;[72] rather, what is emphasized is the practice that theater playing is, which is doubled and divided in itself and in this way is dependent on cognition and engenders cognition. *Vorspielen*, playing as acting (something) out in the theater, in its relation to the spectators, brings "the relation of the performed action to that (action), which is given as such in performing" "to expression" ("zum Ausdruck"),[73] since it unfolds for the relation of both as division and in this way exposes, in both "actions[s]," their non-identity, their difference from themselves. This theater-practice is split and doubled in and with

---

70   (2.), p. 306 [*GS* II, p. 538].
71   To prove why it would be erroneous ("irrig"), to recognize the "Tiecksche Dramaturgie der Reflexion" in the self-distancing of the gestural theater would imply: "auf einer Wendeltreppe den Schnürboden der Brechtschen Theorie erklettern" ([1.], p. 11 [*GS* II, p. 529]). It is kind of funny that thereby the "Volute"—the analog of "the romantic reflection" thanks to which Calderón "[das Drama] immer von neuem zu umrahmen und zu verkleinern verstand" (*Ursprung des deutschen Trauerspiels, GS* I, p. 262)—is let in here as a verticalized metaphor, in order to give no other "ground" as the unstable one of an off-device for stage workers.
72   The setting apart of play and world is put differently in C. Menke, *Tragic Play*, pp. 108–115 [*Gegenwart der Tragödie*, pp. 134–142]. See also Christop Menke,"Das Spiel des Theaters und die Veränderung der Welt," in Olivia Ebert et al., eds., *Theater als Kritik. Theorie, Geschichte und Praktiken der Ent-Unterwerfung* (Bielefeld: transcript, 2018), pp. 37–48. C. Menke distinguishes the action of playing something to someone [Handlung des Vorspielens] from the (concept of) praxis, which derives from *prattein*, which is aim-oriented and completes itself in the achievement of the aim. Ibid p. 45; C. Menke, *Tragic Play*, pp. 98–100, pp. 103–105 [*Gegenwart der Tragödie*, pp. 123–125, pp. 128–129].
73   (1.), p. 11, "Oberste Aufgabe einer epischen Regie ist, das Verhältnis der aufgeführten Handlung zu derjenigen, die im Aufführen überhaupt gegeben ist, zum Ausdruck zu bringen." [*GS* II, p. 529].

itself: it is never *one*, never identical with itself, it is foreign to itself. Brecht's theater referred "to a radicalized *self-foreignness*, or an internal otherness, alterity [...] from which Brecht—in theory—always shrinks away in fear," according to Hans-Thies Lehmann.[74]

Benjamin characterizes the relatedness and division of both actions *in* the play-acting in citing Brecht as the actors' "showing a thing" and "showing themselves":

> Der Schauspieler muß eine Sache zeigen, und er muß sich zeigen. Er zeigt die Sache natürlich, indem er sich zeigt, und er zeigt sich, indem er die Sache zeigt. Obwohl dies zusammenfällt, darf es doch nicht so zusammenfallen, daß der Gegensatz (Unterschied) zwischen diesen beiden Aufgaben verschwindet.

> The actor must show a thing, and he must show himself. He naturally shows the thing by showing himself, and he shows himself by showing the thing. Although these two tasks coincide, they must not coincide to such a point that the contrast (difference) between them disappears.[75]

"Showing a thing" would "coincide" with the actors' "showing themselves" in the *Vorspielen*, in playing (as acting out) taking place, thus exactly the play is thus split and doubled in itself.[76] The "ongoing setting-apart ["Auseinandersetzung"] between the action on the stage ["Bühnenvorgang"] which is shown and the behavior on the stage ["Bühnenverhalten"] that shows,"[77] in such a way that "the one who is showing, is shown" is what constitutes gestural theater. Actors "bring to expression," as Benjamin has it, "the relation of the performed action to the other (action) given in performing

---

**74** Lehmann, *Das Politische Schreiben*, p. 231.
**75** Brecht, cited in (1.), p. 11 [*GS* II, p. 529]; see (2.), p. 306 [*GS* II, p. 538].
**76** (1.), p. 11 [*GS* II, p. 529].
**77** Ibid.

as such,"[78] insofar as they *block* the relationship between
the two in the gesture; thus the two distinct tasks and
actions do not collapse into one another. It should be
understood that the gesture is not a form of expression,
whether involuntarily or historically conventionalized.
The gesture is not the expression of something that supposedly preceded it; it is not at all (as in the common
discussion of gesture in the field of theater studies) a
sign bound to semantics;[79] it contradicts the representational model and asserts itself *as* an act in its *dynamis*
intransitively against anything that it would "carry."[80]
It is an "element" of a stance (*Haltung*) as a halt (*Halt*),
an interruption of the course of events that "retards"
them and sets itself off (from them), which is incompat-
ible with any interest in the coherence of action.[81] As
one proceeds with words: they "want to be practiced,
that means first noticed, and later understood"; this
also applies to gestures.[82] Benjamin's text from 1939
proceeds from the presentation of speech—"'one waited
until the crowd had laid the sentences on the scale.' In

**78** Ibid.; see (2.), pp. 306–307 [*GS II*, pp. 538–539].
**79** Regarding the common understandings, see Petra Maria Meyer, "Die
Geste als intermediale Vergleichskategorie. Zur Umwertung von
Sprachgesten und Gestensprachen zwischen dem 18. und 20. Jahrhundert," in Christopher Balme and Markus Moninger, eds., *Crossing Media – Theater – Film – Fotographie – Neue Medien* (Munich:
ePODIUM, 2004), pp. 55–73, here p. 61.
**80** See also, very close to Benjamin, Giorgio Agamben, "Notes on Gesture," in Giorgio Agamben, *Infancy and History: The Destruction of
Experience* (London and New York: Verson, 1993), pp. 133–140. (This
essay also appears in Giorgio Agamben, *Means Without End: Notes on
Politics* [Minneapolis: University of Minnesota Press, 2000], pp. 49–
54.) Gestures' are conceived as becoming intransitive also by Henri
Bergson and Roland Barthes, see Meyer, "Die Geste als intermediale
Vergleichskategorie," pp. 56–57.
**81** See also (1.), pp. 3–5 [*GS II*, pp. 521–523]; until now it was missed,
"dass zwischen dem, was Brechts Idee des Gestus anzielt, und seinem
Konzept der Fabel [...] ein vielleicht sogar unüberbrückbarer Gegen-
satz bestehen könnte." Lehmann, *Das Politische Schreiben*, p. 231; see
also pp. 214–216, and Lehmann, *Brecht Lesen*, p. 159.
**82** Benjamin, "Bert Brecht," *GS II*, pp. 660–676, here 662, in English,
in Michael W. Jennings, Howard Eiland and Gary Smith, eds., *Walter Benjamin: Selected Writings, vol. 2, part 1, 1927–1930* (Cambridge
MA: Belknap Press of Harvard University Press, 2005), pp. 365–371.

short the play was interrupted" ("'abgewartet wurde, bis die Menge die Sätze auf die Waagschale gelegt hatte.' Kurz das Spiel wurde unterbrochen")—to the "interruption [as] one of the fundamental procedures of all form-giving."[83] In a gesture of casualness, Benjamin highlights this in citation: "To cite a text also means: to interrupt its context."[84] "The epic theater, which is organized by interruption, [is therefore] a citable (theater) in a specific sense" ("das epische Theater, das auf die Unterbrechung gestellt ist, [ist] ein in spezifischem Sinne zitierbares"), not only in the sense of the "citability of its texts," but rather with respect to the "gestures that have their place in the course of the play"[85] (even though Benjamin at the same time defined critique or criticism as a mode of *citation*, which as "a single medium has the survival of works").[86] With gesture, there is *no form* specified that critique (or criticism) could assume (as the proposal for "Critical Stances" would have it); rather, it is (to use a different formulation from the proposal), an "entry of form" and *as entry* it is disruptive, form-*giving*, but not an established form. It is an act of giving, that is suspended before becoming present.[87] This, that there isn't anything given or established, must also be

83   (2.), p. 305 [*GS* II, p. 535–536]; these are the first sentences under the subtitle "The citable gesture."
84   Ibid. [*GS* II, p. 536]
85   Ibid.
86   On "the highest level of the investigation" of critique/criticism, "the theory of citation" ["die Theorie des Zitats"] has to be developed. See Benjamin, ›Fragmente zur Kritik‹, *GS* VI, pp. 170–171 [fr. 135 and 136], also pp. 161–162, p. 169. In "Karl Kraus" (1931), Benjamin sets the task of "unbinding" the "force" ["Kraft"] in citation: "to expurgate, to destruct, the only one (force), which gives hope" ["zu reinigen, zu zerstören; die einzige, in der noch Hoffnung liegt"]. *GS* II, pp. 334–367, here p. 365; this relates to citation in Benjamin's concept of historiography, see Walter Benjamin, *Das Passagen-Werk*, *Gesammelte Schriften V* (hereinafter referred to as *GS V*), ed. Rolf Tiedemann (Frankfurt am Main: Suhrkamp, 1982), p. 595, note 113.
87   This is how Derrida conceives of the gift. See Jacques Derrida, *Given Time: I. Counterfeit Money* (Chicago and London: University of Chigaco Press, 1992) pp. 23–27, pp. 111–112, pp. 100–102, pp. 12–15, pp. 38–42; see also (referring to Jean-Luc Nancy) Lehmann, *Das Politische Schreiben*, pp. 367–368.

opposed to concepts of theory as a content that might be taught (or learned) (opposed to Brecht and even, at times, Benjamin).[88] The position of theory itself is affected. Precisely Brecht's *Lehrstücke*, "Dichtung für Übungszwecke,"[89] instead of using (the production of) *gestures* merely as a means to an end, make them "one" of their "most immediate ends."[90]

"'Making gestures citable' is the actor's [or the epic theater's] most important accomplishment; he must be able to space out his gestures as the typesetter spaces out words" ("seine Gebärden muß er sperren können, wie ein Setzer die Worte"),[91] according to Benjamin's stunning phrase, which models the theater according to the spatial arrangement of letters and the typeface of books.[92] Gestures are not only produced by means of the interruption of an action; rather, they interrupt the course, set themselves off, as an extended—retarding—interruption, as the typesetter spaces out the words by expanding the spaces between letters into interstices, which in turn separate the letters (from each other), in such a way that the words space out: *sperren*, or block the course

---

88 The "relation between theory and practice" refers to the "dialectic that reigns between teaching and learning comportment," (1.), pp. 11–13 [*GS* II, p. 529]. "The learning that the *Lehrstück* promises through the theater, does not consist in the transmission of contents, but rather in a stance [*Haltung*]: in a stance of trying [versuchenden] making it oneself and interpretating oneself." C. Menke, *Tragic Play*, p. 117 [*Gegenwart der Tragödie*, p. 145].

89 Cited in Müller-Schöll, *Das Theater des "konstruktiven Defaitismus"*, p. 325; it was revisable, see (2.), p. 306 [*GS* II, p. 537].

90 (2.), p. 305, "Was im epischen Drama überhaupt ein Kunstmittel der subtilsten Art ist, wird im besonderen Fall des Lehrstücks zu einem der nächsten Zecke." [*GS* II, p. 536].

91 (1.), p. 11 [*GS* II, p. 529].

92 Similarly, Benjamin characterizes the baroque Trauerspiele: "daß die Situationen nicht allzu oft, dann aber blitzartig wechselten wie der Aspekt des Satzspiegels, wenn man umblättert." *Ursprung des deutschen Trauerspiels, GS* I, p. 361; see also pp. 300–302. The "literalization" of the theater connects there: "Auch in die Dramatik ist die Fußnote und das vergleichende Blättern einzuführen." Brecht, cited in (1.), p. 7 [*GS* II, p. 525], instead of "Dekorationen zu Szenen" surfaces of representation are assembled: with "Beschriftungen," "Plakaten" (placards) relating to the different "Nummern." (1.) pp. 6–7 [*GS* II, pp. 524–525]; (2.), p. 303 [*GS* II, p. 533].

of the sentence by inserting intervals (in themselves) and setting themselves off from the course of the sentence: dissociating it. Gestures are made "citable" insofar as they are spaced out, so that they "bring to expression" the "relation of the performed action to the action given in performing as such," by interrupting it, and as the damming-up or stasis in the course.⁹³ *Gesperrt sperrend*: spaced out, barred, and blocking, they set themselves off as "citable."⁹⁴ And, conversely they are as such *given* by being remarked by their repetition or citation: therefore precisely where and insofar as they are not themselves.⁹⁵ Benjamin emphasizes in Brecht's *Mann ist Mann*: "One and the same gesture summons Galy Gay, first to change his clothes, and then to be shot, against the wall."⁹⁶ Set off in the repetition as gesture (that is) as citable, precisely there, where it (always already) will not have been able to be "one and the same" thing, it interrupts, by referring back and potentially ahead to what is to come (a repetition elsewhere, sometime); it is cit*able* as other (to itself). And, to give another example, Brecht's *Lehrstück*, *Die Maßnahme*, cites gestures in a kind of "play in the play,"⁹⁷ so that according to Benjamin, "not only the report from the communists, but

93 (1.), p. 11 [*GS* II, p. 529]; (2.), pp. 306–307 [*GS* II, pp. 538–539]. Benjamin points out Kraus's way of letterspacing in his citation of a notorious scene and line from Shakespeare's *Romeo and Juliet*: "die dort im G r a n a t baum saß" ("Karl Kraus," *GS* II, p. 363) and claims that Kraus's citations decontextualize the cited parts, at the same time destroying (the context) and saving (the quote).
94 See also Meyer, "Die Geste als intermediale Vergleichskategorie," pp. 60–61.
95 On the foreignness of the gesture to itself, insofar as it is repeated or lends itself to imitation, see also Bergson's observation in *Le rire* : "An imitation of our gestures can begin only where we cease to be ourselves. […] To imitate anyone is to separate the part of automatism that has fixed itself in him from his person." Henri Bergson, *Laughter: An Essay on the Meaning of the Comic* (New York: Macmillan, 1911), p. 33. The imitative process is split in itself from the beginning. See Müller-Scholl, *Das Theater des "konstruktiven Defaitismus"*, p. 156.
96 (1.), p. 12 [*GS* II, p. 530].
97 See C. Menke, *Tragic Play*, p. 118 [*Gegenwart der Tragödie*, p. 146].

through their acting ("Spiel") also a series of gestures of their comrade whom they took action against are brought before the party tribunal" ("nicht nur der Bericht der Kommunisten, sondern durch deren Spiel [werden] auch eine Reihe von Gesten des Genossen, gegen den sie vorgingen, vor das Parteitribunal gebracht").[98] In acting, playing what has happened before the tribunal and before the spectators in the theater, at each time one of those who have returned plays/acts (*spielt vor*) the absent one, whom they killed, for whose effacing they seek a judgement.[99] In playing/ acting out what occurred , they play/act their playing/acting out (it's a *Vorspielen* of *Vorspielen*)—ex-citing the dead,[100] the one they effaced—they play/act out (*vorspielen*) his gestures. They cite them and make them citable, perform them *as* citable, by showing them *as* gestures. "Making gestures citable" is here the "action performed." Since each time one of the returned agitators acts out before the tribunal the role of the absent person, of the one killed and disfigured far-away, who precisely *cannot* become present (again), in these gestures-citations—spacing these gestures in themselves—*otherness* prevails. And their entry, which in drama must be integrated as a transition *into* the performed dramatic person, is hindered as a problematic—provisional: conditional—passage *into* the performance (*Vorspielen*). Here we can recall the word *episodion* in its significance for the ancient theater, which names the entrance: *Zutritt*, of the protagonists as a stepping-into-the-way: as going between (the

98 (2.), p. 305 [*GS* II, p. 536].
99 See Lehmann, *Das Politische Schreiben*, pp. 256–257; also pp. 264–266; and Lehmann, "Die Rücknahme der Maßgabe," in Lehmann, *Brecht Lesen*, pp. 165–180.
100 This is to recall the (rhetorical) figure of ex-citare of the absent, of the dead, of the faceless, that is prosopopeia. The "separation of actors and spectators as the dead from the living" ["Spieler vom Publikum wie die Toten von den Lebendigen"] which has become inoperable ([1.], p. 1 [*GS* II, p. 519]; [2.], p. 307 [*GS* II, p. 539]) must indeed be held to be the threshold that *Die Maßnahme* folds onto/on the stage in its playing.

choruses), and the *Hinzutritt*: opening up another space of speech, which disruptively opens the *episodion* of each entry between the choruses' songs. The fissure or gap that opens up theatrical presentation is remarked, held up. And its "episodic character" is pointed out, given by framings as disruptive-retarding setting-offs of its parts,[101] so that the theatrical presentation is to be viewed as a disjunctive assemblage of dissociated separated "panels" ("Tafeln").[102]

Every (stage) entry has the character of an interrupting intrusion by a stranger. Benjamin cites this access, which as an interruption gives and sets off episodes, with the entrance of the stranger, who in interrupting a situation brings it to a standstill (*stillstellen*), which is exposed. The epic theater that is interested in "the state of things" ("Zustände") is *gestural,* because the "Zustände" are *not* available (objects) so that they, as naturalistic theorems would have it, only would have to be represented or imitated: *wiederzugeben* or *nachzuahmen*; rather, they had first to be "discovered" by being distanced.[103] The discovery, in Brecht's notorious vocabulary the "alienation" ("[Verfremdung] von Zuständen"), is performed as interrupting the "Abläufe": the course of things, is brought to a halt.[104] The sudden entry of a stranger is gesture, that interrupts the course of things, that inserts the distance of *another regard* and, in effecting a standstill, brings forth "a state" ("einen Zustand"), which one runs into:

101 (1.), pp. 4–6 [*GS* II, pp. 521–523]. With the "episodic character of the framework," the gesture intervenes against the dramatic action. ([2.], pp. 303–305 [*GS* II, pp. 533–535]). On the *Reyen* (a kind of German Baroque chorus) as "frames" for the acts as separated "Bestandstücke einer bloßen Schaustellung" ("component pieces of a mere exposition") see Benjamin, *Ursprung des deutschen Trauerspiels, GS* I, p. 367.
102 The theater as "a series of panels" ["eine Folge von Tafeln"], according to Brecht, cited in Müller-Scholl, *Das Theater des "konstruktiven Defaitismus"*, p. 165.
103 (2.), p. 303 [*GS* II, p. 533]; (1.), pp. 4–5 [*GS* II, pp. 521–522].
104 (2.), p. 304 [*GS* II, p. 535].

Das primitivste Beispiel: eine Familienszene. Plötzlich tritt da ein Fremder ein. Die Frau war gerade im Begriff, ein Kopfkissen zu ballen, um es nach der Tochter zu schleudern; der Vater im Begriff, das Fenster zu öffnen, um einen Schupo zu holen. In diesem Augenblick erscheint in der Tür der Fremde. "Tableau"—wie man um 1900 zu sagen pflegte. Das heißt: der Fremde stößt jetzt auf einen Zustand: zerknülltes Bettzeug, offenes Fenster, verwüstetes Mobiliar. Es gibt aber einen Blick, vor dem auch die gewohnteren Szenen des bürgerlichen Lebens sich nicht viel anders ausnehmen.

The most primitive example: a family scene. Suddenly a stranger enters. The wife had just been about to clench a pillow, in order to throw it to the daughter; the father had just been about to open the window, to call a policeman. In this moment the stranger appears in the door. A "tableau"—as one called it around 1900. That means: the stranger now runs into a situation: rumpled bedding, open window, ravaged furnishings. But there is a gaze before which even the familiar scenes of bourgeois life do not look much different.[105]

The state of things ("Zustände") that, in the moment ("Augenblick") of the interruption by a sudden entry or of the coming into the gaze of the spectators, is brought forth to a pause (*Innehalten*), and set off,[106] the spectators "cognize" ("erkennen") "as the real state of things ["als die wirklichen Zustände"], not [recognizing it] as in the theater of naturalism, smirking, but rather with wonder" ("nicht, wie auf dem Theater des Naturalismus, mit

---

**105** (1.), p. 5 [*GS* II, p. 522]; in the second text it is: "verstörte Mienen, offenes Fenster, […]" (2.), p. 305 [*GS* II, p. 535].

**106** It is the gaze, which makes those stop who come fleeing onto the scene: "Der Augenblick, da sie Zuschauern sichtbar werden, lässt sie einhalten. Der Flucht der dramatischen Personen gebietet die Szene halt." Benjamin, *Einbahnstraße*, p. 77. The gaze that constitutes the theater, and precedes all representation, allows the dislocated who are appearing to pause, interrupting the movement of fleeing.

Süffisance sondern mit Staunen").[107] This is made possible by the theater which keeps "incessantly a living and
productive awareness that it is theater." For the "wirkliche Zustände", the "real state of things" is cognizable
where and insofar as it precisely is not available as something to be *re*presented and cannot be imitated (*nach*-
geahmt), but rather insofar as it, to use a phrase from
Lehmann, is pre-mitated ("*vor*-geahmt"),[108] and only
"at the end, not at the beginning of this experiment"
("Versuch"), that is conducted tentatively (*probeweise*),
set on trial, in a revisable manner in the theater.[109] The
difference between cognition and recognition (*Wieder-
erkennen*, which nevertheless all cognition must also
always be) manifests itself in "wonder" ("Staunen").
"Wonder," as Benjamin's text from 1931 quotes in an
extraordinarily long passage of Brecht, is the effect of
(this) theater, because "that man ["der Mensch"] is not
completely ["ganz"], nor definitely ["endgültig"] to be
(re)cognized, but rather is not so easily exhausted, holding and hiding within him many possibilities ["viele
Möglichkeiten in sich Bergendes und Verbergendes"][...]
is a delighting cognition ["lustvolle Erkenntnis"]."[110] It
is made possible through the theater, which deals with
"the elements of the real in the sense of an experimental
disposition" ("im Sinne einer Versuchsanordnung"),[111]
whose "stance" or tenor is that all represented and all
those who are presenting are possible otherwise or possibly are not,[112] which is practiced in theater-playing,
in an acting in rehearsal (*Probehandeln*). In this way,
theater refers "productively" to itself as a *space of the*

107 (1.), p. 4 [*GS* II, p. 522]; see also (1.), p. 13 [*GS* II, p. 531], (2.), p. 304
[*GS* II, p. 535].
108 Lehmann, *Das Politische Schreiben*, p. 366.
109 (1.), p. 4 [*GS* II, p. 522]; see also (2.), p. 305 [*GS* II, p. 535].
110 (1.), p. 13 [*GS* II, p. 531].
111 (1.), p. 4 [*GS* II, p. 522].
112 (1.), p. 7 [*GS* II, p. 525].

*possible*,[113] in which what is presented and the present-ers are not self-contained, are not given as identical with themselves, in which every tentative or experimental arrangement, in which the "wirkliche Zustände" ("the real state of things") may be (re)cognized retrospec-tively, as always—and this applies to the events on the stage as to reality—an uncountable multitude of other "possibilities holding and hiding in themselves" (which have not become real), becomes cognizable.

"Der Zustand, den das epische Theater aufdeckt, ist die Dialektik im Stillstand" ("The state that the epic theater uncovers is dialectics at a standstill") as Benja-min puts it with that phrase he uses here for the first time for the theater's interrupting *Stillstellung* or put-ting-to-a-halt,[114] which he then works out in notations on history and historiography.[115] "Immanent dialecti-cal behavior is what in the 'state of things' is cleared up in a flash".[116] That is what effects the "wondering," the "Staunen," that Benjamin, motivated by the signi-fiers' relation between wondering: *Staunen*, and dam-ming-up: *Stauen*, characterizes as the "backwards tide" of a "swell in the real flow of life" ("Stauung im realen Lebensfluß"), in the "instant that its course comes to a standstill" ("Augenblick, da sein Ablauf zum Ste-

---

**113** In particular the Lehrstück discovers the "Möglichkeitsraum" in "setting free of potential, play, fantasy, provisionality, openness." Lehmann, *Das Politische Schreiben*, p. 368; see also C. Menke, *Tragic Play*, pp. 117–119 [*Gegenwart der Tragödie*, p. 145].

**114** (1.), pp. 12–13 [*GS* II, pp. 530–531]; see also Müller-Scholl, *Das Thea-ter des "konstruktiven Defaitismus"*, p. 160.

**115** Benjamin, "Über den Begriff der Geschichte," in: Walter Benjamin, *Werke und Nachlaß. Kritische Gesamtausgabe, vol. 19*, ed. Christophe Gödde and Henri Lonitz (Berlin: Suhrkamp, 2010), p. 104, pp. 102–105; see also *GS* I, p. 1236, p. 1250; *Das Passagen-Werk, GS* V, pp. 577–578 (N2a,3, N3, p. 1), p. 1001, p. 55.

**116** (1.), p. 12. "Immanent dialektisches Verhalten ist es, was im Zustand [...] blitzartig klargestellt wird". [*GS* II, p. 530]. Thus Galy Gay (in *Mann ist Mann*) is "nothing other than a stage of contradictions, which constitute our society." Brecht has "in a mediated, dialectical way" let "unsere Zustände", "our state of things", "criticize an-other, play their various elements logically against each other" (1.), p. 8 [*GS* II, p. 526].

hen kommt");[117] there, where at the same time—in the breaking-up of the metaphors—"the stream, current of things breaks itself" on the "cliff of wonder" ("Fels des Staunens"), that allows "Being [to] spray up high out of the bed of time and, shimmering, in an instant ["Nu"] [to] stand in emptiness, in order to bed it anew".[118] The *dynamis* of the rupture, in the damming-up as a broken movement trembles inside of the "Zustände" (state of things), brought forth by interrupting and retarding. The "mother" of "dialectics at a standstill," that is Benjamin's rather irritating metaphor, is "not the course of contradictions" but rather "gesture itself"; dialectics manifests itself "already in gestural elements, that underly every temporal sequence, and that one can only improperly call elements,"[119] and indeed because they are not indivisible elements, but rather are already split and doubled *in* themselves, differ from themselves, are not themselves and are not identical with themselves, but rather are *citable*. The force of the form-giving interruption putting to a halt (*stillstellend*) conveys itself to that which it gives, without this attaining any identical givenness. Benjamin conceives the "dialectics at a standstill" within the "dialectical image," as the "readable image," in the epistemology, or more precisely, the procedure of historiography[120] which ties "(re)cog-

---

117 (1.), p. 13, [*GS* II, p. 531]; "das Staunen ist diese Rückflut. Die Dialektik im Stillstand ist sein eigentlicher Gegenstand." There is an analogy in Benjamin's approach to the language of the Baroque: it is the inhibition, the barring, the damming ["Hemmung", "Stauung"] (in/ of the flow of language) that comes to expression in/by the expression's inhibition. *Ursprung des deutschen Trauerspiels, GS* I, pp. 376–378, pp. 383–384.

118 (1.), p. 13: "das Dasein aus dem Bett der Zeit hoch aufsprühen und schillernd einen Nu im Leeren stehen, um es neu zu betten," [*GS* II, p. 531]; here there is "no difference between a human life and a word." The broken metaphor continues and transforms Brecht's cited verses ("Beharre nicht auf der Welle, / Die sich an deinem Fuß bricht, solange er / Im Wasser steht, werden sich / Neue Wellen an ihm brechen.").

119 (1.), p. 12.

120 Benjamin, *Das Passagen-Werk, GS* V, p. 570, pp. 576–578, pp. 591–592.

nizability," as "readability," to citation, which rips out and makes readable what has been (*das Gewesene*) in its broken bits cited into the text of the present.[121] As in a flash, the "readable image," that is the "historical object," appears in the "now of readability" ("Jetzt der Lesbarkeit"),[122] that must be grasped as the moment: *Augenblick*, of (re)cognizability of a constellation, and that is in danger of being missed "already in the next moment."[123] The so-called "image" *is* "dialectics at a standstill," "in its interior" a "field of tension" that is polarized into "pre- and post-history by the effects of 'actuality' ("Aktualität")."[124]

If the gestural theater is characterized by Benjamin as "a way of acting that directs him [the actor] to cognition" ("eine Art zu spielen, die ihn [den Schauspieler] auf Erkenntnis anweist"), this, which is "produced"[125] in the play-acting or theater-playing, is nothing one would have already known in advance, or which could be stated. But here cognition is a matter of performing gestures of opening, breaches that hold open ruptures in the inside, turns and gaps.[126] If the actors, according to the text from 1939, "insist on presenting the one reflect-

---

**121** Ibid., p. 595 [N11,3]. What has been "is" not what one might be used to conceiving as facts. See Benjamin, "Über den Begriff der Geschichte," and compare Werner Hamacher, "JETZT. Benjamin zur historischen Zeit," in Helga Geyer-Ryan, ed., *Perception and Experience in Modernity* (Amsterdam and New York: Rodopi, 2002), pp. 147–183. In English: "'Now': Walter Benjamin on Historical Time," in Andrew Benjamin, ed., *Walter Benjamin and History* (London and New York: Continuum, 2005), translation by N. Rosenthal, pp. 38–68.
**122** Benjamin, *Das Passagen-Werk, GS* V, N1,1, N3,1, N9,7; see also (1.), p. 12 [*GS* II, p. 530].
**123** Benjamin, *Das Passagen-Werk, GS* V, p. 592 [N9,7].
**124** Ibid., pp. 594–596 [N10,3; N10a,2; N10a,3; N11,5], pp. 587–588 [N7a,1; N7,7]; pp. 577–578.
**125** (1.), p. 11 [*GS* II, p. 528].
**126** The Lehrstück places more weight on "the reality and the occurrence of the act of representation itself" than on the completion of representation and content. Lehmann, *Das Politische Schreiben*, p. 368. That, as an act without completion, contradicts Austin's concept of performatives. See Werner Hamacher, "Das eine Kriterium für das, was geschieht. Aristoteles: *Poetik*. Brecht: 'Kleines Organon'," in Ebert et al., *Theater als Kritik*, pp. 19–36.

ing (about his *part*)" ("[sich] nicht nehmen lassen, den [über seinen *Part*] Nachdenkenden vorzumachen"),[127] they do so insofar as—with their distance to what is represented and at the same time to "the way in which it is represented," "in their […] acting" ("in ihrem Spiel"), and in its difference from itself—they display the "intervals" which give the spectators occasion (*Anhalt*) to take "critical stances" ("kritische Stellungnahmen"): between/*in* the theater-playing that is doubled and split in itself, which inserts spectatorship into itself, turns actors into spectators, so that spectatorship sees itself let into the acting [*Schauspielen*] as *other*.[128] The (Brechtian) task, which the text from 1931 is dissecting, to bring the "Denkenden" (the one who is "thinking") to "existence on the stage" ("Dasein auf der Bühne"), is on the one hand solved by an "impartial third one" ("inappropriate" according to the ordinary concept of the theater from the perspective of drama).[129] On the other hand, distance *to itself* (and also to one's own action)[130] is taken and given—opened—in and as behavior (*Verhalten*) *in* play-acting (*Schauspielen*), that refers critically to the "actions on the stage" that it shows and to itself, *as* this showing (*Zeigen*). Theater-playing ("Theaterspielen") is a "critical practice," not by virtue of something that may be said or meant, but rather by means of the giving of distance as a gift, through which it becomes theoretical, (potentially) everywhere, by referring everything that is shown elsewhere, to the

---

**127** (2.), p. 307 [*GS* II, p. 538].

**128** In particular in the Lehrstück: "*The act of spectating is brought into the play*. The actors ["Spieler"] […] are actors ["Akteure"] and spectators at once and thus strictly speaking are acting spectators and spectating actors." Lehmann, *Das Polische Schreiben*, p. 372. This is formulated the other way around in Benjamin: "Every spectator will be able to become an actor ["Mitspieler"]." (2.), p. 305 [*GS* II, p. 536].

**129** (1.), pp. 5–7 [*GS* II, pp. 523–525]; the actor "finds himself in the epic theater by the side ["an der Seite"] of the philosopher." (1.), p. 12 [*GS* II, p. 530].

**130** One's own action is also interrupted. (1.), p. 3 [*GS* II, p. 521].

other, that it is not, to the fissure that makes it possible and that the gesture holds open.

It is thus a matter not so much of "critique as praxis," as was suggested for "Critical Stances," but rather of theater *as* critical praxis, as the setting-apart of acting in itself, as a praxis that splits/doubles itself: *entzweit sich*, from and in itself,[131] that *as* the *act* of the performing performs the action (supposedly identical with itself), which is staged, *as* split/doubled in itself. The theater can be called *critical* because, according to C. Menke, with its non-identity it counters the repression of the non-identical, through which alone the supposedly self-contained identity, and the necessity of the world asserts itself as given.[132] Identity *is* solely through the exclusion, always undertaken again, or through the repression of differences from itself, of hidden (other) possibilities (which split actions, figures, and worlds in themselves), through the making-forgotten of non-form for the sake of the supposedly self-contained, "finished" form,[133] through the repression of the margins of (other)

131 Praxis "reflected and thereby transformed in drama" opens "a tension in the inside of praxis": between completion and possibility. C. Menke, "Das Spiel des Theaters und die Veränderung der Welt," p. 45, p. 41. But C. Menke develops the "paradox" of theater-playing as that of playing (something to someone) [Vorspielen] and imitating something (pp. 37–48).

132 "The critique of the theater goes against the defense, the immunization of life against the transformation that it experiences in the theater." "The theater criticizes [...] the immunization against paradox, and thus against the theater; for the theater is the implementation of paradox." C. Menke , "Das Spiel des Theaters und die Veränderung der Welt", pp. 45–46. Since the "praxis reflected and thereby transformed in drama" creates a "'tension' on the inside of praxis" between completion and possibility (p. 45, p. 41), "theater fundamentally *changes* both elements, which it joins together through the paradox of its action. The theater brings forth in its bringing-forth of form, and indeed through its paradox, an *other play* and indeed *another life*. That always already happens when there is theater. [...] The theater transforms life (or the world)." (p. 44).

133 Playing is, with Nietzsche, the taking-place of form-giving out of formlessness, in which the forms, in becoming, dissolve themselves again and again, and as "bringing forth out of the abyss of formlessness" "meet the abyss, the emptiness and the potential of formlessness." C. Menke ties this to imitation [Nachahmen]: in the play, form

possibilities, cut off by the figuration, for the sake of the supposedly realized figure. The theatrical taking of distance of the presentation and of those presenting/acting to/in themselves contests self-identity and completion, refers the represented or performed action on the stage, just like the act of performing (suspending it in its becoming), to their *margins*, refers form to (excluded) *other* possibilities (not having become reality), to the *shadows* of the otherwise-possible, excluded in every instance of form-giving, which accompanies the respectively constituted form and from which the form will not have been able to release itself (completely), which (according to Benjamin and Brecht) it "holds" [*birgt*] in its interior, so that conversely form is divided and virtualized by it. The potential being other of what is provisionally: *probeweise*, cited from the space of the possible forms part of "what is shown" in its difference from showing, as its gaps, ambivalences, ambiguities; as its trembling.[134]

What is at stake in theater-playing is not distinction that ends in judgment, as is the case for criticism,[135] but rather it is "critical" as performing or as taking place that will have no instance installed that may state or

is the imitated "form of life" ("Das Spiel des Theaters und die Veränderung der Welt," p. 41). But if one would suppose that what is represented finds its form given in reality as that which can be imitated, "the imitation [Nachahmung] of another, preceding form" (p. 42) is however just a *retroactive* effect, as is with Benjamin the "recognizability" of "real states" (der "wirklichen Zustände").

134 Lehmann, *Das Politische Schreiben*, pp. 376–378; "the trembling of its contours still reveals from which inner proximity they have torn themselves in order to become visible" ["das Zittern ihrer Umrisse verrät immer noch, aus welcher innigen Nähe sie sich gerissen haben, um sichtbar zu werden"]. (1.), p. 7 [*GS* II, p. 525]; see also Müller-Scholl, *Das Theater des "konstruktiven Defaitismus,"* pp. 162–164.

135 See also C. Menke, "Das Spiel des Theaters und die Veränderung der Welt," pp. 37–38, p. 48. Still, what theater does is "critique": "The theater criticizes [...] the immunization against paradox" (p. 46). Therefore "the insight that can be gained from reflection (Nachdenken) about the theater for a theater of critical judgments [is]: that one can criticize in the name of paradox, decide in the name of undecidability." (p. 48).;

judge, but which rather consists (undecidably) *in* the event or *in* the becoming[136] in which it does not coincide with itself: potentially at any moment, in every place, it differs from itself and opens gaps. The behavior or acting (*Verhalten*) *in* "theater-playing" or acting, the "stance" as *Haltung* toward acting *in* playing, contests the instituting of such instances.[137] Their *halt* is without place, it *comes* from a (non)place of difference— and gives the interrupting intervals as an occasion and *An-Halt* for "critical" spectatorship, attaining no unity.

Therefore, instead of "criticism as form," however, neither should there be expected a "scene of criticism," if the critical procedure wants to do justice to the gestural theater and thereby to Benjamin's theoretical reach. After all, the scene (as homogeneous as it may be considered to be) is not itself; after all, the entry's place is (only) given by a separation, a cutting by the *skēnē*, that at the same time produces other spaces of what is secluded, not visible, and not knowable, out of which one may come forth, because one can exit or disappear into them. It is this separation that relates the place of entry or the scene to the absent, so that the scene is split *in* itself, not homogeneous, not self-contained,[138] no established place for the grand entrance of criticism or

---

136 "'[E]s gibt' [...] ist im Modus des Entstehens da;" "[es] besteht in einem Ankommen." Lehmann, *Das Politische Schreiben*, p. 368, (and referring to Nancy) p. 367.

137 According to Benjamin, Brecht attempts "to move [the one thinking – den Denkenden,] to existence on the stage" ["zum Dasein auf der Bühne zu bewegen"], whose wild genealogy he presents as "the search for the untragic hero" – in the not-easy-to-read relation to the wise person as "undramatic hero" ([1.], pp. 4–6, p. 8 [*GS* II, pp. 522– 524, p. 526]; [2.], p. 304, [*GS* II, p. 534]). Keuner, "der Denkende" (the one who is thinking), would have, according to Brecht's recommendation, "to be carried lying down onto the stage (so little is he drawn to it)" ([1.], p. 5 [*GS* II, p. 523]); Plato led the (untragic) sage (der Weise) onto the threshold of the stage ([1.], p. 6 [*GS* II, p. 524]).

138 See also Bettine Menke, "Agon und Theater. Fluchtwege, die Sch(n)eidung und die Szene – nach den aitiologischen Fiktionen F.C. Rangs und W. Benjamins," in Bettine Menke and Juliane Vogel, eds., *Flucht und Szene. Perspektiven und Formen eines Theaters der Fliehenden* (Berlin: Theater der Zeit, 2018), pp. 203–241, here pp. 206–211.

of judgment. The gestural theater holds up the disruptive opening act, hinders its closure; it has an "episodic character,"[139] so that the theatrical presentation (quite different from any supposition of dramatic coherence of action) is a disjunctive assemblage (as in other forms of that theater-kin, whose "mule track" "today—however unkempt and wild"—emerges in the Brechtian theater). When in the gestural theater (as in *Die Maßnahme*/*The Measures Taken*) the playing/acting (*Vorspielen*) of the entry to the stage is played (*vorgespielt*) or performed as a disruptive, citational form-giving, then the transgression of the threshold to the "delimited space" of playing/acting, to the "podium" of the stage ("on" the stage)[140] or merely (as in Tabori's staging of Beckett's *Endgame*) to a field of a rehearsal stage marked off with stage-chalk, is suspended and held up, the threshold is extended into the theatrical timespan: *Zeit-Raum*. The act of giving, the fissure or gap, that it opens, is held open: *in* the performed—played and shown—provisional (*probeweise*) transition into playing, and *in* this transition from showing into what is shown, which does not detach itself from *showing* that performs/shows and that is performed/shown: it is not completed, closed up in itself. The absent (one) can gain no presence in the transition to the stage: the separation of "the dead from

---

**139** To the "episodic character of framing" ([1.], pp. 4–6 [*GS* II, pp. 521–523]; [2.], pp. 303–305 [*GS* II, pp. 533–535]) corresponds the fact that the "episodic theater", "comparable to the images of the film strip", "advances in jolts" ("den Bildern des Filmstreifens vergleichbar, in Stößen vorrückt"). Similarly, in the allegorical mourning play, its action advances into the allegorical framing ["Rahmen"]: always altered "in jolts" ("in den die Handlung stets verändert, stoßweise einrückt"); it is thus characterized by "the intermittent rhythm of (interrupting) ever-repeated pausing, sudden reversal and new stiffening" ("die intermittierende Rhythmik eines beständigen Einhaltens, stoßweisen Umschlagens und neuen Erstarrens"). Benjamin, *Ursprung des deutschen Trauerspiels*, *GS* I, p. 373); on the assemblage of the allegorical interludes (*Reyen*) and the acts that the interludes frame and separate see p. 301, p. 367.

**140** (1.), p. 1 [*GS* II, p. 519]; in the second text the last section reads: "The theater on the podium" ([2.], p. 307 [*GS* II, p. 539]).

the living"[141] remains to be recalled as the self-foreign-ness of the gesture, as non-self-presence of the theater. The "arrangement" on the "podium," which is the task of the gestural theater thereby setting itself into relation to the stage, will only ever be experimental (*versuchs-weise*), tentative, provisional, (always still and again) revisable. The gesture of form-giving remains in reser-vation before and against every givenness (also that of reality). It will, detaching itself from the darkness of the formless, and of the contingent bodies, recall the fissure (that makes possible): in "the trembling of the contours" ("Zittern der Umrisse")[142]—in the shadows of the other-wise possible, which virtualize what is shown.

*Translated by Jason Kavett*

---

**141** (1.), p. 1 [*GS* II, p. 519; (2.), p. 307 [*GS* II, p. 539].
**142** (1.), p. 7 [*GS* II, p. 525].

Mimmi Woisnitza

# The Stakes of the Stage

Piscator's Scenography as a Practice of Critique and
Benjamin's Discontent with the "Zeittheater"

Walter Benjamin's two studies on epic theater, written 1931 and 1939, are important sources for an understanding of Bertolt Brecht's conception of dramaturgy
and acting as well as for Benjamin's understanding of
theater in general.[1] It is well established that, in these
studies, Benjamin worked out the deictic function of
Brecht's acting technique and the political significance
of gestural theater, in which "'the performer' [*der Zei-
gende*]—or the actor as such—'is made visible' [*gezeigt
werde*]," and which Benjamin presents as analogous to
Marxist pedagogy.[2] That is to say, the two studies also
bear witness to a turbulent and crisis-ridden historical
period, during which artistic practices were increasingly

---

1    Walter Benjamin: "What is Epic Theatre?" (1) and (2), in Walter
     Benjamin, *Understanding Brecht*, ed. Stanley Mitchell, trans. Anna
     Bostock (London and New York: Verso, 1998), pp. 1–14 and 15–22
     respectively. The first version was commissioned by Siegfried Kra-
     cauer in 1931 as a review for the *Frankfurter Zeitung* of the recent
     performance of Brecht's *Mann ist Mann*; the revised second version
     was published anonymously in 1939 in the bimonthly publication
     *Maß und Wert*. Cited in the following as "Epic Theatre" (1) and
     "Epic Theatre" (2). If not specifically referenced otherwise, all trans-
     lations from German texts by Mimmi Woisnitza.
2    "The general educational approach of Marxism is determined by the
     dialectic at work between the attitude of teaching and that of learn-
     ing: something similar occurs in epic theatre with the constant dia-
     lectic between the action which is shown on the stage and the atti-
     tude of showing an action on the stage." Benjamin, "Epic Theatre"
     (1), p. 11. In her essay in this volume, Bettine Menke suggests that the
     notion of a gestural theater which Benjamin develops with regard
     to Brecht's epic theater implicates a more general sense of theater as
     critical practice.

confronted with the question of their ability to intervene in society. In this article, I seek to expand on the
intersection of theory and practice in Benjamin's studies
and discuss them in the context of the theater culture in
Berlin at the time. My starting point is Benjamin's initial
assessment that the stage had become a "podium"—a
well-noted observation that provides the framework for
both studies, in the literal sense of the word. While the
1931 manuscript begins with the insight that the contemporary theater of the "podium" can be "more accurately defined in relation to the stage than to the play,"[3]
the essay that Benjamin eventually published in an exile
magazine in 1939, shortly before the outbreak of the Second World War, ends with the sentence: "The didactic
play and epic theatre set out to occupy [*sich einrichten
auf*] this podium."[4] What in Benjamin's rather militant
reflections from 1931 represents the actual possibility
of a new, politically effectual theater of the "podium,"
offers a more sober outlook in 1939, from an ominous
present into an unpredictable future that concerns politics just as much as the theater.

A first indication of the particular theatrical practice that Benjamin invokes with the "podium" can
be inferred from the opening lines of the 1931 manuscript: The contemporary "podium" stage, Benjamin
writes, distinguishes itself by the fact that the constitutive element of the bourgeois theater of illusions, the
"abyss which separates the actors from the audience like
the dead from the living" and "whose silence heightens the sublime in drama, whose resonance heightens
the intoxication of opera" has lost its function.[5] It is
exactly there, Benjamin continues, on this "podium,"
albeit "elevated," but not separated from the audience
by Diderot's *fourth wall* or by Wagner's hidden orches-

---

3   See Benjamin, "Epic Theatre" (1), p. 1.
4   Benjamin, "Epic Theatre" (2), p. 22.
5   Benjamin, "Epic Theatre" (1), p. 1.

tra pit, that it is necessary to establish oneself [*sich ein-richten*]. From this determination of the current "state" [*Lage*] of the theater, the question follows whether a drama for such a "podium" is possible and, if so, what kind. This line of questioning provides the grounds for Benjamin's reflections on Brecht's epic theater in the early manuscript. He differentiates it from the so-called "Zeittheater," a trend of Berlin's contemporary theater at that time.[6]

This prerequisite of the stage as podium in the form of a new, decidedly anti-illusionist theater practice, as well as the reference to "Zeittheater,"[7] bring to mind another Berlin theater-maker whom Benjamin must have known about, but notably never refers to by name: Erwin Piscator. To be sure, a clear attribution of the term "Zeittheater" is difficult in this case, since Piscator distanced himself from certain kinds of "Zeittheater" in an article that same year, 1931.[8] However, his documentary theater practice, which explicitly aims at radical contem-

6 Ibid., p. 2.
7 Piscator positions himself with caution in relation to the notion of "Zeittheater" in *The Political Theatre* (1929) and then again in the essay "Die Krise des Zeittheaters," (1931): "As the 'Zeittheater', the drama of current events [*Aktualitätsdrama*] political theater became commercial. It goes without saying that I draw a clear dividing line between this kind of theater and my own, otherwise the essence of all of my work would be falsified. It is one thing for a theater to turn topical problems into 'art'; it is another thing for a theater to take art and use it in the struggle to achieve important political results." Erwin Piscator, *The Political Theatre: A History, 1914–1929*, ed. Hugh Rorrison (New York: Avon, 1978), p. 323.
8 A more precise investigation of how conceptions of temporal relations, contemporaneity and the documentary manifest themselves in Piscator's theater practice and how this relates to the conceptions of "Zeittheater" (translated here as theatre of current events) and "Zeit-stück," (translated here as current event play) still needs to be carried out. It should be noted that the often unquestioned connection between the term "Zeittheater" and Piscator is first and foremost the result of Manfred Brauneck and Peter Stertz's editorial decision to use the title "Zeittheater" for the new edition of a selection of Piscator's writings. See Erwin Piscator, *Zeittheater."Das politische Theater" und weitere Schriften von 1915–1966*, ed. Manfred Brauneck and Peter Stertz (Hamburg: Rowohlt, 1986). Thus said, it can be assumed that Benjamin refers to the discursive context of Berlin theater practice which Piscator had decisively influenced.

poraneity, is clearly related to the term. I thus propose to read Benjamin's studies on epic theater as an implicit discussion of Piscator's theater practice.

The claim that it was the "Zeittheater" "in the form of political [thesis] plays [*Thesenstücke*]" that, until then, had represented the only possibility of "doing justice" [*gerecht zu werden*] to the "podium" suggests that Benjamin's point of reference was the dramatic structure rather than the concrete staging practice. A key addendum, however, obscures this apparent distinction: "The functional relations between stage and audience, text and performance, producer and actor remained almost [*fast*] unchanged."[9] "Text" here appears as a register of theatrical realization alongside other elements whose restructuring is obviously of great importance to Benjamin. What does "almost" refer to here? To what extent might Benjamin's narrowing of the "Zeittheater" to "political Thesenstücke" be insufficient? Considering that here, as in much of Benjamin's writing, it is difficult to separate his theory formation from its historical context, what could have led Benjamin to this assessment in 1931, when Piscator had already given up his theatrical endeavors in Berlin (and where he would not return for the next 30 years, as it turned out)? And what may have prompted Benjamin to withdraw his implicit criticism of Piscator's theater practice in the version published in 1939?

Citing examples from Piscator's stagings, I will elaborate on the hypothesis that his scenographic experiments go beyond "political Thesenstücke" in so far as they—much like what Benjamin finds in Brecht's epic theater—put on display the act of theatrical *showing* as such, or rather its crisis, if not through the dramaturgy of text and performance, then via scenography and stage technology. Piscator's productions at non-theatrical venues, particularly in the early 1920s, fundamentally questioned the exclusive bourgeois theater space, its insti-

---

**9** Benjamin, "Epic Theatre" (1), p. 2.

tutionalization and the established relationship to the audience. This ultimately led to a radical rethinking of the theatrical conception of space and of stage design, based on principles of montage, during the time Piscator worked at established theaters; a rethinking, in other words, that provided the foundation for the notion of the stage as "podium." Piscator's increasing dramaturgical use of media and technology not only had an atmospheric effect. Light, sound, film, and projected images increasingly appeared as stage elements that would deliberately interrupt the dramatic plot. These technological effects began to interact, if not compete, with the performers on stage, and thereby opened up a new, dynamic stage language, as well as a new logic of representation with a deliberately socio-critical function.[10] Thus, as we will see, the formal elements of Piscator's stage have neither a purely representational nor a merely symbolic function. It is in the principles of construction and montage, of quotation, and of interruption that the constitutive situatedness of the stage-action, and thus its social localization, finds manifestation.

## Piscator's Stage Practice and the Act of Showing

It is possible to establish an at least indirect relationship between Benjamin and Piscator through the lens of a woman who knew both Brecht and Benjamin, and who had also repeatedly collaborated with Piscator.[11]

---

10  Joachim Fiebach notes the pivotal cultural and historical significance of Piscator's stage language. See Joachim Fiebach, "Piscator, Brecht und Medialisierung," in *Bertolt Brecht und Erwin Piscator. Experimentelles Theater im Berlin der Zwanziger Jahre*, ed. Michael Schwaiger (Vienna: Brandstätter, 2004), pp. 112–126, especially p. 113–114.

11  Lacis met Piscator and Brecht through her partner Bernhard Reich during their first trip to Berlin in 1922. She subsequently worked with Brecht on various occasions in Berlin and Munich. See Karin Burk, *Kindertheater als Möglichkeitsraum. Untersuchungen zu Walter Benjamins "Programm eines proletarischen Kindertheaters"* (Berlin: Transcript, 2015), pp. 20–22.

Alongside theater projects in Orel, Moscow, and Riga in the 1920s, the Latvian theater practitioner Asja Lacis visited Berlin in the mid-1920s, where she contributed to the exchange between Soviet and German avant-garde theater. Strongly influenced by Vsevolod Meyerhold's theatrical experimentation, poet Vladimir Mayakovsky's agitprop endeavors and the emerging Soviet documentary film practice, she was committed to the idea of a Bolshevik-oriented, proletarian theater. It is therefore not surprising that she quickly found her place in the Berlin theater scene, which had been infused with revolutionary ideas since the end of the First World War and where she was soon acquainted with Piscator and Brecht. In the summer of 1924, Lacis met Benjamin on the artists' resort island of Capri and, a few years later, established contact between Brecht and Benjamin, initiating the renowned exchange between the two.[12] Letters and memoirs testify not only to her intense personal and intellectual relationship with Benjamin, but also to her demonstrable influence on his thinking at the time.[13] Various references indicate that Benjamin's friendship with Lacis must have provided important input for his reflections on contemporary political theater.[14] With this constellation in mind, it is hard to conceive that Lacis' encounters with Piscator, in the early 1920s at the Berlin Volksbühne and in Moscow between 1931 and 1933 as the assistant production manager on

---

12  See Jean-Michel Palmeier, *Walter Benjamin. Lumpensammler, Engel und bucklicht Männlein. Ästhetik und Politik bei Walter Benjamin* (Frankfurt am Main: Suhrkamp, 2006), p. 338–339. Lacis and Benjamin's encounter was discredited by Scholem and Adorno to such an extent that it was ultimately written out of his biography over several decades. See Burk, Kindertheater, pp. 29–31.
13  Lacis contributed to a number of Benjamin's essays, such as "Naples" and the "Passagenwerk."
14  "I received letters from Walter. [...]ut he also wrote about Berlin's greatest theatrical productions (Jessner, Piscator, Brecht)." Asja Lacis, *Revolutionär im Beruf. Berichte über proletarisches Theater, über Meyerhold, Brecht, Benjamin und Piscator*, ed. Hildegard Brenner (Munich: Rogner und Bernhard, 1971), p. 71.

his film project *Der Aufstand der Fischer von St. Barbara* (1934), would not have made their way into her correspondence with Benjamin.

In light of the concrete theater practice that Benjamin alludes to with his reference to the "podium stage" and his critique of the "Zeittheater," it is worth taking a look at the description of Piscator's "proletarian theatre" that Lacis provides in *Revolutionäres Theater in Deutschland* (1935, Moscow).[15] She particularly emphasizes the importance of the political revues that Piscator organized on behalf of the KPD at various venues of Berlin's local political scene,[16] the exceptional "success and effect" of which she describes as "unprecedented" in an increasingly depoliticized theater culture:

> "The bourgeoisie now had to acknowledge this 'proletarian theater' and admit that something new and remarkable was offered here, from a formal point of view as well."[17]

From her succinct and detailed accounts, for example of the *Rote Revue Rummel* (1924), it becomes clear that the "proletarianization" of theater that Piscator was striving for was inseparable from a new conception of the theater space, including the stage. The review by theater critic Jakob Altmaier, quoted in full below (and in Lacis' article), clearly indicates the profound impact that this new theatrical form had on the audience, in terms of both dramaturgy, and the conditions of production and

---

15  Lacis' "Revolutionäres Theater in Deutschland" (1935), originally in Russian, appeared in German translation in the second part of Lacis, *Revolutionär im Beruf*, pp. 81–120. All translations from this volume are my own.
16  Piscator's "Proletarian Theatre" took place at venues dedicated to local culture and politics, such as the Festsaal in the Hasenheide, the Gesellschaftshaus Moabit or the Pharussälen in what was then "der rote" Wedding, a regular meeting place of the KPD.
17  "Piscator, Initiator des Agitprop-Theaters," in Lacis, *Revolutionär im Beruf*, pp. 81–86, here p. 85.

performance. According to Altmaier, "the masses pil-grimaged" to the *Rote Revue*:

> When we got there, hundreds were standing on the street, demanding to be let in to no avail. The workers fought for seats. The hall was crowded and narrow, and the air could knock you out. But their faces beamed and glowed after the start of the performance. Music. The lights went out. Silence. In the audience two people argue, people are frightened, the quarrelling duo moves down the middle aisle, the ramp brightens, and the two emerge from below and appear in front of the curtain. They are two workers talking about their predicament. A gentleman in a top hat joins them. Bourgeois. He has his own world view and invites the disputants to spend an evening with him. Curtain up! Scene one. And now it happens in quick succession. Acker-straße—Kurfürstendamm. Tenements—champagne halls. Blue gold clad porter—begging war cripple. Potbelly and fancy watch chain. Match seller and cigarette butt collector. Swastika—Femicide—What are you doing with your knee, dear Hans—Hail you with the laurel wreath. Between the scenes: Screen, cinema, statistical numbers, images! New scenes. The begging war victim is thrown out by the porter. A gathering in front of the restaurant. Workers force their way in and demolish the hall. The audience joins in. They whistle, scream, romp, cheer, throw their arms up and help out in their minds … unforgettable![18]

Altmaier's account of his experience testifies to the enormous turnout for the *Rote Revue*, tens of thousands of proletarians gathered in Berlin's various local district assembly rooms, making the performances a mass attraction that already indicates a change in the institutional framework. Furthermore, the description makes tangible the unconventional dramaturgy of the production. The rapid sequence of scenes seems to be inscribed in the

**18**  Ibid., p. 83.

staccato of sentence fragments. Particularly noteworthy for our context is the report of the production's beginning, which emerges out of the audience "in front of the curtain"; a movement that "frightened people." The initial stage entrance thus did not occur from a theatrical "off" behind the stage, but from the "off" of the spectator's reality.[19] That is to say, the opening sequence can be called performative in that it constituted a new form of theatrical space. The scene ostentatiously abolished the separation between the audience and the stage—a stage that, at such non-theatrical venues, in fact already served as a podium.

With Benjamin, it can be concluded that this initial act of quarreling, which the "liminal figure" of the bourgeois representative (the gentleman with the top hat) eventually guides into the space of theatrical action, is precisely what *shows* [*zeigen*] the transgression of the gap between stage and audience. At the same time, the theatrical space itself is identified as the venue for *showing* [*Zeigen*] the conditions that the Russian and later Soviet proletarian movement, drawing on Marx, were concerned with: When the reality of the workers in the auditorium is transposed into theatrical reality, with its bourgeois connotations, what becomes apparent is the very act of exposing the present conditions, their outlines and forms.[20] The transparency of the very act of

19  The performance thus proceeds from a place that already belongs to the "here and now" of the spectators and actors, whereby the shift in register results from the theatrical framing of the literal passage onto the stage. See Bettine Menke, "On/Off," in *Auftreten. Wege auf die Bühne*, ed. Juliane Vogel and Christopher Wild (Berlin: Theater der Zeit, 2014), pp. 180–188, especially p. 180.

20  Following Karl Marx's claim that "reality must itself strive towards thought" in order to reconcile the theoretical foundations of the revolution with the practical needs of the people, Vladimir Ilyevich Lenin calls for an appropriate "tribune" and an "auditorium" for "arousing in every section of the population that is at all politically conscious a passion for *political* exposure" in his essay "Where to Begin?" (1901), which was fundamental to the proletarian avant-garde movement. See Karl Marx, "Contribution to the Critique of Hegel's Philosophy of Law. Introduction," in *Marx and*

theatricalizing the reality of the proletarian spectators thus results in the persistence of both the link between and the differentiation of audience and stage. The separation, in other words, is bridged at the same time that it is marked. This operation implicates a dialectical logic that echoes Benjamin's notion of gestural "setting apart" [*Auseinandersetzung*] between that which is shown and the act of showing [*Gezeigtem* and *Zeigen*].²¹ The initial conflict in the *Rote Revue* is brought onto the stage as a kind of quotation that lifts the struggle from the context of everyday life without completely abandoning the reference to its original context. In both Realism and Naturalism, the connection to reality was claimed from within the self-contained dramatic space. Piscator's decision, by contrast, to showcase the very act of *mise-en-scène* of the workers' struggle, pointedly reveals the technique of *showing* and display, i.e. of theatrical practice per se, in its "manifest relation" to the off of the audiences' lived realities.²²

A similar mode of citational representation applies to the radically new use of news media on the stage, which brought everyday reality in as quotations, as Altmaier puts it, that interrupt the plot: "between the scenes: Screen, cinema, statistical numbers, images." The dramatic scenes were thus confronted with signs of reality, the referentiality of which seemed undeniable while the theatrical context rendered them contingent at the

*Engels Collected Works*, Vol. 3 (London: Lawrence & Wishart, 1975), pp. 175–187, pp. 182–183; V.I. Lenin, "Where to Begin?," in *Lenin Collected Works*, Vol. 5 (Moscow: Progress Publishers, 1960), pp.13–24, here p. 21. (Originally published in *Iskra* 4, May 1901).

21  Benjamin, "Epic Theatre" (1), p. 11–12.
22  Compare Menke, "On/Off," p. 184: "Every performance is a crossing of a threshold into the dramatic frame, that which is excluded and cut off by the framing, that which is off, is carried with it and brought in, in relation to or as an attitude towards that which it must develop. This is the potential crisis of the performance: as a manifest relation of everything that shows itself in the performance space towards the off beyond and on this side of the frame, the factual off of the stage, the backstage, or its back side, as well as the off of representation, the amorphous."

same time. Although on the one hand, these "images" vouched for an extra-theatrical reality, on the other hand they demonstrated the medialization of all reality, and insisted on the possibility for material intervention. The use of editing, cutting, and montage—the techniques of filmic representation—support this insight.[23] It can thus be said that Piscator's scenography created new constellations of both extra- and inner-theatrical realities that aimed at mobilizing the audience to participate in a communal theater experience that radically broke with bourgeois theater conventions.

### The Constructivist Stage, Media Technology, and the Drama of the Individual

What I described as Piscator's theatricalization of the "podium" in reference to the *Rote Revue Rummel* (1924) gave way to attempts at using established theater spaces as political forums, thus transforming actual theater stages into "podiums." For example, the revue *Trotz Alledem!*, which the KPD commissioned a year later, in 1925, and which was composed of documentary material from the March Revolution of 1918 and quotes from Karl Liebknecht, took place on the stage of the Große Schauspielhaus. Hans Poelzig had converted the venue from a circus into a gigantic, 3000-spectator theater for Max Reinhardt fifteen years earlier. Together with his stage designer, the Dada artist John

---

**23** Sergei Eisenstein's groundbreaking work "The Montage of Attractions" (1923), written for the theatre, testifies to the proximity of these new theatrical forms of representation to the film arts, the theorization of which Eisenstein would soon develop out of the same principle of montage. Sergei Eisenstein, "The Montage of Attractions," in *S.M. Eisenstein: Selected Works, Vol. 1, Writings, 1922–34*, ed. Richard Taylor (London: British Film Institute, 1988), pp. 33–38. See Erika Fischer-Lichte, *Die Entdeckung des Zuschauers. Paradigmenwechsel auf dem Theater des 20. Jahrhunderts* (Tübingen and Basel: Francke, 1997), pp. 125–129.

Heartfield, Piscator installed a multi-story scaffolding, which resembled the Russian constructivist stages of Meyerhold and Eisenstein, onto the revolving stage that had been specially installed for Reinhardt's immersive theater festivals.[24] Piscator's scaffold, with slopes, stairs and platforms on both sides, was intended to be used for individual scenes either staged simultaneously or in rapid alternation. In addition to such a dynamic stage construction, Piscator again employed slide projections and film material. Images of wartime destruction from the *Reichsarchiv* confronted the spectators with a past they themselves had experienced ten years earlier and might have repressed in the meantime: "flame thrower attacks, piles of mutilated bodies, burning cities [...]."[25] Piscator described the motivation for using media technology as the creation of a kind of reality effect: The spectators saw "their fate, their own tragedy being acted out before their eyes," and hence the performance "had become reality" for them.[26] This effect transformed their mere "willing receptivity" into "active participation: the masses took over the direction." By the end, the theater had become "one big assembly hall, one big battlefield, one massive demonstration," dissolving the distinction between "stage and audience."[27] Hence, the stage was to be turned into a "podium" in the sense of a site of direct

24  Fischer-Lichte discusses Piscator's new conception of the theatrical space in the context of the avant-garde theater of Reinhardt, Eisenstein, and Meyerhold. Even though the profound differences in their conceptions of theater fade into the background here, the account nonetheless testifies to the temporal consolidation of various theater experiments between 1910 and 1930 that radically rethought the theatrical space and the relationship between audience and stage. Fischer-Lichte, *Die Entdeckung des Zuschauers*, p. 125.

25  See Piscator's *Political Theatre*, the original version of which was published in 1929 as a programmatic account of the beginnings and aspirations of the theatrical enterprise that Piscator envisaged. Piscator authorized a reworked and redesigned edition in 1966. Erwin Piscator, *The Political Theatre*, ed. Hugh Rorrison (London: Eyre Methuen, 1980), p. 94.

26  Ibid., p. 96.

27  Ibid., pp. 96–97.

address and participation at the same time. It should be stressed that the claim to realness implied here by no means refers to an "unmediated" experience of reality, but is conceived rather as theatrical reality. As Piscator himself points out, it is not the realism of the individual that concerns him, but rather a "political reality" in the sense of "being of general concern." [28]

After his fallout with the Volksbühne directorate, Piscator expanded his production experience with his own theater at Nollendorfplatz, which he managed between 1927 and 1931.[29] In the opening production from September 1927, the intersection of scenography and dramatic text played a decisive role. Within a few weeks, Piscator and his dramaturgical team, which included Brecht for the first time, collaborated on the five-act piece *Hoppla, wir leben!*, based on a drama by Ernst Toller. By his own account, Piscator was primarily interested in connecting Toller's expressionist drama about the fate of a former revolutionary of the Munich Soviet Republic, who in 1927 was released from nine years of confinement in an insane asylum into a completely changed world, with the theatrical rendering of "war and revolution."[30] For this purpose, Piscator had another multi-story stage built, which provided multiple simultaneous performance locations, and again used film and slide projections. The play's unity of dramatic action, which presents the revolution as an idea that is good in principle but no longer adequate, was thus

---

**28** Piscator, *Political Theatre*, p. 96. Piscator's rhetoric of realness is often associated with the claim of a direct, unmediated reference to reality, contrary to text references which clearly state the opposite. See Michael Schwaiger, "Einbruch der Wirklichkeit. Das Theater Bertolt Brechts und Erwin Piscators," in Schwaiger, *Brecht und Piscator*, pp. 9–15.

**29** Before Piscator's membership at the Volksbühne was suspended after the theatrical scandal surrounding the "Gewitter über Gottland," which was considered too political, he had worked on similarly influential productions between 1924 and 1927, such as Alfons Paquet's *Fahnen* (1924) and *Sturmflut* (1926), and Schiller's *Räuber* (1926).

**30** Piscator, *Political Theatre*, p. 201.

intentionally interrupted by documentary film material and confronted with the multiperspectivity and technicality of the stage. This example of interweaving a dramatic narrative with historical imagery illustrates what Piscator might have been interested in with regards to the notion of "Zeittheater."

Piscator envisioned a theater of radical contemporaneity that features the playwright, who presents a self-contained storyline, as only one element of the production process.[31] As a "helper," the dramatist provides "the material" which a "constructively producing arrangement of performance" [*konstruktiv produzierende Spielanordnung*] is built upon. It is the "stylistic will of the *mise-en-scène*" [*Stilwillen der Inszenierung*] that sets the drama's subject matter [*Stoff*] in motion in the first place, with the help of various theatrical devices that "permeate" the material.[32] Piscator thus declares the process of *mise-en-scène* of dramatic content, which transforms the drama into theatrical form, to be the fundamental principle of his "Zeittheater." This emphasis of the processual quality of scenography points to the dialectics of deixis, as discussed above in regard to the *Rote Revue Rummel*. Far beyond the reference to an alienated acting style that is reminiscent of Brecht,[33] Piscator reaches for the use of stage construction and technology.

For the production of *Hoppla, wir leben!*, Piscator commissioned Traugott Müller to build an 11m wide and 8m high "konstruktivistisches Simultangerüst."[34] As can be seen from the stage design sketches as well as from

---

31  The following remarks are taken from the essay "Das Zeittheater in der Krise," which appeared in 1931 in *Blätter der Piscator-Bühne*. It was republished in Piscator, *Zeittheater*, pp. 263–266.

32  Ibid., p. 264.

33  "This kind of performance requires a kind of mentally trained actor, who must also be willing to subordinate language and gestures to the necessity of a purely dialectical dialogue, against the often obvious temptation of performing oneself personally." Ibid., p. 265–266.

34  See Fischer-Lichte, *Die Entdeckung des Zuschauers*, p. 161, who situates Piscator's stage aesthetics in the context of the Russian theatrical avant-garde, in particular the Jewish collective GOSET and Eisen-

**Fig. 1:** Erwin Piscator, *Hoppla, wir leben!* [IX], 1927, stage design by Traugott Müller, photography, 8.6 x 11.5 cm, Theatre-Historical Collection, Free University Berlin.

**Fig. 2:** Erwin Piscator, *Hoppla, wir leben!* [XI] – II, 2. Szene, 5. Bild, 1927, stage design by Traugott Müller, photography, 16.8 x 23 cm, Theatre-Historical Collection, Free University Berlin.

stage photography (figs. 1 and 2), the scaffold consisted of three vertical sections, of which the left and right sections were each divided horizontally into three floors of different heights, and the central section was covered by a dome-like structure. The scaffolding featured a total of up to eight performance spaces, which could be used in addition to the surrounding stage area, either simultaneously or in quick alternation. This stage construction revealed the concurrency of everyday spaces—the office, the bedroom, the assembly hall—where the performers were to take on different roles. For Piscator, the possibility for multiple settings epitomized the "cross section of society" and "social order" in which individuals had to compete.[35] The front and back of the stage scaffolding, on which living and office rooms, as well as prison cells, were located, functioned in a similar manner. A rotating mechanism allowed for the scaffold to shift from the front side to the back. The stage construction was anti-illusionary in the sense that the theatrically-constructed nature of the dramaturgical space was not denied, but rather emphasized.[36] The language of forms that emerges here was dynamic and designed for the experience of transformation, while—unlike Reinhardt's analogy between theater and dream—the technicality of the dynamic stage remained visible at all times.

Alongside the multitude of possibilities of performing movement, the scaffolding also provided an array of projection surfaces for slides and film material [fig. 3]. The back side was made from a translucent screen that could be projected onto from both sides. A white projection screen could be lowered in front of the scaffolding,

stein's recourse to Meyerhold, who exposed the construction of the stage design, its materiality, mechanics, and technicity.

35 Piscator, *Political Theatre*, p. 202.
36 Piscator's former stage manager Otto Richter impressively describes the logistical challenges associated with the construction, assembly and dismantling of the four-ton stage scaffolding. See *Erwin Piscator. Eine Arbeitsbiographie in zwei Bänden*, ed. Knut Boeser and Renata Vatková, Vol. 1 (Berlin: Fröhlich & Kaufmann 1986), p. 153–154.

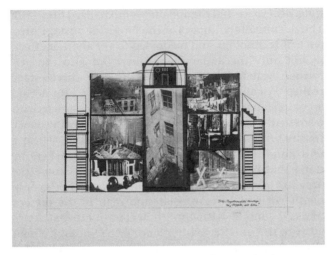

**Fig. 3:** Traugott Müller, *Hoppla Wir Leben!* [III] – projection image montage, 1927, stage design sketch, 49.7 x 67.8 cm, Theatre-Historical Collection, Free University Berlin.

and fixed projection screens could be mounted in front of the individual performance spaces. That the use of new media technology, which enhanced the rapid set changes and transformed the performances into spectacular light shows, must have felt overwhelming to a contemporary audience can be inferred from the responses of theater critics: Alfred Kerr described the visual effect as a "chaotic shimmering of implied phenomena,"[37] and Ernst Heilborn emphasized that "the film, the music (which is strangely provocative [...])" had "the same function" as the drama.[38]

The projection surfaces on the various levels of the stage brought about a completely new entanglement of

---

[37] Alfred Kerr, *Berliner Tageblatt* 419, 5 September 1927. Quoted in Hugo Fetting, *Von der freien Bühne zum politischen Theater*, Vol. 2 (Leipzig: Reclam, 1987), pp. 361–366, here p. 365.

[38] Ernst Heilborn, *Frankfurter Zeitung* 662, 6 September 1927. Quoted in Fetting, *Von der freien Bühne*, pp. 358–361, here p. 358.

theatrical space and the audience's medialized lifeworld. The documentary impact of the powerful onstage presence of technology and media led to yet another effect, as not only the audience members but also the performers were faced with a new technology-driven stage reality. Piscator's performers had to move and act on a complicated scaffold, and they had to compete with oversized images. This challenging new performance setting brings to mind Benjamin's remarks in "Theater und Rundfunk" [*Theatre and Radio*] (1932), where he states that Brecht's epic theater suffices "to expose the present" [*die Exponierung des Anwesenden*], the "experiments" of which "revolve around man in the present crisis."[39] Among other things, Benjamin attributes this crisis to the unreflected influence of technology: "man eliminated by radio and cinema, a person, to put it somewhat drastically, as the fifth wheel of technology."[40] For Benjamin, it is Brecht's "dramatically experimental" attempts that are capable of bringing onto the stage this "reduced, cold" human being and the conditions of possibility of his or her actions.[41] I propose that Piscator pursued a similar "exposure" of the human in an increasingly technological environment with his stage constructions and highly complex productions in terms of media technology.

In response to repeated criticism regarding the inadequate performances in *Hoppla, wir leben!*, Piscator argues that "actors who are accustomed to acting within the stable framework of the old bourgeois stage will be slow to find the style that suits my stage architecture [*Bühnenapparatur*]."[42] To the actors, this "apparatus"

39 Walter Benjamin, "Theater and Radio: On the Mutual Supervision of Their Educational Roles," in Walter Benjamin, *Radio Benjamin*, ed. Lecia Rosenthal, trans. Jonathan Lutes (London and New York: Verso, 2014), pp. 365–358, here p. 367.
40 Ibid.
41 Walter Benjamin, "The Author as Producer" (1934), in Benjamin, *Understanding Brecht*, pp. 85–103.
42 Piscator, *Political Theatre*, p. 213.

appears "strange, even hostile," and they feel "lost amid the gigantic mechanical structures, which leave them little peace to unfold their virtuoso individual performances." Even though Piscator admits that this kind of interplay can be improved upon with "many years [...] of training and experience," he still considers the "disharmony" between human and machine to be a necessary, if not symptomatic, step towards a new form or "style" of acting. The observation that "the effect of placing live actors against a filmed background is always lively and provocative" further points to a new logic of representation, in which contemporary "conditions" appear to be profoundly determined by media technology. That is to say, Piscator does not aim at reproducing the "conditions" by way of self-contained dramatic narratives, as would be the case with Benjamin's contemptuously-termed "political thesis plays," but he does in fact aspire to "reveal them" by way of his experiments with stage technology.[43] One could even say that, in Piscator's productions, the technological conditions *show* themselves, to a certain extent, as supremacy and power, exposing the vulnerability of the human beings that Benjamin assumes to be at the "centre" of epic theater's "experiments."[44]

The fact that this kind of "human being in crisis" on the stage, in spite of being at the mercy of the theatrical apparatus, always reveals him or herself as a protagonist and agent, as a performer, and thus as changeable as well as changing, echoes the dialectics of *showing* and being *shown* that Benjamin points at regarding Brecht's epic theatre. Similar to how the Brechtian gesture interrupts

---

**43** Benjamin, "The Author as Producer," p. 100; Benjamin, "Epic Theatre" (1), p. 4: "Epic theatre, then, does not reproduce conditions but, rather, reveals them."

**44** Benjamin writes about Brecht: "He opposes the dramatic laboratory to the finished work of art. He goes back, in a new way, to the theatre's greatest and most ancient opportunity: the opportunity to expose the present. At the centre of his experiments stands man." Benjamin, "The Author as Producer," p. 100.

a drama and thus manifests as a theatrical act, Piscator's use of stage and media technology interrupts the dramatic plot as much as it obstructs the performance of acting. The technologized stage exposes scenographic representation as such, in terms of the spatial elements as well as the performers.[45] When Benjamin describes "interruption" as being "one of the fundamental methods of all form-giving" in his 1939 study, and cites quotation and gesture as the most important examples,[46] a kinship between Piscator's and Brecht's theater practice can be assumed, in that they both *show* the stage as a place of *showing*, which is both form-shaping and form-dissolving at the same time.[47]

Brecht himself hints at a conceptual affinity with Piscator on various occasions, with the distinction that he derived his understanding of epic theater primarily from acting, while Piscator developed his notion of "epic form" from scenography.[48] For Brecht, it is the quotation-like gesture of the actors which makes "the usual conspicuous, the familiar surprising" and thereby reveals the "socio-historical process" to which humans

---

45  Fischer-Lichte emphasizes the new "space-time" relationship in Piscator's constructed stage: "Piscator's stage constructions functioned on the one hand as moving technical architecture and in this sense as dynamic, 'four-dimensional' spaces. On the other hand, they enabled the simultaneous and concurrent perceptible execution or simultaneous presentation of events that take place or have taken place at a spatial and/or temporal distance from one another." It is questionable whether this could be described as a "perfect portrayal and allegory" of the mechanized world, however. Fischer-Lichte, *Die Entdeckung des Zuschauers*, p. 163.

46  Benjamin, "Epic Theatre" (2), pp. 19.

47  This ties in to Christoph Menke's reflections on the paradoxical formal references of theater: "In the interweaving of performance and imitation, theatre is both the de-foundation [*Entgründung*] and foundation [*Gründung*] of form (without being able to be both at the same time): the foundation of form in life and the de-foundation of form in the play." Christoph Menke, "Das Spiel des Theaters und die Veränderung der Welt," in *Theater als Kritik*, ed. Olivia Ebert et al. (Bielefeld: Transcript, 2018), pp. 37–48, here p. 43.

48  See Bertolt Brecht, "On Experiments in Epic Theatre" (1935/36), in *Brecht on Theatre*, ed. Marc Silberman et al. (London: Bloomsbury, 2018), pp. 139–141, here p. 141.

are subjected, but compared to which theatrical representation [the German "vorstellen" refers to both "imagination" as well as "performance"] proves them to be "changeable":[49]

this person is like this [*so und so*] because the conditions are like that [*so und so*]. And the conditions are like that [*so und so*] because the person is like this [*so und so*]. But this person can be imagined [vorstellbar] not only as he is but also otherwise [*anders*], as he could be, and the conditions too can be imagined [*vorstellbar*] other [*anders*] than they are.[50]

Piscator, on the other hand, conceives of the notion of such a "Vorstellung" (in the double sense of "imagination" and "performance") of the "like this and that" [*so und so*] and "otherwise" [*anders*] in terms of the design and formation of the theatrical space, i.e. in terms of scenography. In his essay "Theater und Kino" (1933), he describes the "epic" of theater as the dissolution of the "earlier arrangement of scenes" into "countless frames that should appear in parallel spatially [*rauminhaltlich nebeneinander*], but are torn apart by the change of performance sites [*durch den Wandel der Spielplätze*]."[51] The use of slide projections has a similar effect. The images and film sequences expand the "narration" of events

---

**49** Bertolt Brecht, "Episches Theater, Entfremdung" (1936/37), in Bertolt Brecht, *Ausgewählte Werke in sechs Bänden*, Vol. 6 (Frankfurt am Main: Suhrkamp, 1997), pp. 243–244, here p. 243.

**50** Bertolt Brecht, "On Experimental Theatre" (1939/40), in *Brecht on Theatre*, pp. 157–170, here p. 168. To what extent the criticality of Brecht's gestural theater is based on the dynamics of forms has been worked out by Werner Hamacher with reference to an "ethics of gestural dramaturgies," "through which a multitude of mutually paralyzing identifications could become a society that allows everyone to become an other, and different from the one for whom he thinks he is, or for whom he is thought to be." Werner Hamacher, "Das eine Kriterium für das, was geschieht. Aristoteles: Poetik. Brecht: 'Kleines Organon'," in Ebert et. al., *Theater als Kritik*, pp. 20–38, here p. 32.

**51** Erwin Piscator, "Theater und Kino" (1933), in Piscator, *Zeittheater*, pp. 267–271, here p. 268.

and, as non-theatrical material, establish a reference to the audience members' everyday realities. It is essential, Piscator stresses, to dismantle the "architectonic shapes of the theatre" which in bourgeois theater resulted in "the sharp separation of the stage from the audience" as well as "the opening of the stage only towards one side." The constructivist stage and the disruptive use of media thus provide the stage-technological framework for the concept of epic theater, the development of which Brecht himself explicitly traced back to his collaboration with Piscator in the mid-1930s.[52] Piscator's theater no longer posits the site of illusion as a prerequisite for the depiction of a drama's narrative, but rather reveals itself as a site of the labor of theatrical *showing* in all regards: its performance, its spatial construction, and its technologies. Through such an execution of scenographic *showing*, the stage reveals itself as an element that is fundamental to the theatrical process of altering and building form and identity.

## Conclusion

The goal of Piscator's decidedly political theater practice was to put the established bourgeois theater industry into the service of a concrete *practice* of political and social *critique*. Alongside the emphasis on collective working methods, Piscator used scenography, in the sense of shaping the theatrical space, as a means of criti-

---

**52** In 1935 Brecht writes: "The advent of the Third Reich cut short the numerous experiments in Germany that we can best refer to from a technical standpoint as experiments in epic theatre. They were conducted primarily by Piscator and me, and in large public theatres." Brecht, "On Experiments in Epic Theatre," p. 139. Four years later, in 1939, he describes the radical break that Piscator's stage experiments represented with regard to established theater as "chaos," out of which a politicized theater had developed into a "parliament" in terms of both content and techniques of representation. See Brecht, "On Experimental Theatre," p. 160.

cal intervention. As illustrated with regard to the above examples, he developed a new, technically dynamic language of forms for the theater stage. This language of forms was not intended to create a synesthetic, atmospheric environment. Rather, the constructivist stage, with its simultaneous performance sites and projection surfaces, offered a multi-perspectival and highly differentiated performance framework. Piscator used such a constructivist, architectural framework to stage a kind of montage of theatrical elements, comprised of dramatic narrative, sound, and projected images. He thereby confronted performers and spectators alike with an interplay of theatrical and extra-theatrical realities. Piscator's consciously scenographic dramaturgy, in other words, put on display the inseparable yet dichotomous relationship between life and theater practice.[53] As a result, the audience witnessed Piscator's performers become elements of dynamic stage constellations that can be described in terms of individual scenographic graphemes (in the sense of sceno–graphy), which belong to different theatrical systems of signs: dramatic dialogue and plot, as well as choreography, but similarly, if not more importantly, stage architecture, light, sound and music, as well as the use of visual media.[54] Piscator's theatrical language of forms stands for the use of the stage in terms of space and technology in the service of political intervention, and, consequently, as a *practice of critique*.

This brings us back to the initial question: Given Piscator's importance for the development of the podium stage

[53] The fact that Piscator's concept of theater is based on a rethinking of this relationship can be further substantiated by the "primal scene" of political theater as he staged it in his book *Das politische Theater*, with regard to the frontline theater he joined in 1917. On the paradox of life and theater practice, see Menke, "Das Spiel des Theaters," p. 48.

[54] For more on constructivist stage composition as language, which demonstrates the specificity of the convergence of different sign systems and their interaction for theatrical performance, see Fischer-Lichte, *Die Entdeckung des Zuschauers*, p. 123.

and for Brecht's conception of epic theater, how can we understand Benjamin's conclusion that the "functional relationship between the stage and the audience, text and performance, director and actor [...] has remained almost unchanged" in the "Zeittheater"? The "almost" in Benjamin's analysis echoes Asja Lacis' observation of a "rift" in Piscator's theater "between the further development of existing principles on the one hand and the introduction of new elements on the other."[55] I suggest that Benjamin's "almost" and Lacis' "new elements" refer to Piscator's scenographic practice, which might not have been able to change the production apparatus in an immediately perceptible way. Yet the new language of forms that Piscator developed nevertheless provided a fundamental impulse for the advancement of epic-gestural theater and a critical theater aesthetic that is still at work today. Those who unequivocally juxtapose Brecht's conception of "distance" and "alienation" with Piscator's "claim to reality" lose sight of the latter's theatrical practice, in which stage construction and the use of media and stage technology allowed for everything but an "unmediated" recourse to reality.[56] More significant than the polemical efforts of the two theatermakers to differentiate themselves in the years during and shortly after their collaboration are, in my opinion, the expressly appreciative words that Brecht voiced for Piscator in the 1930s.[57] Brecht's conclusion that Piscator

---

55  Lacis, *Revolutionär im Beruf*, p. 86.
56  See, among others, Klaus Völker, "Das politische Theater Piscators und das epische Theater Brechts," in *"Leben – ist immer ein Anfang!" Erwin Piscator 1863–1966*, ed. Ullrich Amlung (Marburg and Berlin: Jonas-Verlag, 1993), pp. 47–58. Similarly, in Schwaiger, *Brecht und Piscator*, p. 14.
57  In "On Experiments in Epic Theatre," Brecht uses the third person plural to delineate early experiments with the new theatrical form, referring to himself and Piscator and thus viewing their differing perspectives as complementary: "We marched separately for a time. Piscator turned his attention to the subject matter and revolutionized the stage. I was more concerned with individual persons, or more accurately: with their relationships, and I revolutionized the

was one of the "most influential people in theatre" of all time, as someone who "electrified the theatre," suggests that the theatrical densification of the medialized, technified "human being in our crisis," as Benjamin defined the aim of Brechtian gestural theater, would have been inconceivable without Piscator's experiments with stage and media technology.[58]

Beyond the discussion of theory, the historical context of Benjamin's studies on epic theater must not be forgotten. The years between 1931 and 1939 mark the most intensive intellectual exchange between Brecht and Benjamin on form and the possibilities of critical thought and action. At the same time, they mark a period of extreme political and cultural crisis, which forced Piscator and Brecht to abandon their theater work in Berlin, and drove Benjamin into exile. After the parliamentary elections in September 1930 (when the NSDAP became the second most powerful party for the first time) and the ensuing pogroms in Berlin, the National Socialist and anti-Semitic mobilization of the German population became increasingly apparent, which in turn mobilized political dissidents, and in particular Jewish cultural practitioners and intellectuals. This political climate provided the immediate context for Brecht's productions following his breakthrough in 1928 with *Die Dreigroschenoper* and the theatrical scandal of *Aufstieg und Fall der Stadt Mahagonny* in Leipzig in March 1930.[59] After repeated disruptions of his productions by

---

art of acting. The stage itself became actor and performer." Brecht, "On Experiments in Epic Theatre," p. 141.

**58** Joachim Fiebach emphasizes the fact that Piscator's last productions in Berlin during the Weimar Republic were, with their reduced stage structures, surprisingly similar to Brecht's theater. See Fiebach, "Piscator, Brecht und Medialisierung," pp. 116 and 120.

**59** The first performance of *Aufstieg und Fall der Stadt Mahagonny* at the Leipzig Opera House on March 9, 1930 had the effect that Brecht and Weill had hoped for in that they subverted the visual expectations of its bourgeois audience. See Jan Knopf, *Brecht Handbuch: Theater. Eine Ästhetik der Widersprüche* (Stuttgart and Weimar: Metzler, 1996), p. 71.

the National Socialists, a performance of *Die Maßnahme* in Erfurt in January 1933 was shut down by the police and Brecht was accused of high treason.[60] The day after the Reichstag burned, he left Germany and travelled to Zurich via Prague and Vienna. Piscator, on the other hand, had left Berlin already in 1931, shortly after yet another bankruptcy of his theater at Nollendorfplatz (due in part to the high costs of stage construction and the dwindling numbers of spectators). He went to Moscow to shoot the film project *The Revolt of the Fishermen*, on which Asja Lacis worked as production assistant, before emigrating first to France, in 1936, and then to the U.S. in 1939.

Thus, Benjamin's first manuscript on epic theater was written at a time when Brecht was one of the few still trying to resist the rise of National Socialism, while Piscator's theater work in Berlin had already come to an end. At that time, Piscator blamed the "crisis" of the "Zeittheater" (1931) on the increasing depoliticization of the theater landscape. The return to "atmospheric theatre," Piscator writes, produced a "Zeittheater" of the "individual" [*Zeittheater des einzelnen*] that he explicitly contrasts with a socially-oriented "Zeittheater."[61] When Benjamin finally published his revised study on Brecht in 1939, Brecht's gestural theater had also become subject to the constraints of National Socialist cultural policy. After stays in Zurich and Denmark, where Benjamin visited Brecht for the last time in 1939, Brecht's epic theater had in fact become an almost purely theoretical theater. It now came to represent a practice that was itself forced into exile and thus rendered "impossible," at least momentarily.[62] Conceived from the posi-

60 Brecht left Berlin a few weeks after the book burnings that had been organized at numerous German universities, which included his writings. See Jan Knopf, *Bertolt Brecht – Lebenskunst in finsteren Zeiten* (Munich: Hanser, 2012) p. 271–272.
61 See Piscator, *Das Zeittheater in der Krise*, p. 263.
62 This argument seeks to further complicate the ongoing debate about the "impossibility" of Brecht's theater conception, especially regard-

tion of exile in 1939, the possibility of a theater of critical impact originated in not much more than a vague
hope for a better future.

*Translated by Angela Anderson*

ing the "Lehrstücke," and what such a notion of "impossible theater"
might mean with regard to Brecht's theater practice in particular
and, more generally, the practice of political theater in Germany at
the time. See Nikolaus Müller-Schöll, *Das Theater des "konstruktiven
Defaitismus". Lektüren zur Theorie eines Theaters der A-Identität bei
Walter Benjamin, Bertolt Brecht und Heiner Müller* (Frankfurt am
Main: Stroemfeld, 2002), pp. 322–324.

Sebastian Kirsch

# Why Streets Are No Longer Paved with Theater Gold

**Critique and Stage Form(s)**

## 1

Walter Benjamin's *One Way Street*, published in 1928, contains among others a remarkable vignette on the problem of criticism, entitled "These Spaces to Rent."[1] Here it is in a slightly shortened version:

> Fools, who bewail the decline of criticism. The fact is, its time expired long ago. Criticism is a question of correct distance. Criticism is at home in a world where perspectives and prospects matter, where it was still possible to adopt a stance. Things have now begun to chivvy human society much too urgently. "Impartiality" and the "open outlook" have become lies if not the wholly naive expression of straight non-competence. The name of the most intrinsic quality today, the mercantile look penetrating to the heart of things, is advertising. Advertising eliminates the free leeway of consideration, bringing things dangerously close, right in our face, the way a car, in the cinema, hugely increasing in size on the screen, comes quivering towards us. [...] With that, "objective reality" is eventually left behind, and faced with huge illustrations on the sides of houses, where "Chlorodont" and "Sleipnir" lie within easy

1 Walter Benjamin, *One Way Street and other Writings*, trans. J.A. Underwood (London and New York: Penguin, 2009), p. 97.

reach of giants, recovered sentimentality is set free, American-style [...]. What is it, ultimately, that makes advertising so superior to criticism? Not what the red electric text up on the moving screen says—the pool of fire that mirrors it on the asphalt.[2]

Like other texts by Benjamin, "These Spaces to Rent" has been hugely commented on. However, bearing in mind most recent debates on today's possibilities or impossibilities for critical practices, it may be interesting to see it with fresh eyes. After all, there seem to be remarkable resemblances between this ninety-year-old diagnosis of a long-expired criticism and several so-called "post-critical" claims which have become very prominent in the twenty-first century. Benjamin's questioning of the primacy of critical distance especially catches the eye here, since a very similar problem has been hugely discussed for instance in the light of so-called immersive art forms.[3] But also his steering towards "things" which have begun to "chivvy human society much too urgently" seems at least at first sight reminiscent of a well-known tendency of the last decade: namely the renewed interest in "non-human" entities that many post-critical theories have come to consider as active agents. However, regarding Benjamin's "things" themselves, that is, the object culture he locates beyond criticism, one cannot but start to wonder about the differences between the situation depicted in *One Way Street* and the "post-critical" condition of the twenty-first century. There seems to be an enormous shift between Benjamin's "chivvying" objects, that spring from a world of camera cranks and cars, and the "internet of things," with all its digital

---

2  Ibid.
3  With respect to theater, compare particularly James Frieze, ed., *Reframing Immersive Theatre: The Politics and Pragmatics of Participatory Performance* (London: Palgrave Macmillan, 2016) and Josephine Machon, *Immersive Theatres: Intimacy and Immediacy in Contemporary Performance* (London: Palgrave Macmillan, 2013).

gadgets that are often perceived as having outrun the critical subject's abilities in velocity, efficiency and precision. But how can this shift be located exactly? And what might it tell about the conditions under which a "decline of criticism" is being experienced today?

In this essay I'd like to take "These Spaces to Rent" as a starting point for developing a specifically theater-theoretical perspective on these questions. This choice is mainly for two reasons. First, it is not difficult to discuss Benjamin's text in a theater horizon, since it does after all explicitly mention "perspectives and prospects." But second, by revisiting this classical problematization of criticism by a "critical theorist," I'd also like to open a broader perspective on the issue of criticism (or its expiring), avoiding the traps of a somewhat fashionable fare-well to critical traditions, such as we may find, for example, in Bruno Latour's often-quoted "Why has critique run out of steam?"[4] This seems all the more apposite precisely because I want to ask what might separate our contemporary situation from the one Benjamin sought to portray in *One Way Street*. In the following I will take up both of the "post-critical" motifs mentioned above—the questioning of critical distance and the importance of things and non-human entities—and connect them to the history of two poles that inform different historical shapes of theater. In the first part I want to comment on Benjamin's relation to Bertolt Brecht, whose "counter-critical" theater work suited the conditions of *One Way Street* in an exact manner. However, in trying to

---

4   Compare Bruno Latour, "Why Has Critique Run out of Steam? From Matters of Fact to Matters of Concern," *Critical Inquiry* 30:2 (2004): pp. 225–248. One problem of the current "post-critical" discourse is that it often doesn't differentiate properly between criticism and critique. Benjamin's "These Spaces to Rent" for example can be read as a (Marxist) *critique* of the traditions of a (bourgeois) *criticism*, but this division points also to the difference between a Kantian sense of critique (as for example in *Kritik der reinen Vernunft*) and then "applied" or "practical" criticism. This double meaning often gets blurred in English translations of Benjamin's texts.

understand what might have changed since then I will take a kind of detour: In the second part of this essay I will consider ancient Greek theater and especially its stage form, to outline a somehow astonishing closeness of its main aspects to questions at stake in today's "post-critical" times.

## 2

When publishing *One Way Street*, Benjamin was already well aware of Brecht's work of the same era. Therefore it is certainly not by chance that he associates the outdated tradition of criticism with perspectives and prospects which point to the modern picture frame stage. In fact, Brecht's theater of the 1920s treated criticism in the aforementioned sense like ashes of the bourgeois age. That may come as a surprise, since Brecht is still often made to serve today as a particularly desolate example of the very idea of criticism that has long expired. However, according to Benjamin, the innermost kernel of Brecht's *Attempts* [*Versuche*][5] was indeed a radical rejection of this very type of criticism, as a dense passage of his essay "What is Epic Theatre?" makes clear:

> The moment when [...] the false and deceptive totality called "audience" begins to disintegrate and there is new space for the formation of separate parties within it—separate parties corresponding to conditions as they really are—at that moment the critic suffers the double misfortune of seeing his nature as agent revealed and, at the same time, devalued.[6]

5   *Versuche* was the title of a series which contained lyrics, plays, and theoretical essays by Brecht who also edited the series. It appeared from 1930–1957.
6   Walter Benjamin, "What is Epic Theatre?" (First version), p. 10, in Walter Benjamin, *Understanding Brecht*, ed. Stanley Mitchell, trans. Anna Bostock (London and New York: Verso, 1998), pp. 1–14.

Paraphrasing this as briefly as possible,[7] epic theater exposes the "chief critic" who likes to explain the state of world affairs to an alleged homogeneous mass, the "audience." This character type indeed depends on the possibility of "correct distance." Then again, with his abdication, the mass audience turns out to be split and divided into multiple parties and interest groups, so much so that no reconciliation between them could possibly be in sight. On the contrary: In Benjamin's view, it was one of Brecht's main ambitions to prove each and every harmonization of that kind to be ideological, a harmonization which in theater would equal the transformation of the audience into a unity applauding uniformly. Insofar as Brecht's theater is counter-critical, it gives a critique of a reductive version of criticism that therefore can't draw any longer on its traditional forms and standards. Indeed, a closer reading of Brecht's theater pieces can legitimize this view, for example *A Man is a Man*, which was of great importance for Benjamin.[8] On the one hand, this "comedy" draws its humor from *The provability of any and every contention*,[9] which results directly from the impossibility of correct distance, proper stances and the related forms of subjectivity. Then again, this play about Galy Gay, a "man reassembled like a car, / Without his losing anything by it,"[10] is one of Brecht's first attempts to create a stage

---

7    For a more detailed discussion, see Nikolaus Müller-Schöll, *Das Theater des "konstruktiven Defaitismus". Lektüren zur Theorie eines Theaters der A-Identität bei Walter Benjamin, Bertolt Brecht und Heiner Müller* (Frankfurt am Main: Stroemfeld, 2002), pp. 19–44.

8    See for example Benjamin's persistent notes on the play in "What is Epic Theatre?" (First version), pp. 2–3 and 8–13. On this essay see also the articles by Bettine Menke and Mimmi Woisnitza in this volume.

9    *The Elephant Calf or The provability of any and every contention* is a small piece Brecht wrote as a separate part of *A Man is a Man*, in Bertolt Brecht, *The Jewish Wife and other short plays*, trans. Eric Bentley (New York: Grove Press, 1965), pp. 57–73.

10   This is relatively the closest translation of the original verse "Hier wird heute abend ein Mensch wie ein Auto ummontiert / Ohne daß er irgend etwas dabei verliert", cited from Brigid Doherty, "Text and

form for a modern "mass man" [*Massemensch*][11]: a "Nobody"[12] who is a close relative to the lead characters of Joyce's *Ulysses* or Musil's *Man without Qualities*. This "rubber man" [*Gummimensch*][13] can't be a classical bearer of criticism any longer, since Galy Gay is a man "who can't say no."[14] At the same time, the "mass man" Galy Gay is basically divided in himself: Not an individual, but a "dividual" [*Dividuum*],[15] he moves persistently through changing orders and environments, affirming them without any difference, but then again subverting them exactly because of his inability to say no. In this sense Galy Gay is no longer a humanist "man."

I don't want to repeat here the readings that have been given of this play.[16] Instead I would like to return to the question of what might in fact separate today's "post-critical" conditions from those *A Man is a Man* and *One Way Street* reacted to. To do so it seems wise to first change from problematizing critical distance, to regarding the very nature of the things and non-human entities Benjamin and Brecht dealt with. I have already mentioned the camera cranks and cars Benjamin talks about in "These Spaces to Rent." To generalize, it is fair to say that these objects stand in for a world of optical media and engine-powered machines. But this is obviously also the world of the early twentieth century's urban masses, whose forces Benjamin captures in the impressive image of the non-human giants reaching for the vast billboards.

Gestus in Brecht and Benjamin," *MLN* 115:3 (April 2000): pp. 442–481, here p. 455.
11  Brecht comments on the term "Massemensch" in a short note to Helene Weigel from 1928, in Bertolt Brecht, *Briefe 1913–1956, Band 1* (Berlin and Weimar: Aufbau,1983), p. 125.
12  See Benjamin, "What is Epic Theatre?" (First version), p. 5.
13  See for this expression Brecht's introduction to his *Hauspostille*, *Gedichte 1, Sammlungen 1918–1938, Werke 11* (Berlin and Weimar: Aufbau, 1988), p. 39.
14  Quoted from Benjamin, "What is Epic Theatre?" (First version), p. 8.
15  See for this Brecht's short note "Individuum und Masse," *Schriften 1*, Werke 21 (Berlin and Weimar: Aufbau, 1992), p. 359.
16  See particularly Müller-Schöll, *Das Theater des "konstruktiven Defaitismus,"* pp. 201–230.

Benjamin even names the environment adequate to all of this: The emblematic pool on the asphalt that mirrors the red billboard letters hints metonymically at *the environment of the street*, which gave *One Way Street* its title. The same holds true for Brecht: His construction of the "dividual" as a non-human and counter-critical other of criticism relates, exactly like Benjamin's *One Way Street*, to the street and the according object culture. As already quoted, Galy Gay is "reassembled like a car," and the original book design for the play showed photographs of urban masses next to images of a parking lot densely covered with cars. One could even argue that all of Brecht's polemics against the logic of bourgeois interiors—empathy, pity, and the very position of the allegedly impartial critic—relied heavily on an exterior defined by the street. This explains for instance the tremendous importance of "asocial" stage personnel for Brecht's plays, all the notorious hoodlums and prostitutes who populate his earlier pieces especially. It likewise explains Brecht's choice of a "Street Scene" [*Straßenszene*] as "a Basic Model for an Epic Theatre."[17] But first and foremost it illuminates the very relevance of the car, which has even been described as a heraldic figure for Brecht's whole project.[18]

However, Galy Gay does not just intermingle with the car. Brecht's "rubber man" is also an obvious reformulation of the Harlequin: the infernal comical stock character who was most prominent within *commedia dell'arte*, the street theater of the sixteenth century, and was then from the eighteenth century banished from theater in the name of enlightenment and an alleged

17  Bertolt Brecht, "The Street Scene. A Basic Model for an Epic Theatre," in *Brecht on Theatre: The Development of an Aesthetic*, ed. and trans. John Willett (London: Methuen, 1964), pp. 121–129.
18  See in more detail Freddie Rokem, *Philosophers & Thespians: Thinking Performance* (Stanford CA: Stanford University Press, 2010), pp. 141–176.

more realistic "portrayal of men."[19] *A Man is a Man* thus connects two "non-human" vectors that both refer to the street, interweaving the twentieth century with the early modern age and putting in parentheses the intervening bourgeois era. This hints directly at the historical and epistemological frame Brecht's and Benjamin's counter-critical move was embedded in: It is crucial to connect the outstanding role of the street in their texts *to the specific conditions of modern visibility*, which were first formulated within Italian city states during the Renaissance, particularly in Florence. It was those cities that decided to make the street their defining exterior, especially using it as a trade and traffic route, and they did this as they began to invent themselves as intramundane formations horizontally connected to coequal spots and to other cities.[20] This connection also leads to a more general assumption: It appears fair to say that Brecht's and Benjamin's counter-critical opening of theater to the street reinvented something that had been constitutive for theater during its modern period: *The defining other of the picture frame stage, and thus the exterior that served theater as a primal reference milieu from its early modern reformulations in the Renaissance and Baroque, was the street in all of its richness.* If epic theater, then, tried to mobilize this reference for the purpose of overcoming bourgeois inwardness and subjectivity, this was only possible because the corresponding aesthetics since Gottsched or Lessing had attempted to blur the relation between theater and street. By contrast the street is manifest in pre-bourgeois theater, not only in the *commedia dell'arte*, but more generally in Renaissance market stages, in Shakespeare, and even in the earliest indoor stages, where scenographers like Sebastiano

---

**19** See also Rudolf Münz's influential essay "Das Harlekin-Prinzip," in Rudolf Münz, *Theatralität und Theater. Zur Historiographie von Theatralitätsgefügen* (Berlin: Schwarzkopf & Schwarzkopf, 1998), pp. 60–65.
**20** See Ulrike Haß, *Das Drama des Sehens. Auge, Blick und Bühnenform* (Munich: Fink, 2005), pp. 218–227.

Serlio first sought to rebuild and emulate the scene of the urban street crossing.[21]

This topic is more complex than one might suppose, considering these more or less historical facts. First of all, one has to take into account a deep ambivalence toward the street that has been apparent since early modern times, an ambivalence that was still of huge relevance for the twentieth century. On the one hand, the street was certainly the genuine environment for the Harlequin and all modern nomads, vagrants and tramps, including the Beatniks who wanted to live "on the road." On the other hand, it was also a leading medium for the one-sided European conquest that constituted the modern globe, becoming the Hegelian "military road of culture" [*allgemeine Heerstraße der Kultur*].[22] Thus, the street is ultimately two-sided. It has a "nomadic" side, but it is also an imperialistic instrument intrinsic to a formation Martin Heidegger called the "Age of the World Picture"[23]—and this is where things start to get complicated.

One of the most convincing arguments in Heidegger's famous essay on the "Age of the World Picture" is that the modern attempt to conceive (and conquer) the "world as a picture" went along with the necessity to position oneself against a "picture of the world," and thus with all the well-known divisions between subject and object, me and other, and also *res cogitans* and *res extensa*. But this also means that the modern instatement of the world picture enabled the very kind of criticism dependent on correct distances, prospects and perspective that Benjamin and Brecht reacted to with their counter-critical moves. However, attacking the

21  Ibid., pp. 188–200.
22  Georg Friedrich Wilhelm Hegel, "Aufsätze aus dem kritischen Journal der Philosophie," in *Werke 2. Jenaer Schriften 1801–1807* (Frankfurt am Main: Suhrkamp, 1979), p. 121.
23  Martin Heidegger, "The Age of the World Picture," in Martin Heidgegger, *The Question Concerning Technology and Other Essays*, trans. William Lovitt (New York: Harper and Row, 1977).

coordinates of the "world picture" by in turn referring to the street—even to its nomadic vector—turns out to be a quite paradoxical project: It means to remain within the frame of the world picture, trying to convert it from there, while simultaneously acknowledging that every attempt to tackle it from a distinct outside would in fact reproduce its own conditions. In this light it is not difficult to draw a parallel between Benjamin's and Brecht's counter-critical strategies and Heidegger's notion of "Verwindung" (instead of "Überwindung" in the sense of an agonistic overcoming). And of course one is very close here to the oscillating movements and flip-flop images deconstruction doesn't grow tired of exposing. However, the question remains whether this is really all there is. What about the intuition that something about referring to camera cranks, cars and urban masses doesn't really fit the "post-critical" conditions of the twenty-first century? Trying to find an answer to this question, I will now change my frame of reference and turn away from the Benjamin-Brecht discussion.

## 3

With respect to our present age it seems in fact fair to say that the street has increasingly lost its world-building functions, parallel to the implementation of an "electronic globalization" and "internetization" that has led to the possibility of steering and controlling global movements by means of digital satellite signals.[24] If, therefore, the contemporary crisis of criticism seems to even exceed its early twentieth century formulation, this can also be understood as the other side of an escalating loss of contours which the street has sustained

---

[24] For a discussion of the control effects of internetization, see the works of Alexander Galloway, starting with his 2004 monograph *Protocol: How Control Exists after Decentralization* (Cambridge MA: MIT Press, 2004).

due to capitalism becoming planetary.[25] One result of these dynamics is that today a counter-critical turn against criticism in terms of an opening to the street and its milieus seems to work less and less and, if still relied on, produces mainly nostalgic effects. However, I do not want to go into the details of this change by discussing the everyday world of the twenty-first century. Instead I will make a contrary move: Keeping this "decontouration of the street" in mind, I will take a look at ancient Greek theater and also sharpen the question of "The Scene as Form."

If modern theater was connected to the exterior environment of the street, regardless of intermediate attempts to enclose it in a picture frame stage, ancient Greek theater played between two poles in a similar and yet totally unlike manner. The differences begin with the important fact that the ancient stage was explicitly bipartite: It was put together from two completely heterogeneous stage parts, *skené* and *orchéstra*, which moreover were reserved for the two outstanding types of figure this theater knew: the protagonist entering from the stage building (*skené*) and stepping onto the *proskénion*, the narrow stage area in front where he engaged in the tragic events, and then the chorus moving into the *orchéstra* from the surrounding space of the *pólis* at the beginning of the theater feast, opening the play and going along with the events.[26] Protagonist and

---

25  In fact Benjamin already touched on this topic, as *One Way Street* closes with a text on modern technique entitled "To the Planetarium," and in 1938 Brecht also referred to his new form of drama as the "planetarium type" (P-Typus), as opposed to the "merry-go-round type" (K-Typus). See Bertolt Brecht, *The Messingkauf Dialogues*, trans. John Willett (London: Methuen, 1965).

26  There has been a rich discussion of the chorus in recent years, which I am taking up in this section. See especially Evelyn Annuß, ed., "kollektiv auftreten," special issue of *Forum Modernes Theater* 28:1 (2013); Evelyn Annuß, ed., "Volksfiguren," *Maske und Kothurn* 2 (2014); Julia Bodenburg, Katharina Grabbe and Nicole Haitzinger, eds., *Chor-Figuren. Transdisziplinäre Beiträge* (Berlin and Vienna: Böhlau, 2016); Genia Enzelsberger, Monika Meister and Stefanie Schmitt, eds., *Auftritt Chor. Formationen des Chorischen im Gegen-*

SEBASTIAN KIRSCH

chorus for their part belong to two totally different histories. Even a superficial look shows that the protagonist only developed with the younger rules of the *pólis*,
namely in the context of the *tyrannís* and on the threshold of the "classical" period from the fifth century BC.
Speculations even concentrate on a name and a date:
It is Thespis who is said to have shown the first actor
around 534 BC and thus "invented" the tragic form as
such. In extreme contrast the far older chorus has multiple origins vastly scattered in space and time. Its traces
lead (and disappear) into the more rural surroundings
of the *pólis*, and then from the pastures of the "archaic"
centuries into diverse directions and cultures, for example Minoan, Egyptian, Persian or Semitic. The appearance of the chorus in the surviving plays resembles a
process of emergence: The chorus is adopted in the new
theater frame like a foreign body with many origins, or
like an erratic boulder that no poet has come up with,
but which nevertheless seems to be constitutive for the
whole structure one is forced to account for. Hence
whoever wanted to take part in the tragic contest was
obliged to at first "apply for a chorus" and assure its
financing, while the state apparatus only paid the protagonists, that is the actors who were already profession-
alized in some degree.[27]

Now, a closer look shows that the tragic protagonists
mainly have to sustain the impossibilities and the aporia of groundings. Unlike the chorus they are endowed
with a strong will to found or, like Oedipus, re-erect
cities and houses on their own. They are also used to
say "I," as Aischylos's Xerxes does, when he enters the

*wartstheater, Maske und Kothurn* 1 (2012); also recent essays by Ulrike Haß, particularly "Die zwei Körper des Theaters. Protagonist und
Chor," in *Orte des Unermesslichen. Theater nach der Geschichtsteleol-
ogie*, ed. Marita Tatari (Zurich and Berlin: diaphanes, 2014), pp. 139–
159, as well as my own research, particularly my book *Chor-Denken.
Sorge, Wahrheit, Technik* (Paderborn: Fink, 2020).
**27** For more detail see Theo Girshausen, *Ursprungszeiten des Theaters.
Das Theater der Antike* (Berlin: Vorwerk 8, 1999), pp. 348–349.

stage of the *Persians* with the word "Ego"—irrespective of the fact that he has only just lost a millennial war. At the same time the protagonists tend to define themselves by genealogical trees and to transfer them into the political sphere, as one can again learn from Sophocles's *Oedipus*. However, this logic remains strange to the chorus, but also to all the other non-protagonist figures that are close to it, especially the messengers. That is because the chorus is often not just a many-headed environment that precedes the protagonists' entrances and also enables them in the first place. Especially in its songs, the chorus appears to be a bearer of an eminently different knowledge that isn't centered around an ego. It is a knowledge of multiple beginnings that does not allow for the idea of *one* grounding, since each and every beginning is always already permeated by immeasurable environmental forces. In the context of ancient tragedy these forces are interpreted in terms of a widespread mythological horizon, populated by countless human-animal-god-landscape hybrids, and furthermore in many regards resemble the logics of a rhizome—what tragedy calls *hýbris* is ultimately the protagonist's attempt to replace these rhizomatic layers by younger arborescent logics. So it's fair to say that those aporetic internal structures which evolve along with the protagonists will much later shape the modern subject, whereas all the non-human and non-personal environmental variables the subject will stay connected to, like it or not, will come to articulation through the chorus and/or the messengers. The chorus and messengers are thus equivalent to the constellation which in modern times was reformulated under the banner of the street. However, there are at least two fundamental differences resulting from the specific epistemological frame of ancient Greek theater that could be of enormous interest for a present that has reached the "end of the street."

First, there is a very different state of visibility, precisely because ancient Greek theater does not yet fall into the "age of the world picture." The reason for this is ultimately a totally different idea about what it means to see, since antiquity in general conceptualized seeing as a physiological process between bodies being in each other's presence.[28] Notably, the modern theory of light refraction cannot emerge in this frame, and it was only this theory that enabled the modern attempts to visualize and represent (the) world. As a direct result of its strictly somatic conception of seeing, the ancient stage can't be apprehended in terms of confrontation or a mirror-relation. Its three parts, *skené*, *orchéstra* and *théatron*, don't front each other, but lie side by side.[29] They elude the modern dualism, and this is also the reason why later times didn't know whether to count the somehow "superfluous" chorus among the actors, or to make it part of the audience. However, today it's becoming clearer that it's more appropriate to approximate the play between the three stage parts in terms of contagion and bodily affection. Donna Haraway's concept of "becoming-with"[30] is not far away here.

The second difference concerns the reference milieu of ancient Greek theater, its exterior, since not a single surviving play refers to the other of the *pólis* in terms of the street. This allows for my second assumption: *The defining exterior of ancient Greek theater was not the street, but the landscapes of Greek mythology, and thus a spherical cosmos that exceeds human measures and particularly arborescent logics in space and time.* The failing of protagonists like Oedipus is thus grounded in their futile attempts to cut themselves off from these cosmic landscapes, which also characterize the great power politics of the fifth century BC *pólis*. In this respect it's the function of the chorus to insist on a primordial relationality

**28** See in detail Gérard Simon, *Der Blick, das Sein und die Erscheinung in der antiken Optik* (Munich: Fink, 1992).
**29** Compare Haß, "Die zwei Körper des Theaters," p. 142.
**30** See Donna Haraway, *Staying with the Trouble: Making Kin in the Chthulucene* (Durham NC and London: Duke University Press, 2016).

and to evoke its irreducibility against all tendencies of closure.

Seen from today, it is fascinating that this relationality "beyond the street," apart from being embedded in mythological horizons, does not differ too much from the relationality at stake in today's post-critical debates on environmentality.[31] It even carries technological knowledges that strangely resemble current theories about today's "ecotechnological" condition.[32] There are for example mantic techniques, mastered in *Oedipus* by the blind seer Teiresias who serves here as a messenger. Since Teiresisas "has a natural bond with the truth,"[33] his technique does not relate to an absence or lack. Instead he is busy to "nourish the truth in me,"[34] relying on particular somatic techniques of reflecting that include an openness to being affected by swarming events like the flight of the birds. Oedipus on the contrary invents a new, heuristic technique which presupposes a lack of knowledge and furthermore concentrates just on human traces, which is also the reason for him to deny overall the technical character of Teiresias's activities. But there are also more earthly techniques. Aischylos's *Oresteia* opens with a nameless warden who is watching the sky brighten up. This is certainly a hint at the actual sunrise, since tragedies regularly open with a reference to cosmic events going along with the time of the stage performance. However, the warden describes the brightening as the approaching fire signal indicating the fall of Troy: The Greeks built a chain of bonfires from Troy

---

31  See for this discussion Erich Hörl, ed., *General Ecology: The New Ecological Paradigm* (London: Bloomsbury Academic, 2017).

32  See for this expression Erich Hörl, ed., *Die technologische Bedingung: Beiträge zur Beschreibung der technischen Welt* (Berlin: Suhrkamp, 2011).

33  Cited from Michel Foucault, *On the Government of the Living: Lectures at the Collège de France 1979–1980*, trans. Graham Burchell (London and New York: Palgrave Macmillan, 2014), p. 54. Foucault gives here an extended lecture on *Oedipus*, discussing particularly the question of different techniques and knowledges.

34  Ibid.

to Argos, being gradually lit now. Thus, the sunrise as a cosmological event interleaves here with an eminently connective technology, and both effects unroll within an anonymous intermediate sphere that persists below the threshold of the protagonist's entrance. One could speak of ancient Greek internet here. But isn't this also a perfect counterpart to Benjamin's pool of fire on the asphalt, implying that due to the dominance of optical media in modern times the street was like a filter sitting on the landscapes?

## 4

To return to the initial question: What can this difference between street and landscape tell about the conditions under which today's "decline of criticism" is being experienced? Our present seems to relate strangely to that "pre-critical" threshold period when men first began to see themselves as human beings. By contrast, the modern "age of the world picture," including its counter-critical reactions, looks more and more like a "story-within-the-story." I tried to illustrate this here with the examples of Brecht, Benjamin and ancient Greek tragedy. But in fact, this constellation has been formulated in various ways by quite different theories, however persuasive the single approaches may be. I mentioned Haraway and Latour, but one could also think of similar "ecosophical" ideas by Félix Guattari,[35] or even Peter Sloterdijk's *Spheres* trilogy and its distinction between a pre-Copernican spherical cosmos, a modern "terrestrial"

---

[35] See particularly his construction of the "three paradigms" in Félix Guattari, *Chaosmosis: an ethico-aesthetic paradigm*, trans. Paul Bains and Julian Pefanis (Bloomington: Indiana University Press, 1995), pp. 98–118. See also Félix Guattari, *The Three Ecologies*, trans. Ian Pindar and Paul Sutton (London: Continuum, 2008), p. 29.

globalization and today's electronic globalization, starting at least after 1945.[36]

Furthermore, this seems to be the reason why the chorus and everything correlating with its logic has been gaining more and more interest in recent theater. One might also consider the very famous example of Elfriede Jelinek, who has been consistently re-writing ancient plays to confront the crises and catastrophes of our time:[37] The second Gulf War on Iraq and Aischylos's *Persians*; Fukushima and Sophocles's *Tracking Satyrs*, the so-called "refugee crisis" and Aischylos's *Suppliant Women*, the election of Donald Trump and *Oedipus*, etc. However, one can hardly ignore the fact that theater experiences the breaking away of the street as its reference milieu mainly as a vacuum. This helplessness became manifest with the end of Frank Castorf's "Volksbühne," which was a theater that had indeed once more gained its force from the street, as its logo, the "robbers' wheel," already made clear enough. Even so, the task seems evident: If Brecht was able to screw together the Harlequin and the car during the 1920s, then theater today will have to carry on interconnecting the chorus and the satellite control system.

---

**36** See Sloterdijk, *Spheres. Bubbles – Globes – Foams. Trilogy*, trans. Wieland Hoban (Los Angeles: Semiotext(e), 2011, 2014, 2016).

**37** All plays by Jelinek are (in parts exclusively) published on her website: https://www.elfriedejelinek.com.

# List of Illustrations

### Oona Lochner: "To Arlene on Wings of Love"

**1** Arlene Raven / Ruth Iskin, "Through the Peephole: Toward a Lesbian Sensibility in Art," *Chrysalis: A Magazine of Women's Culture*, 4 (1977): p. 22, photo: Independent Voices. An Open Access Collection of an Alternative Press. **2** Arlene Raven / Ruth Iskin, "Through the Peephole: Toward a Lesbian Sensibility in Art," *Chrysalis: A Magazine of Women's Culture*, 4 (1977): p. 30, photo: Independent Voices. An Open Access Collection of an Alternative Press. **3** Arlene Raven / Mary Beth Edelson, "Happy Birthday America," *Chrysalis: A Magazine of Women's Culture*, 4 (1977): pp. 52–53, photo: Independent Voices. An Open Access Collection of an Alternative Press. **4** *From Where I Stand on Tour*, Washington D.C., September 2018, Instagram screenshot, photo: Oona Lochner. **5** *Arlene Raven's Study, Bookshelf*, Brooklyn, October 2018, Courtesy of The Estate of Arlene Raven.

### Beate Söntgen: Decorating Charleston Farmhouse

**1** *Exterior view*, Charleston, from: Quentin Bell & Virginia Nicholson, *Charleston. Ein englisches Landhaus des Bloomsbury-Kreises* (Munich: Christian, 1998), plate 15. **2** *Interior view*, Charleston, from: Quentin Bell & Virginia Nicholson, *Charleston. Ein englisches Landhaus des Bloomsbury-Kreises* (Munich: Christian, 1998), plate 67. **3** *Interior view*, Charleston, from: Quentin Bell & Virginia Nicholson, *Charleston. Ein englisches Landhaus des Bloomsbury-Kreises* (Munich: Christian, 1998), plate 23. **4** *Interior view*, Charleston, from: Quentin Bell & Virginia Nicholson, *Charleston. Ein englisches Landhaus des Bloomsbury-Kreises* (Munich: Christian, 1998), plate 25. **5** Duncan Grant, *Interior*, 1918, oil on canvas, 163 x 174.8 cm, National Museums Northern Ireland, from: Quentin Bell & Virginia Nicholson, *Charleston. Ein englisches Landhaus des Bloomsbury-Kreises* (Munich: Christian, 1998), plate 34. **6** Duncan Grant, *Lessons in the Orchard*, 1917, oil on canvas, 18 x 20 cm, The Charleston Trust, from: Quentin Bell & Virginia Nicholson, *Charleston. Ein englisches Landhaus des Bloomsbury-Kreises* (Munich: Christian, 1998), plate 129. **7** *Interior view*, Charleston, from: Quentin Bell & Virginia Nicholson, *Charleston. Ein englisches Landhaus des Bloomsbury-Kreises* (Munich: Christian, 1998), plate 64. **8** Vanessa Bell: *Omega Workshops. Model for a Nursery*, 1913, from: Christopher Reed, *Bloomsbury Rooms. Modernism, Subculture, Domesticity* (New Haven/London: Yale University Press, 2004), plate 17. **9** Roger Fry, *Still Life with Omega Flowers*, 1919, oil on canvas, 59.9 x 44.2 cm, Tatham Art Gallery, from: Shone, Richard, *The Art of Bloomsbury. Roger Fry, Vanessa Bell and Duncan Grant* (Princeton, NJ: Princeton University Press, 1999), plate 135. **10** Henri Matisse, *Red Room (Harmony in Red)*, 1907, oil on canvas, 180 x 220 cm, Eremitage, St. Petersburg, photo: Archiv des Instituts für Kunstgeschichte der LMU München. **11** *Interior view*, Charleston, from: Quentin Bell & Virginia Nicholson, *Charleston. Ein englisches Landhaus des Bloomsbury-Kreises* (Munich: Christian, 1998), plate 49. **12** Henri Matisse, *La Danse I.* 1909, oil on canvas, 259.7 x 390.1 cm, Museum of Modern Art, New York, photo: Archiv des Instituts für Kunstgeschichte der LMU München. **13** *Interior view*, Charleston, from: Quentin Bell & Virginia Nicholson, *Charleston. Ein englisches Landhaus des Bloomsbury-Kreises* (Munich: Christian, 1998), plate 29. **14** Pablo Picasso, *The Acrobat*, 1930, oil on canvas, 161,5 x 130 cm, Musée Picasso, Paris, from: William

Rubin (Hg.). *Pablo Picasso. Retrospektive im Museum of Modern Art, New York* (München: Prestel, 1980), plate 280. **15** *Interior view*, Charleston, from: Quentin Bell & Virginia Nicholson, *Charleston. Ein englisches Landhaus des Bloomsbury-Kreises* (Munich: Christian, 1998), plate 95. **16** Henri Matisse, *The Painting Lesson*, 1918/1919, oil on canvas, 74 x 93 cm, The Scottish National Gallery of Modern Art, Edinburgh, from: Pia Müller-Tamm, ed., *Henri Matisse. Figur Farbe Raum* (Ostfildern-Ruit: Hatje Cantz, 2005) fig. 93, plate 177. **17** *Interior view*, Charleston, from: Quentin Bell & Virginia Nicholson, *Charleston. Ein englisches Landhaus des Bloomsbury-Kreises* (Munich: Christian Verlag, 1998), plate 82.

### Lynne Tillman: The Horse's Eye

**1** Carroll Dunham, *Study for Horse and Rider (My X) (44)*, 2014, Graphite on paper, 13.3 x 9.2 cm, Copyright Carroll Dunham, Courtesy the artist and Gladstone Gallery, New York and Brussels. **2** Carroll Dunham, *Study for Horse and Rider (My X) (48)*, 2015, Graphite on paper, 13.3 x 9.2 cm, Copyright Carroll Dunham, Courtesy the artist and Gladstone Gallery, New York and Brussels.

### Masha Tupitsyn: Editing as the Practice of Criticism

**1** *Happy Together*, Director: Wong Kar-Wai, color, 96 min., 1997. **2** *Children of a Lesser God*, Director: Randa Haines, color, 119 min., 1986. **3** *The Devil Probably*, Director: Robert Bresson, color, 95 min., 1977; still taken from *DECADES: 1970s*, Masha Tupitsyn, film/video, 2018. **4** Title quotes for the opening of *Love Sounds*, Masha Tupitsyn, 2015. **5** *Deliverance*, Director: John Boorman, color, 110 min., 1972; still from *DECADES: 1970s*, Masha Tupitsyn, film/video, 2017.

### Mimmi Woisnitza: The Stakes of the Stage

**1** Erwin Piscator: *Hoppla, wir leben!* [IX], 1927, stage design by Traugott Müller, b/w photography; silver gelatine; Ermanox photograph, 8.6 x 11.5 cm, Berlin: Theatre-Historical Collection, Free University, photo: Hans Böhm. **2** Erwin Piscator: *Hoppla, wir leben!* [XI] – II, 2. Szene, 5. Bild, 1927, stage design by Traugott Müller, b/w photography, silver gelatine, Ermanox photograph, 16.8 x 23 cm, Berlin: Theatre-Historical Collection, Free University, photo: Sascha Stone. **3** Traugott Müller: *Hoppla Wir Leben!* [III] – projection image montage, 1927, stage design sketch, mixed media (photography, tempera, ink) on cardboard, 49.7 x 67.8 cm, Berlin: Theatre-Historical Collection, Free University.

# Contributors

**Maria Fusco** is an award-winning Belfast-born writer. She works across fiction, criticism, theoretical and performance writing and her work has been translated into ten languages. She is Professor of Interdisciplinary Writing at Northumbria University. mariafusco.net.

**Eva Geulen** is Director of the Centre for Literary and Cultural Research and teaches at Humboldt University in Berlin. She studied German Literature and Philosophy at the University of Freiburg and the Johns Hopkins University. She has held teaching positions at Stanford University, the University of Rochester and New York University, and was Professor of German Literature at the University of Bonn and at Goethe University Frankfurt. Her research focuses on literature and philosophy from the eighteenth century to the present, pedagogical discourses around 1800 and 1900 as well as Goethe's morphology and its reception in the twentieth century. Her publications include *Aus dem Leben der Form. Goethes Morphologie und die Nager* (Berlin: August Verlag, 2016), *The End of Art: Readings of a Rumor after Hegel* (Stanford CA: Stanford University Press, 2006); *Giorgio Agamben zur Einführung* (Hamburg: Junius Verlag, 2005, 3rd edition 2016), *Worthörig wider Willen. Darstellungsproblematik und Sprachreflexion in der Prosa Adalbert Stifters* (Munich: ludicium, 1992), as well as essays on Nietzsche, Benjamin, Raabe, Thomas Mann and others. She has been co-editor of the journal *Zeitschrift für deutsche Philologie* since 2004.

**Thomas Glaser** is research fellow at the Department of Neuere Deutsche Literaturwissenschaft at the University of Erfurt. At the Leuphana University Lüneburg he was visiting professor in the research training group "Cultures of Critique" (2019–2020) and held a professorial chair in Rhetoric with Anselm Haverkamp (2013–2015). He was postdoctoral research fellow at the forum "Texte. Zeichen. Medien" at the University of Erfurt (2010–2013), where he also did his PhD on the problem of aesthetic communication in the works of Kant, Schiller, Friedrich Schlegel and Novalis. Outside university he worked as an assistant director at the Badisches Staatstheater Karlsruhe and as a research assistant at the Landesmuseum Württemberg in Stuttgart. He was a founding board member of the Association of Museum Education Baden-Württemberg. With Bettine Menke he co-edited *Experimentalanordnungen der Bildung. Exteriorität, Theatralität, Literarizität* (Paderborn: Fink, 2014).

**Birgit Mara Kaiser** is Associate Professor of Comparative Literature and Transcultural Aesthetics at Utrecht University. Her research spans literature in English, French and German from the nineteenth to the twenty-first century, with particular focus on poetic knowledge production; the relation of literature, aesthetics and affect; and writing subjectivity in transcultural and post/colonial constellations of power, for which questions of un/translatability, multilingual writing and the materiality of language are especially important. Together with Kathrin Thiele, she founded and coordinates the international research network *Terra Critica: Interdisciplinary Network for the Critical Humanities* and is editor of the book series *New Critical Humanities* with Rowman & Littlefield International. Her publications have appeared in *Comparative Literature*, *Interventions*, *Parallax*, *Textual Practice* and *PhiloSOPHIA: A Journal of Continental Feminism*. She is author of the monograph *Figures of Simplicity: Sensation and Thinking in Kleist and Melville* (Albany: State University of New York Press, 2011) and the recently edited collections *Singularity and Transnational Poetics* (London and New York: Routledge, 2015) and, with Kathrin Thiele and Mercedes Bunz, *Symptoms of the Planetary Condition: A Critical Vocabulary* (Meson Press, 2017).

**Sami Khatib** is Professor of Visual Arts at the American University in Cairo (AUC) and member of the Mellon Foundation research group "Extimacies: Critical Theory from the

Global South." He is also a founding member of the Beirut Institute for Critical Analysis and Research (BICAR). Before joining AUC, he worked as a postdoctoral researcher at the German Research Council (DFG) research training group "Cultures of Critique" at Leuphana University Lüneburg. His ongoing research project "Aesthetics of the Sensuous-Supra-Sensuous" examines the aesthetic scope and political relevance of Marx's discovery of the commodity form. Prior appointments include a Mellon postdoctoral fellowship at the Center for Arts and Humanities at the American University of Beirut (AUB) and visiting professorships at the Department of Fine Arts and Art History at AUB and at the Institute for Art Theory and Cultural Studies at the Academy of Fine Arts Vienna (2017).

**Sebastian Kirsch** is a German theater scholar currently affiliated as a Feodor Lynen research fellow to the Department of German Studies at New York University (until Oct 2020). Having worked particularly on the history of the baroque theater and of the ancient chorus, he holds his PhD and his habilitation from the Ruhr-Universität Bochum. He also held research positions and host professorships at the universities of Vienna and Düsseldorf. His current research focuses on the history of the chorus and on questions of governmentality and taking care. He is the author of *Das Reale der Perspektive: Der Barok, die Lacan'sche Psychoanalyse und das "untote" in der Kultur* (Berlin: Theater der Zeit, 2013) and *Chor-Denken. Sorge, Wahrheit, Technik* (Paderborn: Fink, 2020)
Besides his academic activities he worked as an editor and regular author for the German theater magazine *Theater der Zeit* (2007–2013) and has been cooperating as a dramaturge with directors and performers Johannes Schmit and Hans-Peter Litscher.

**Chris Kraus's** books include *I Love Dick* (1997), *Torpor* (2006), *After Kathy Acker: A Literary Biography* (2017) and most recently *Social Practices* (2018). The German edition of her book *Aliens & Anorexia,* translated by Kevin Vennemann, is published in 2020 by MSB Mattes and Seitz Berlin. She received a Guggenheim Foundation fellowship in 2016. Alongside Hedi El Kholti and Sylvère Lotringer, Kraus is co-editor of the publishing house Semiotext(e), which has introduced much of contemporary French theory to an American audience, and published writers such as Abdellah Taia, Veronica Gonzalez Pena, Natasha Stagg, and Dodie Bellamy. She teaches writing at Art Center College of Design in Pasadena.

**Holger Kuhn** works as postdoctoral researcher at the DFG research training group "Cultures of Critique" at Leuphana University Lüneburg. He is currently working on a book project on "Liquidity: The Cultural Logic of Governmentality in Contemporary Video and Film." From 2012 to 2016 he worked at the Department of Art History at Leuphana University. Recent publications include a book on the "holy kinship" and the construction of family in early capitalism, *Die Heilige Sippe und die Mediengeschichte des Triptychons* (Emsdetten and Berlin: Edition Imorde, 2018), and a book on the depiction of merchants in paintings from the sixteenth century, *Die leibhaftige Münze. Quentin Massys' Goldwäger und die altniederländische Malerei* (Paderborn: Wilhelm Fink, 2015).

**Oona Lochner** is a research assistant at the Institute of Philosophy and Sciences of Art and a PhD candidate in the research training group "Cultures of Critique," both at Leuphana University Lüneburg. Her PhD project focuses on forms of feminist art criticism since the 1960s, asking how writing about art can contribute to a negotiation of subjectivity. Together with Isabel Mehl, she founded the collaborative "From Where I Stand" which addresses the current conditions and possibilities of writing feminist art histories. She was an editor of *Texte zur Kunst* and writes about contemporary art.

**Isabel Mehl** is a writer and an art critic. Since 2016 she is part of the research training group "Cultures of Critique." In her PhD project she explores the fictional art critic Madame Realism , created by writer Lynne Tillman in 1985, and researches the function of fiction for art criticism. Her texts have been published in *Frieze*, *PROVENCE*, *Texte zur Kunst*, and elsewhere. Collaboration and dialogue are at the core of her work—collaborators include among others: art historian Oona Lochner, artists Grażyna Roguski and Lotte Meret Effinger, media theorist Lotte Warnsholdt and graphic designer Sascia Reibel. In 2012 she co-founded the Feminist Working Collective (FAK) and was co-editor of their publication *Body of Work* (2015). Currently she is developing a radio play for WDR Klassik with opera singer Pauline Jacob and musician Georg Conrad; and plans an anthology as well as a critical, experimental study on digital addiction with critic and writer Masha Tupitsyn.

**Bettine Menke** is Professor for Comparative Literature at the University of Erfurt since 1999. She has also taught at the University of Konstanz, the Europa-Universität Viadrina Frankfurt (Oder), the Goethe-Universität Frankfurt (Main), the Philipps-Universität Marburg, as well as the University of California, Santa Barbara. She directed (together with Joseph Vogl, Friedrich Balke, and Bernhard Siegert) the research training group "Mediale Historiographien" (funded by DFG, in Erfurt and Weimar 2004–2014). She has held fellowships at the International Research Institute for Cultural Technologies and Media Philosophy (IKKM) at the Bauhaus Universität Weimar, at Kulturwissenschaftliches Kolleg University of Konstanz, and at the International Research Center for Cultural Studies (IFK) in Vienna (in 2020). Her recent publications include the co-edited volumes *Flucht und Szene. Perspektiven und Formen eines Theaters der Fliehenden* (Berlin: Theater der Zeit, 2018), *Experimentalanordnungen der Bildung. Exteriorität – Theatralität – Literarizität* (Paderborn: Fink, 2014), and *Allegorie. DFG-Symposium 2014* (Berlin and New York: de Gruyter, 2016).

**Beate Söntgen** is Professor of Art History and was Vice President of Research and Humanities in the Presidential Committee (2012–2019) at the Leuphana University Lüneburg. She heads, together with Erich Hörl, the research training group "Cultures of Critique" as well as, together with Susanne Leeb, "PriMus – PhD in Museums." Before joining the Leuphana University in 2011, she held a professorship in Art History at Ruhr University of Bochum (2003–2011), where she directed, together with Ulrike Groos, the postgraduate program "Art Criticism and Curatorial Knowledge," and was Laurenz Professor for Contemporary Art at the University of Basel, Switzerland (2002–2003). She is a member of the Advisory Board of *Texte zur Kunst* and of the Board of Trustees of the Volkswagen Foundation. She has published on modern and contemporary art, art theory and art criticism. She co-edited *Judgement Practices in the Artistic Field* (in print, München: Edition Metzler, 2020), was guest editor of *Der Ort der Kunstkritik in der Kunstgeschichte* for the *Zeitschrift für Kunstgeschichte* (78:1, 2015), and with Ewa Lajer-Burchardt co-edited *Interiors and Interiority* (Berlin and New York: de Gruyter, 2016).

**Heiko Stubenrauch** is Research Assistant at the Institute of Philosophy and Science of Art at Leuphana University Lüneburg. He studied philosophy, sociology, economics, cultural studies and art history in Frankfurt, Lüneburg and Hamburg. From 2016 to 2019 he worked as a researcher and PhD student within the DFG research training group "Cultures of Critique." He has published on critical theory, political philosophy and philosophy of technology. He is co-editor of *What's Legit? Criticism of Law and Strategies of Rights* (Zurich: diaphanes, 2020). His main research interests are the Frankfurt School, poststructuralism, German Idealism, Marxism, aesthetics and theories of the unconscious. In his PhD thesis, he examines the relationship between critique and affect, especially in the works of Kant, Adorno and Deleuze.

**Kathrin Thiele** is Associate Professor of Gender Studies and Critical Theory at Utrecht University. Trained trans-disciplinarily in gender studies, sociology, literary studies and critical theory, her research focuses on questions of ethics and politics from queer feminist, decolonial and posthuman(ist) perspectives. Her published work intervenes in contemporary feminist debates around (sexual) differences, de/coloniality and new materialism/posthumanisms, with specific attention to questions of relationality, implicatedness and entanglements. Together with Birgit M. Kaiser, she founded and coordinates the international research network *Terra Critica: Interdisciplinary Network for the Critical Humanities*. Kathrin Thiele's most recent publications are "Biopolitics, Necropolitics, Cosmopolitics: Feminist and Queer Interventions," a special issue of the *Journal of Gender Studies* 29:1 (2020), co-edited with Christine Quinan, and "The Ends of Being Human? Returning (To) The Question," a special issue of *philoSOPHIA: A Journal of Continental Feminism* 8:1 (2018), co-edited with B. M. Kaiser). Her most recent co-edited book publications are, with Birgit M. Kaiser and Mercedes Bunz, *Symptoms of the Planetary Condition: A Critical Vocabulary* (Meson Press, 2017) and, with Rosemarie Buikema and Liedeke Plate, *Doing Gender in Media, Art and Culture* (London and New York: Routledge, 2017).

**Lynne Tillman** writes novels, short stories, and nonfiction. Her novel *No Lease on Life* was a Finalist for a National Book Critics Circle Award in Fiction, and her essay collection *What Would Lynne Tillman Do?* a Finalist for the National Book Critics Circle Award in Criticism. She is the author of *The Velvet Years: Warhol's Factory 1965–67*, with photographs by Stephen Shore. Her sixth novel, *Men and Apparitions*, was recently published by Soft Skull. Tillman's stories and essays appear frequently in artists' books and museum catalogues, including, recently, those of Raymond Pettibon, Joan Jonas, Cindy Sherman, Liz Deschenes and Anne Collier. Her column "In These Intemperate Times" appeared bimonthly in *Frieze* magazine from 2012–2019; and she still writes regu-

larly for the magazine. Tillman is a recipient of a Guggenheim Fellowship, and a Creative Capital/Warhol Foundation grant for arts writing. She lives in Manhattan with bass
player David Hofstra.

**Masha Tupitsyn** is a writer, critic, and multi-media artist.
She is the author of several books, the latest, *Picture Cycle*,
forthcoming with Semiotext(e) in 2019. In 2015, she completed the 24-hour film, *Love Sounds*, an audio-essay and history of love in English-speaking cinema, which concluded
an immaterial trilogy. The film was accompanied by a catalogue, published in 2015 by Penny-Ante Editions, and has
been exhibited and screened in the United States, Canada,
Europe, and Australia. In 2017, she completed the first
installment, the 1970s, of her ongoing essay-film, *DECADES*.
The second installment, the 1980s, was completed in 2018.
*DECADES* composes a history of cinematic sound and score
for each twentieth century decade. Her writing has appeared
in numerous journals and anthologies. She teaches film, literature, and gender studies at The New School in New York.

**Mimmi Woisnitza** is a postdoctoral research associate at
the Institute of Philosophy and Sciences of Art at Leuphana
University Lüneburg. She holds a PhD from the Department
of Germanic Studies at the University of Chicago for a dissertation on the intersection of eighteenth-century German
theater praxis and aesthetic theory, forthcoming in 2020 as
*Dramaturgies of the Imagination. The Theatre as a Laboratory
of Spectatorial Imagination in Lessing and Kleist* with Rombach Verlag. More recently, she has been doing research on
the history of theater rehearsal, and staging practices and
scenography as a form of critique, in the works and lives of
theater practitioners of the historical avant-gardes.